EPSOM LIB
www.surreycc.gov.uk/libraries

4 FEB 2015

SURREY
COUNTY COUNCIL

Overdue items may incur charges as published in the current Schedule of Charges.

L21

A Philosophical Walking Tour with C. S. Lewis

Why it Did Not Include Rome

Stewart Goetz

Bloomsbury Academic
An imprint of Bloomsbury Publishing Inc

B L O O M S B U R Y
NEW YORK · LONDON · NEW DELHI · SYDNEY

Bloomsbury Academic

An imprint of Bloomsbury Publishing Inc

1385 Broadway	50 Bedford Square
New York	London
NY 10018	WC1B 3DP
USA	UK

www.bloomsbury.com

BLOOMSBURY and the Diana logo are trademarks of Bloomsbury Publishing Plc

First published 2015

© Stewart Goetz, 2015

All rights reserved. No part of this publication may be reproduced or transmitted in any form or by any means, electronic or mechanical, including photocopying, recording, or any information storage or retrieval system, without prior permission in writing from the publishers.

No responsibility for loss caused to any individual or organization acting on or refraining from action as a result of the material in this publication can be accepted by Bloomsbury or the author.

Library of Congress Cataloging-in-Publication Data
A catalog record for this book is available from the Library of Congress.

ISBN: HB: 978-1-6289-2316-2
PB: 978-1-6289-2317-9
ePDF: 978-1-6289-2320-9
ePub: 978-1-6289-2319-3

Typeset by Deanta Global Publishing Services, Chennai, India
Printed and bound in the United States of America

In Memory of Rich Craven
1954–2014

"*Men must endure their going hence*"
From *William Shakespeare's* King Lear

SURREY LIBRARIES	
Askews & Holts	20-Feb-2015
230.092 REL	£19.99

Oddly enough as time goes on the vision of J [Jack] as he was in his later years grows fainter, that of him in earlier days more and more vivid. . . . Perhaps it has been sharpened by the fact that I am reliving something of the middle years by going through our old walking tours in my diaries, and I can see him almost as if he was visible, on a path in front of me, striding along with stick and pack in his shapeless old fisherman's hat. I am glad to remember that J himself re-read these chronicles only a few weeks before his death and got a great deal of pleasure from them.
        Warren Hamilton Lewis, *Brothers and Friends: The Diaries of Major Warren Hamilton Lewis*, 255.

Contents

Acknowledgments	ix
Introduction	1

Part One

1 Hedonistic Happiness — 17
- Common sense and happiness — 17
- The nature of happiness, good, and evil — 21
- Euthyphro and action — 29
- Hedonism — 35
- The relation between happiness and morality — 38
- Eudaemonism — 46
- Possible objections to Lewis's understanding of happiness — 52
- Natural law — 57
- Joy or *Sehnsucht* — 59
- Can we really understand the nature of perfect happiness? — 65

2 Supernatural Persons — 69
- The body and happiness — 69
- Lewis's view of the body — 70
- Mental-to-mental causation — 74
- Mental-to-physical causation — 84
- The soul is the person — 90
- Once more on common sense — 94
- The pleasure of the soul — 98

Part Two

3 Privation and Goodness — 103
- Augustine, Aquinas, and Lewis — 103
- Augustine's understanding of evil — 104

Aquinas's understanding of evil	107
Is pain evil?	108
Aquinas's account of pleasure, happiness, and goodness	114
Eudaemonism and "Good"	121
Lewis and Aquinas	122

4 Body and Soul — 131
- Cartesian dualism — 131
- Aquinas's view of the soul — 132
- Aquinas's view of the body — 135
- What would Lewis have thought? — 138
- The resurrection body's relationship to pleasure and happiness — 141
- Lewis, Aquinas, and the soul — 145
- A section not strictly necessary — 148

Part Three

5 A Rational Journey — 151
- Why not Roman Catholicism? — 151
- Conversion and mere Christianity — 152
- Firmly an Anglican — 154
- Lack of exposure — 161
- Homegrown prejudices — 162
- Vocational aspirations — 164
- Ignorance of history — 165
- Difficulties based in reason — 166
- Thomas Aquinas and Roman Catholicism — 168
- Common sense, mere Christianity, and Roman Catholicism — 177
- Conclusion — 179

Bibliography — 181
Author Index — 189

Acknowledgments

I am indebted to several people who read and discussed the manuscript with me. Those who deserve special mention are my son, Andrew, Charles Taliaferro, Jerry Walls, and especially my wife, Carolyn, who kept pushing me to make "this stuff" accessible to the layperson.

I am grateful to Marjorie Mead and staff of the Marion E. Wade Center at Wheaton College for their warm welcome and friendliness. The late Christopher Mitchell, former director of the Wade Center, was extremely welcoming to Carolyn and me, even having us up to his office for afternoon tea, in the true spirit of Lewis. For help in providing Lewis materials at the Wade Center, I especially acknowledge Laura Schmidt. I also thank Walter Hooper for emailing with me at the outset of my writing about an obscure matter of Lewisania.

While writing this book, I benefitted from a research fellowship at Biola University's Center for Christian Thought, which was made possible through the support of a grant from the John Templeton Foundation. The opinions expressed in this publication are mine and do not necessarily reflect the views of the John Templeton Foundation or Biola's Center for Christian Thought.

Finally, Mary Al-Sayed and Anita Singh were extremely helpful with the preparation of the manuscript. And I thank Haaris Naqvi of Bloomsbury for his support. As always, it has been an absolute delight to work with him.

Introduction

How do you come to be in this benighted part of the country?
'I'm on a walking-tour,' said Ransom ....
'God!' exclaimed Devine, his corkscrew still idle. 'Do you do it for money,
or is it sheer masochism?'
'Pleasure, of course,' said Ransom ....[1]

For most of my adult life, I avoided reading the works of C. S. Lewis. My reason for not reading Lewis went back to my time as a graduate student at Oxford, where Lewis had taught for much of his life. When I arrived in Oxford in the late 1970s, there was an interest in Lewis that bordered on the obsessive. A book entitled *A Severe Mercy* by Sheldon Vanauken, which recounted his time in Oxford as a graduate student and friendship with Lewis in the 1950s, was all the rage. This book and many other works about Lewis seemed to me to be servings in a literary sacrificial meal shared by members of a Lewis cult, and I was determined not to become a member of a cult.

When I say that I avoided reading Lewis's books for much of my adult life, I do not mean to imply that prior to the late 1970s I had never read anything by him. By that time, copies of *Mere Christianity*, *Miracles*, and *The Problem of Pain* had been on my bookshelf for several years. Fingering through them now, it is evident that I had read the last in its entirety and the first two in bits and pieces. But that was pretty much it. Then, in October 2006, my wife, Carolyn, and I wandered into a used-book store in Hyannis, Massachusetts. We were on Cape Cod for our customary five days of relaxation during my college's fall break and looking for something to read. As a philosophy professor, it is hard for me to stay away from bookstores generally and their philosophy sections in particular. Because many Boston academics retire on the Cape and not infrequently sell off some or all of their libraries, I found the philosophy section of this used-book store to be especially well stocked. After examining the philosophy collection, I moved, as I almost always do in any bookstore, to the religion section (I am a Christian who has a serious interest in thoughtful literature about Christianity), where I found several Lewis books. Then in the literature and biography sections I came across some works by and about J. R. R. Tolkien. I called Carolyn over (she always

---

[1] C. S. Lewis, *Out of the Silent Planet* (New York: Scribner, 2003), 18.

makes a beeline to the children's literature in bookstores) and we ended up buying several paperbacks by Lewis and a book of selected letters of Tolkien. I can't recall all of the titles by Lewis that I picked up that day, but I remember *The Screwtape Letters*, *Reflections on the Psalms*, and *That Hideous Strength* were among them. By this time in my life, I was well beyond worrying about becoming part of a Lewis cult, so I could read his books without my old inhibition. We left the bookstore that day and headed to Nauset Beach for a time of sitting by the ocean and reading.

The day passed quickly as it always does when one becomes lost in a good book. As I read Lewis's *Reflections on the Psalms*, I remember turning to Carolyn and saying something like "This is incredibly good stuff." I was hooked. Over the five days, I finished the books by Lewis and was on my way to becoming a Lewis addict. On subsequent journeys to the Cape, we returned to what was now our favorite used book store and combed the stacks for anything by or related to Lewis. *Out of the Silent Planet*, *Surprised by Joy*, *Perelandra*, *Mere Christianity*, *A Grief Observed*, and many others were there to be had. I even found a copy of *A Severe Mercy* and bought it. Carolyn found Walter Hooper's massive volume *C. S. Lewis: Companion and Guide* and Lewis's *The Oxford History of English Literature: Poetry and Prose in the Sixteenth Century* and *The Allegory of Love*. Now when we visit the bookstore, we buy extra copies of books by Lewis so that we can give them to others.

So I love reading Lewis. But why write a book about him? After all, so much has already been written about his life and thought. What could possibly justify another book about him? As I continued to read more and more of the Lewis corpus, I found myself becoming seriously interested in Lewis's philosophical views about happiness and pleasure, which were issues he often discussed. And as a curious reader, I was also interested in what others had to say about Lewis's ideas on these topics. To my surprise, I discovered that hardly anyone had written about his views of these matters. While I was making this discovery, I was co-writing a book on the history of the soul and researching what Thomas Aquinas had to say about the soul's existence and nature. At this point in time, the idea that Lewis might have had views about the thought of Aquinas was not even on my intellectual radar.

What was coming on my radar was an interest in Lewis's life. I began to read biographies about him and to learn that different details of his life were of special interest to different people. For example, I discovered some individuals were interested in the question of why Lewis did not become a Roman Catholic.[2] Though I found the topic interesting, I was not seriously

---

[2] I read Christopher Derrick's *C. S. Lewis and the Church of Rome: A Study in Proto-Ecumenism* (San Francisco: Ignatius Press, 1981) and Joseph Pearce's *C. S. Lewis and the Catholic Church* (San Francisco: Ignatius Press, 2003).

engaged by it. Then two significant events occurred. First, my best friend for almost thirty years became a Roman Catholic. Second, as I continued to read about Lewis as a person and was working my way through James T. Como's book, *Remembering C. S. Lewis: Recollections of Those Who Knew Him*, I came across a chapter by Dom [Alan] Bede Griffiths, a former student of Lewis, in which he said that Lewis was not attracted to the thought of Aquinas.[3] Suddenly, topics that until then had remained separate in my mind now became connected. Could it be that Lewis's philosophical views about happiness, pleasure, and pain, which I knew were at odds with Aquinas's positions on these matters, also provided the basic elements of an adequate explanation of why Lewis did not become a Roman Catholic? And could it be that Lewis's philosophical views about the soul, body, and person (the self or "I"), which I knew were at odds with Thomas's positions, were also part of an adequate explanation of Lewis remaining within the Anglican Communion?

As I reflected on these questions, I became convinced that the few comments Lewis provided about his not becoming a Roman Catholic were explanatorily incomplete and that a more holistic account would shed light on those that he had given. With this intellectual reordering occurring in my mind, I concluded that I would seek to write a book of my own on Lewis. The discussion would be about his philosophical views of happiness, pleasure, pain, and the soul, body, and self (all of which are interesting and warrant serious treatment in their own right) and how they are relevant to the question of why Lewis did not become a Roman Catholic.

I realized from the outset what others had realized, which is that writing about Lewis's philosophical views concerning the issues mentioned above is difficult because he did not systematically address them. What one must do is cull his thoughts about these topics from what he said here and there in different literary forms. As Gilbert Meilander has written about Lewis's intellectual positions more generally, "anyone attempting to write systematically about Lewis's thought faces the great difficulty of coping with the many genres in which Lewis expresses his ideas. He writes theological treatises, short essays on a variety of topics, science fiction and fantasy, children's stories, myth, and literary criticism."[4]

---

[3] Alan Bede Griffiths, "The Adventure of Faith," in *Remembering C. S. Lewis: Recollections of Those Who Knew Him*, ed. James T. Como (San Francisco: Ignatius Press, 2005), 90.
[4] Gilbert Meilaender, *The Taste for the Other* (Grand Rapids, MI: Eerdmans, 1998), 3. James Como also comments on the lack of system in Lewis's writings: "Many . . . [recent] studies [of Lewis's thought] have sought to systematize . . . Lewis's work, with varying success. But the impulse is understandable—precisely because Lewis was unsystematic and never wrote his own *summa*." *Branches to Heaven: The Geniuses of C. S. Lewis* (Dallas, TX: Spence Publishing Company, 1998), 60.

Given the problem that this multiplicity of written forms creates for systematizing Lewis's philosophical views about topics like happiness, pleasure, pain, and the soul and body, it would be understandable if someone were to take the position that Lewis's views about these topics are difficult to piece together precisely because he never thought philosophically about them. Although I do not know how to decisively refute the suggestion that Lewis never philosophized about these matters, it does not ring true with what I have read by and learned about Lewis. Indeed, for reasons that will become obvious in subsequent chapters, it is positively misguided to think that one can adequately comprehend various aspects of Lewis's thought without understanding that he was, at his core, a philosopher.[5] But many try to do just this. As James Patrick points out, "while Lewis is usually considered an apologist [for the Christian faith] his relation to philosophy [is] ignored."[6]

So what do we know about Lewis's philosophical nature and background? All of the evidence points to his having had a first-rate philosophical mind. For example, Lewis wrote to his father, Albert, in late October of 1914 that "I often wonder how you came to have such a profound and genuine philosopher for your son, don't you?"[7] Moreover, while he taught in the English faculties of Oxford and Cambridge for the vast majority of his professional life, he read philosophy at Oxford as an undergraduate. The biographer A. N. Wilson writes that during 1920–1, the "subject which now interested [Lewis] most was philosophy; it appealed to that side of his nature which was born of the police-court solicitor [Lewis's father, Albert] and nourished at the feet of the Great Knock [Lewis's private tutor from September 1914 through March 1917]. . . . He began to nurse ambitions that he would become a professional philosopher . . . ."[8] Alister McGrath writes "[i]t is . . . clear that Lewis's first love was philosophy."[9] Indeed, Lewis's first academic position in 1924 (at University College, Oxford) was in philosophy.[10] And when

---

[5] For a short and eminently readable overview of Lewis as a philosopher, see Jerry Walls' "Introduction: Jack of the Philosophical Trade," in *C. S. Lewis as Philosopher: Truth, Goodness and Beauty*, eds. David Baggett, Gary R. Habermas, and Jerry L. Walls (Downers Grove, IL: Intervarsity Press, 2008), 13–19.
[6] James Patrick, *The Magdalen Metaphysicals: Idealism and Orthodoxy at Oxford 1901–1945* (Mercer Press, 1985), 165.
[7] C. S. Lewis, *The Collected Letters of C. S. Lewis: Volume I; Family Letters 1905–1931*, ed. Walter Hooper (New York: HarperSanFrancisco, 2004), 85.
[8] A. N. Wilson, *C. S. Lewis: A Biography* (New York: W. W. Norton, 1990), 69–70.
[9] Alister E. McGrath, *The Intellectual World of C. S. Lewis* (Oxford: Wiley-Blackwell, 2014), 33.
[10] Lewis's notes for his lectures in 1924 were entitled "The Moral Good—Its Place among the Values." When one reads through these notes, one finds virtually nothing on the moral good. The notes for the most part are on the epistemologies of Leibniz, Locke, Berkeley, Hume, and Descartes. However, the notes do show that Lewis was well educated in philosophy. The notes are located in the Marion E. Wade Center, Wheaton College, Wheaton, IL. They are cataloged as CSL/MS–76.

Magdalen College, Oxford hired Lewis in 1925 to teach English, it gave him the position because he could teach both English and philosophy. According to Lewis's biographers Roger Lancelyn Green and Walter Hooper, "Lewis had to be always ready [in the Magdalen position] to 'fill in' with a philosophy tutorial or lecture if required. Of the sixteen pupils Lewis had in 1926 only five were reading English."[11] J. A. W. Bennett, who was the successor to Lewis in the Chair of Medieval and Renaissance English at Cambridge, stated about his predecessor in his inaugural lecture that "what was chiefly novel in his equipment was the philosophical mind."[12] Lewis's philosophical mind manifested itself even on his holidays. His brother, Warren, noted in his diary that on a walking tour in early January 1934, Lewis, upon finding the university library in Aberystwyth, Wales, "inspected the philosophical section and found it more than adequate."[13] And in November of the same year, Warren speculated about "what might have happened if [his brother] had never got mixed up with the Greats School [at Oxford]," but he "very quickly realized that [his brother] . . . being what he [was], the study of philosophy was to him as inevitable as death will be."[14] Concerning his religious conversion, Lewis responded in a personal letter to N. Fridama on February 15, 1946, that the first thing that brought him back to Christianity was philosophy.[15] And in his book *Miracles*, Lewis tells the reader that he had had a philosophical education.[16]

So while it is true that Lewis never wrote systematic philosophical treatments about the topics that I will examine in this book, his natural philosophical disposition, academic background in philosophy, and the breadth and depth of his reading make it difficult to hold that he never could have thought systematically in a philosophical way about happiness, pleasure, pain, and the soul, body, and person. Moreover, given the fact that there are many places in his books where he wrote some substantive things about these matters, it is worth the effort of trying to piece together into coherent philosophical positions what he said about them.

The foregoing provides the primary reason for my writing a book about certain aspects of Lewis's thought. But there is another reason for doing so.

---

[11] Roger Lancelyn Green and Walter Hooper, *C. S. Lewis: A Biography*, rev. edn (London: HarperCollins, 2003), 76.
[12] J. A. W. Bennett, "The Humane Medievalist," in *Critical Essays on C. S. Lewis*, ed. George Watson (Aldershot: Scolar Press, 1992), 66.
[13] Clyde S. Kilby and Marjorie Lamp Mead (eds), *Brothers and Friends: The Diaries of Major Warren Hamilton Lewis* (San Francisco: Harper and Row, 1982), 139.
[14] Kilby and Mead (eds), *Brothers and Friends*, 161.
[15] C. S. Lewis, *The Collected Letters of C. S. Lewis: Volume II; Books, Broadcasts, and the War, 1931–1949*, ed. Walter Hooper (New York: HarperSan Francisco, 2004), 702.
[16] C. S. Lewis, *Miracles* (New York: HarperCollins, 2001), 20.

In a recent review of Alister McGrath's excellent biography of Lewis, *C. S. Lewis: A Life*,[17] Anthony Kenny highlights McGrath's point about the growth of an ecumenical readership of Lewis's works in the last fifty years:

> In the 1960s, Lewis almost vanished from view: by the end of the century he had become a cultural icon. Initially, in America, he was read only by Episcopalians, and was upbraided by Evangelicals as a smoker, a drinker and a liberal. But as barriers between mainstream Protestant denominations began to weaken, the author of *Mere Christianity* began to be admired across the spectrum. Roman Catholics, too, began to link him with G. K. Chesterton and Tolkien, and to consider him a fellow traveller. Most surprisingly, . . . Lewis has now become the patron saint of American Evangelicalism.[18]

One result of the trans-denominational readership of Lewis's works is that so many people in different segments of the Christian tradition want to own him. Because they identify with the thread of common sense in his works, they believe their views are also his. And because they want to own him, they run the risk of making him into something other than what he was. An instance of this is what people have said about Lewis's views of happiness, pleasure, and pain. While these topics are rarely addressed by those who write about Lewis, those who do address them inevitably get his view wrong. A brief and tantalizing exception is the following comment and quote of Lewis's work from the pen of the philosopher Richard Purtill:

> Lewis would have begun by arguing [in response to those who claim that Christians are fools for denying themselves present enjoyments] that Christianity can include all that is sane and right in both the hedonistic and the utopian philosophies. Happiness is a perfectly legitimate human desire, and Christianity holds out hopes of infinite happiness. As Screwtape complains to Wormwood about God: "He's a hedonist at heart. All those fasts and vigils and stakes and crosses are only a façade. Or only like foam on the seashore. Out at sea, out in His sea, there is pleasure, and more pleasure. He makes no secret of it; at His right hand are 'pleasures for evermore.'"[19]

---

[17] Alister McGrath, *C. S. Lewis: A Life; Eccentric Genius, Reluctant Prophet* (Carol Stream, IL: Tyndale House Publishers, 2013).
[18] Anthony Kenny, "Faith in Lions," *The Times Literary Supplement*, Number 5751, June 21, 2013, 3–4.
[19] Richard Purtill, *C. S. Lewis' Case for the Christian Faith* (San Francisco: Harper and Row, 1981), 101–2.

If we take our cue from Purtill, we will have serious regard for the idea that Lewis was a hedonist about happiness and maintain that those who would suggest otherwise are mistaken. Indeed, Lewis himself did not hide his hedonistic view of happiness. For example, he wrote the following in 1941 in response to a letter from Canon Oliver Chase Quick, who had raised critical questions about Lewis's *The Problem of Pain*: "I wasn't writing on the Problem of Pleasure! If I had been you might find my views *too* hedonistic."[20] Thus, with Lewis's comments about hedonism as my lead, I will begin by explaining at length why it is reasonable to think that Lewis was what his comments suggest he was—a hedonist about happiness.

In writing the previous two paragraphs, I fully recognize that my claims will raise the eyebrows of some and anger others. For example, when I shared with someone recently that I was writing on Lewis's view of happiness, I was immediately queried whether I thought Lewis was an Aristotelian about the matter.[21] When I explained my belief that Lewis was a hedonist when it came to happiness, an incredulous stare was the response. Thus, I have repeatedly had to ask myself whether it could really be the case that those few who have read Lewis with an eye on his view of happiness have misread and/or misrepresented him.

If the correct answer to this question is yes, as I think it is, then what is the explanation for these individuals' misreading of Lewis? As I mentioned earlier, I do not think it is implausible to hold that they have read their own views into what Lewis had to say about happiness. Lewis believed that we should always be on our guard against people who read their own views into texts. As McGrath has recently written about Lewis and texts, "Lewis . . . insists that texts challenge us as much as they inform us. Insisting that the text conform to our presuppositions, to our way of thinking, is to force it into a mould of our own making, and deny it any opportunity to transform."[22]

At this point, it is instructive to reference a disagreement Lewis had with E. M. W. Tillyard concerning how to read poetry. Tillyard maintained that a poem is about the state of the author's mind. By contrast, Lewis insisted that in reading poetry we seek not to know about the author's mind but to share in his consciousness and to see the world as he sees it:

> I look with his eyes, not at him. He, for the moment, will be precisely what I do not see; for you can see any eyes rather than the pair you see with, and if you want to examine your own glasses you must take them

---

[20] Lewis, *The Collected Letters of C. S. Lewis: Volume II*, 463.
[21] Aristotle's position on happiness will be addressed in Chapters 1 and 2. For now, it will suffice to say that Aristotle was not a hedonist about happiness.
[22] McGrath, *C. S. Lewis: A Life*, 189.

off your nose. The poet is not a man who asks me to look at *him*; he is a man who says "look at that" and points; the more I follow the pointing of his finger the less I can possibly see of *him*.[23]

Over the past several years, it has been my goal to read the works of Lewis and see the world as he saw it with respect to the topics of happiness, pleasure, and pain. I readily admit that much of what I have seen has not been seen by others. It might be that my not having read Lewis earlier puts me in a position to notice themes that have been neglected by long-term readers. I will suggest that some very prominent, highly distinguished readers of Lewis such as McGrath and Meilaender have not in fact appreciated Lewis on topics like happiness, pleasure, and pain. I highly commend the work of McGrath and Meilaender on almost all matters, but in terms of reading Lewis I must respectfully recommend caution. It is because I will be both drawing attention to some overlooked topics in Lewis's thought and challenging popular views of him that I cite and recite his work frequently and sometimes at length in subsequent chapters. In the end, however, even after I have quoted Lewis, I can only ask you, the reader, to read Lewis for the first time or to go back and reread him to see for yourself if I have accurately captured how he saw the topics discussed in this book.

Part One focuses on Lewis's beliefs about happiness, pleasure, and pain, and then his thought about the soul, body, and person. With regard to the soul, body, and person, Lewis was what philosophers and theologians call a "substance dualist," or simply a "dualist." Broadly speaking, dualism is the view that a person is a soul and a human being is composed of a soul and a body, where the former is distinct from and capable of surviving the demise of the latter.

For those who do not read much about what is going on in contemporary academic Christian thought, it might come as a surprise to learn that dualism is under siege.[24] The attack against it is typically formulated in the following way:

> In thinking about the nature of a human being, the fathers of the early Church were unduly influenced by Greek philosophical thought, where by "Greek philosophical thought" is meant first and foremost the thought

---

[23] C. S. Lewis and E. M. W. Tillyard, *The Personal Heresy: A Controversy* (London: Oxford University Press, 1939), 11.

[24] For example, see Warren S. Brown, Nancey Murphy and H. Newton Maloney (eds), *Whatever Happened to the Soul?* (Minneapolis: Fortress Press, 1998); and N. T. Wright, "Mind, Spirit, Soul and Body: All for One and One for All; Reflections on Paul's Anthropology in His Complex Contexts," paper presented at Society of Christian Philosophers Eastern Meeting, March 18, 2011, available at http//www.ntwrightpage.com/Wright_SCP_MindSpiritSoulBody.htm.

of Plato. Plato was decidedly dualist in his thinking about human nature. The authors of Scripture, however, were Hebrews and they viewed a human being in monistic, holistic terms, which means that they believed a human being is not a soul-body composite but a single entity with both psychological and bodily features. Hence, when it comes to the survival of death and the afterlife, we get the idea of the bodily resurrection of the dead as opposed to the Platonic idea of the immortality of the soul in a disembodied state.

Now Lewis would have thought that this contemporary "argument" is not an argument at all but nothing more than balderdash, or in his terminology "Bulverism." In an essay entitled "'Bulverism': or, the Foundation of 20th Century Thought," Lewis wrote: "The modern method is to assume without discussion *that* [a man] is wrong and then distract his attention from this (the only real issue) by busily explaining how he became so silly. . . . I have found the device so common that I have had to invent a name for it. I call it Bulverism."[25] Lewis's point is that telling us how someone came to believe something is not a refutation of the belief. In the case of the contemporary Christian attack against dualism, Bulverism cashes out as follows: the fathers of the early Church erroneously came to embrace belief in the soul as an entity that is separate from its body because they read and were unwittingly blinded by Greek philosophy (Plato), not because they were intellectually convinced by considerations that weigh rationally in favor of dualism.

Were Lewis still alive and a participant in the contemporary discussion about human nature, he would demand of those promoting Hebrew monism that they stop Bulverizing and explain what is wrong with dualism. After all, is it not most plausible and argumentatively charitable to hold that the fathers of the early Church embraced dualism because they believed it is right and not because they had read Plato? Moreover, Lewis would likely go on to make clear that the idea of the soul, whether of a ghostlike entity or not, existing as a thing that has a body, is most certainly *not* a Greek or Platonic idea. Rather, it is a universal, nonphilosophical idea about which many Greeks, including Plato, philosophized. As a nonphilosophical idea, it is found not only among the Greeks but also among the Hindus, Egyptians, and yes, among the Jews. It is an idea of common sense,[26] one that arises out of direct awareness of one's self and one's perception of the external world.

---

[25] C. S. Lewis, *God in the Dock* (Grand Rapids, MI: Eerdmans, 1970), 273.

[26] This point about the commonsensical nature of dualism is emphasized in the following recent works: Jesse Bering, "The Folk Psychology of Souls," *Behavioral and Brain Sciences* 29 (2006): 453–62; Paul Bloom, *Descartes' Baby: How the Science of Child Development Explains What Makes Us Human* (New York: Basic Books, 2004); and Nicholas Humphrey, *Soul Dust* (Princeton, NJ: Princeton University Press, 2011). I will spell out the importance of these works with a bit of detail in Chapter 2.

Lewis was a believer in and defender of common sense. For example, as a philosopher he appealed to common sense in the form of a moral law known by ordinary people in answer to those who suggested that Christianity introduced a new morality into the world. Lewis believed that those who maintained that Jesus and his followers taught a different morality were simply misguided:

> The idea ... that Christianity brought a new ethical code into the world is a grave error. If it had done so, then we should have to conclude that all who first preached it wholly misunderstood their own message: for all of them, its Founder, His precursor, His apostles, came demanding repentance and offering forgiveness, a demand and an offer both meaningless except on the assumption of a moral law already known and already broken.... Essentially, Christianity is not the promulgation of a moral discovery.... A Christian who understands his own religion laughs when unbelievers expect to trouble him by the assertion that Jesus uttered no command which had not been anticipated by the Rabbis— few, indeed, which cannot be paralleled in classical, ancient Egyptian, Ninevite, Babylonian, or Chinese texts.... Our faith is not pinned on a crank.[27]

In Lewis's mind, just as Christianity did not bring a new ethical code into the world, so also it did not bring a new, Hebrew non-dualist view of human nature into the world. Lewis believed it was Christianity's adherence to common sense that made it both intellectually respectable and accessible to people from all walks of life.

What, then, of Aquinas, whose positions on the topics of this book Lewis rejected? What was it about Aquinas's thought that Lewis found so problematic? Not surprisingly, I will maintain Lewis was intellectually at odds with Thomas over fundamental issues of common sense. Aquinas rejected the commonsensical views that Lewis embraced. To make my case, in Part Two I set forth Thomas's views of happiness, pleasure, pain, and the soul, body, and person by citing a significant number of passages to secure an understanding of his positions on these issues. In addition to laying out Aquinas's stances on these matters, I also explain how they differ from Lewis's. The gist of my argument is that Lewis could not intellectually reconcile himself to what he regarded as Aquinas's non-commonsensical understanding of these issues. For Lewis, an intellectual chasm existed that could not be bridged.

---

[27] C. S. Lewis, *Christian Reflections* (Grand Rapids, MI: Eerdmans, 1967), 46–7.

But how did such a disagreement result in Lewis's not becoming a Roman Catholic? Why did Lewis's problems with Aquinas translate into his remaining where he was? Here I can anticipate a chorus of objections from those devotees of Lewis who have read what he wrote about his disagreements with the authority of the Pope and Roman Catholic positions on the Virgin Mary. I am familiar with what Lewis had to say about these matters. Indeed, I will quote his statements concerning them in Part Three. My claim is that while they were real issues for Lewis, their intellectual status was secondary in nature. What more deeply troubled Lewis were Aquinas's, and thus the Roman Catholic Church's, positions on the primary philosophical issues of the nature of happiness, pleasure, pain, and the soul, body, and person. These were more fundamental matters for him because they concern ideas that are conceptually presupposed by theological topics and of interest to ordinary people before they encounter the Christian gospel. The Roman Catholic understanding of the Pope and the Virgin Mary merely added to an already existing deeper intellectual disagreement that Lewis had with Rome.

My earlier emphasis on the fact that Lewis was first and foremost a philosopher warrants repeated stress here, particularly for those who are of an evangelical theological persuasion. Many of them are inclined to hold, if they do not actually believe, that knowledge about good and evil, happiness, morality, the existence of the soul, etc., can be had *only* through reading Scripture and having one's mind enlightened via an understanding of it. Among these evangelicals, the Reformation's *sola scriptura* is a badge of honor. But Lewis was not an evangelical in this sense.[28] As a philosopher, he believed the mind can know something about the just-mentioned topics by means of the natural light of reason alone as it manifests itself in common sense. He defended the soundness of reason with his "argument from reason" (which I discuss in Chapter 2) in part for the purpose of making this point clear. Given his philosophical conviction about the fundamental soundness of reason, which is common to all persons prior to any initiation into theological matters, Lewis regarded theological concerns as secondary in nature when it came to assessing his differences with the Roman Catholic Church.

Whenever I have shared with evangelical friends the distinction between primary and secondary considerations that Lewis had for rejecting Roman Catholicism, some have responded by asking if I think Lewis would have

---

[28] Derrick writes the following about Lewis on Scripture: "[Y]ou can search [Lewis's] published works in vain for any unequivocal statement . . . that Scripture constitutes the sole basis and rule of doctrine. . . . Lewis once agreed with me that the doctrine of *sola Scriptura* is self-contradictory by reason of being itself unscriptural . . . ." *C. S. Lewis and the Church of Rome*, 35, 116.

become a Roman Catholic had the Church never embraced the teachings of Aquinas in the way that it did. They want to know if I believe Lewis would have found a home in a non-Thomistic Rome that nevertheless developed the positions that it has on the Virgin Mary and the Pope. Some of these friends, seeking to distance themselves from their *sola scriptura* brethren, go on to add that they reject Roman claims not only because they have no basis in Scripture but also because there is no historical evidence to support doctrines like Mary's perpetual virginity[29] and her bodily assumption into heaven at death.

None of us knows the answer to my friends' question, though I am convinced that Lewis would still not have become a Roman Catholic for the theological reasons that he gave. But without the philosophical differences with Aquinas in play, Lewis's disagreements with Rome would not have been as intellectually deep. Moreover, while my friends' question is a perfectly legitimate one to raise, it is also characteristically evangelical in nature in the sense that it bespeaks a compartmentalized view of philosophical and religious beliefs. If I understand Lewis's thought at all about such matters, he would have responded that the question dubiously supposes that the Roman Catholic Church might have come to its religious views about Mary and the Pope in a philosophical vacuum. Lewis would have gone on to point out to my friends that their appeal to the lack of historical evidence for Mary's perpetual virginity and bodily assumption into heaven is itself commonsensical in character. It *is* the kind of consideration that weighs heavily with a person of common sense. Lewis would likely have added that my friends fail to realize that Roman Catholicism conceptually left common sense behind long ago. For example, as I will discuss in Chapter 3, the Roman Church left it behind philosophically quite early (in the late fourth and early fifth centuries) with Augustine's development of the privationist view of evil (which Aquinas subsequently embraced and Lewis rejected). So while there is nothing logically incoherent about a Roman Catholicism that does not embrace the philosophical positions of Aquinas yet affirms the accepted teachings about Mary and the Pope, the development of such a view is not all that easy to envision.

Despite the differences that I will discuss between Lewis and Aquinas and Roman Catholicism, Lewis stressed what he called "mere Christianity" and he prayed for and sought unity among Christians of different denominations.

---

[29] The individuals I have in mind often point out that not only is there is no non-Scriptural historical evidence for Mary's perpetual virginity, but also Scripture itself is a historical source of evidence for the fact that Jesus had younger blood brothers and sisters. Here they cite verses and passages like Mk 6.3, Mt. 13.55, Jn 7.3-10, Acts 1.14, and Gal. 1.19.

This was particularly the case with Roman Catholics. As his letters reveal, Lewis derived edification from relationships with Roman Catholic friends and expressed frustration with those who tried to "convert" him to the Roman Catholic Church. Hence, given Lewis's own attitudes about Roman Catholicism, one might wonder why I spend time writing about the disagreements that he sought to downplay.

I can assure the reader that my motive in writing about Lewis's relationship to Roman Catholicism is not that of stirring things up. I would take no delight in doing such a thing. Like Lewis, I hope and pray for the unity of the Christian church. But there is no way to achieve unity unless there is an understanding of the differences that separate those involved. The status of Thomas Aquinas in the Roman Catholic Church created a barrier between Lewis and Roman Catholicism that Lewis saw no way of surmounting. To overlook this fact is to stick one's head in the sand.

In reading this book, it is important to keep two things in mind. First, I am a philosopher. Hence, rightly or wrongly, when I read Lewis I read him as a fellow philosopher. While in recent years some philosophers have shown serious interest in Lewis's thoughts about the problem of evil and his refutation of naturalism with the argument from reason,[30] there has been no serious interest in his thought about the topics of this book and how they help to provide an explanation of Lewis's relationship to Roman Catholicism. Alan Jacobs, a biographer of Lewis, has recently written that "[l]ong ago the writers of books and articles concerning 'What C. S. Lewis Thought About X' ran out of subjects . . . ."[31] While I understand his reason for writing this, I think he is seriously mistaken about Lewis's thought concerning the topics of this book. In what follows, I hope to plug what is a gaping hole in the literature about Lewis.

Second, this is a book that is principally about the philosophical thought of C. S. Lewis, thought that he developed and sharpened with friends during many of his walking tours.[32] While I discuss the views of Thomas Aquinas in Chapters 3 and 4, I do so only because of their relevance to understanding Lewis. Hence, the greater length and depth of my discussion of Lewis's

---

[30] For example, on the problem of evil see Michael Murray's *Nature Red in Tooth and Claw: Theism and the Problem of Animal Suffering* (Oxford: Oxford University Press, 2008). On Lewis' refutation of naturalism, see Victor Reppert's *C. S. Lewis' Dangerous Idea: In Defense of the Argument from Reason* (Downers Grove, IL: InterVarsity Press, 2003).
[31] Alan Jacobs, *The Narnian: The Life and Imagination of C. S. Lewis* (New York: HarperSanFrancisco, 2005), x.
[32] See *The Collected Letters of C. S. Lewis: Volume II*, 572 and *The Collected Letters of C. S. Lewis: Volume III; Narnia, Cambridge, and Joy 1950–1963*, ed. Walter Hooper (New York: HarperSanFrancisco, 2007), 1636.

philosophical views as compared to those of Thomas in no way arises out of a lack of respect for and appreciation of the latter's thought.

Finally, a short word about the book's title. According to Walter Hooper, "Lewis had always liked walking" but "'Walking *Tours*' . . . involved going with several friends to a pre-arranged place by train or car and then walking for several days. . . . [I]t was essential that they spend the nights in village pubs or small hotels where they could get supper, drinks and beds for the night."[33] Hooper points out that Lewis wrote the following on the dust jacket of the original American edition of *Perelandra*: "My happiest hours are spent with three or four old friends in old clothes tramping together and putting up in small pubs."[34] Therefore, it is most appropriate to begin this philosophical walking tour with Lewis's thoughts about happiness.

---

[33] Walter Hooper, *C. S. Lewis: Companion and Guide* (New York: Harper Collins, 1996), 794–5.

[34] Hooper, *C. S. Lewis: Companion and Guide*, 794.

Part One

1

Hedonistic Happiness

The characteristic of Pains and Pleasures is that they are unmistakably real, and therefore, as far as they go, give the man who feels them a touchstone of reality.[1]

Common sense and happiness

How should any of us begin to assess happiness, pleasure, and pain? Should we begin with a purely scientific, perhaps neurological account of human nature? Or perhaps ought we to start with what is experienced in the course of everyday life? Lewis believed that the best starting point for our inquiry is common sense. Thus, if common sense says start with an austere contemporary scientific picture of happiness, pleasure, and pain, then that is the place to start. If it tells us to begin with experiences embedded in daily life, then begin there.

But what is common sense? Or better yet, what did Lewis think it is? While to the best of my knowledge Lewis never provided a formal definition of the notion, he seems to have had in mind the idea of beliefs that are directly grounded in or derived from sources such as self-awareness (e.g., one just believes that one is experiencing pleasure or pain, that one is a soul, that one should not do to others what one believes they should not do to oneself, and that one is thinking), sense perception (one just believes that one has a body, that the car is there on the street, that the apple is red), memory (one just believes that one had cereal for breakfast, that one promised to go to the store later), and reason (one just understands that $1 + 1 = 2$, that if A>B and B>C, then A>C). These and other beliefs like them are part and parcel of everyday life and held by people by virtue of their being human beings. Anyone who is familiar with Lewis's work knows that he believed all people, both Christian and non-Christian, have commonsense beliefs. He also maintained that Christians hold commonsense beliefs prior to any

---

[1] C. S. Lewis, *The Screwtape Letters* (New York: Macmillan, 1961), 58.

beliefs they might embrace on the basis of Scripture and that Scripture itself presupposes this is the case.

Evidence of Lewis's commonsensical attitude can be found in different contexts. For example, in a letter to his father in 1925, in which he explained why he abandoned professional employment in philosophy for that in English, Lewis conveyed his dislike for questioning what ordinary people take for granted:

> As to the other change—from Philosophy to English—I . . . think you are mistaken in supposing that the field is less crowded in Philosophy: it seems so to you only because you have more chance of seeing the literary crowd. . . . On other grounds I am rather glad of the change. I have come to think that if I had the mind, I have not the brain and nerves for a life of pure philosophy. A continued search among the abstract roots of things, a perpetual questioning of all that plain men take for granted . . .—is this the best life for temperaments such as ours?[2]

Lewis told his father in this letter that the ongoing questioning of everything that ordinary people take for granted did not suit his temperament (one might wonder if such questioning is really at the heart of what philosophy is or should be, but that is a matter for another day). In his preface to *The Screwtape Letters*, we find another instance of Lewis's appeal to ordinary folk and what they believe. About his belief in the reality of Satan and devils, Lewis wrote as follows:

> I believe this not in the sense that it is part of my creed, but in the sense that it is one of my opinions. My religion would not be in ruins if this opinion were shown to be false. Till that happens—and proofs of a negative are hard to come by—I shall retain it. It seems to me to explain a good many facts. It agrees with the plain sense of Scripture, the tradition of Christendom, and the beliefs of most men at most times.[3]

Most people at most times believe in disembodied, morally evil souls or spirits. Hence, this belief should be taken seriously. In *A Preface to Paradise Lost*, Lewis appealed to common sense in rejecting the suggestion that Milton affirmed the doctrine of latent evil in God:

> The only basis for [ascribing this view to Milton] is [*Paradise Lost*] v, 117-19, where Adam tells Eve that evil "into the mind of God or Man" may "come and go" without being approved and "leave no spot or blame".

---

[2] Lewis, *The Collected Letters of C. S. Lewis: Volume I*, 648.
[3] Lewis, *The Screwtape Letters*, vii.

Since the whole point of Adam's remark is that the approval of the will alone makes a mind evil and that the presence of evil as an object of thought does not—and since our own common sense tells us that we no more become bad by thinking of badness than we become triangular by thinking about triangles—this passage is wholly inadequate to support the astonishing doctrine attributed to Milton.[4]

The common sense that infuses *A Preface to Paradise Lost* could get Lewis into trouble with literary critics. Thus Elmer Edgar Stoll protests that Lewis "strangely treats the superhuman character" of Satan in Milton's *Paradise Lost* "in the light of common sense. . . . Mr. Lewis demands too much in the way of common sense."[5] However, Lewis would have defended his treatment of Satan on the very grounds that it accorded with common sense. Thus, J. A. W. Bennett writes of Lewis that "[t]he whole man was in all his judgments and activities . . . for [on behalf of] <common life>."[6]

When we turn to Lewis's discussions of ethics, we get a similar appeal by him to what most people believe. Thus, when describing what Jesus came to teach, Lewis made clear that he did not come to proclaim something new about morality. Jesus simply presupposed commonsense morality (the common moral law) or what Lewis in *The Abolition of Man* called the *Tao*. Had Jesus done otherwise, Lewis believed that he would have failed to connect with the ordinary person. His message would have fallen on deaf ears. In a passage that is reminiscent of that which I cited in the Introduction, Lewis stressed that Jesus was not a moral innovator:

> The first thing to get clear about Christian morality between man and man is that in this department Christ did not come to preach any brand new morality. The Golden Rule of the New Testament (Do as you would be done by) is a summing up of what every one, at bottom, had always known to be right. Really great moral teachers never do introduce new moralities: it is quacks and cranks who do that. . . . The real job of every moral teacher is to keep on bringing us back, time after time, to the old simple principles which we are all so anxious not to see; like bringing a horse back and back to the fence it has refused to jump or bringing a child back and back to the bit in its lesson that it wants to shirk.[7]

---

[4] C. S. Lewis, *A Preface to Paradise Lost* (Oxford: Oxford University Press, 1942), 84.
[5] Elmer Edgar Stoll, "Give the Devil His Due: A Reply to Mr. Lewis," in *Critical Essays on C. S. Lewis*, ed. George Watson (Aldershot: Scolar Press, 1992), 182, 187.
[6] Bennett, "The Humane Medievalist," 74.
[7] C. S. Lewis, *Mere Christianity* (New York: HarperSanFrancisco, 2001), 82. Lewis appeals to common sense throughout *Mere Christianity*. For example, see 23, 93, 125, 195–6.

Another example of Lewis's belief in shared human convictions concerned myth. Because common sense undergirded myths about dying gods, he did not dismiss them as silly nonsense produced by the human imagination. Rather, he understood them as real insights into the nature of reality. Thus, the dying and rising of Christ was not just a myth, but *the* true myth: "The Divine light, we are told, 'lighteneth every man.' We should, therefore, expect to find in the imagination of great Pagan teachers and myth makers some glimpse of that theme which we believe to be the very plot of the whole cosmic story – the theme of incarnation, death, and rebirth."[8] As McGrath says, in Lewis's view there ought to be similarities between pagan religions and Christianity. "In fact, the problems would arise if such similarities did *not* exist, as this would be to imply that 'God's myth' left 'human myths' untouched. The great pagan myths, Lewis suggested, were 'dim dreams or premonitions' of the greater and fuller truth of the Christian gospel."[9] Because Lewis was convinced that ordinary views about happiness, pleasure, pain, and the existence of the soul and body were, like views concerning morality and insights expressed in myths about dying and rising gods, commonsense convictions that ordinary people possessed prior to reading the Bible, he believed that calling these beliefs into question would undermine confidence in the integrity of the human mind and the credibility of Christianity.

Christopher Derrick recognizes Lewis's conviction about common sense, which, somewhat amusingly, he thinks is a trait of the English people in general:

> One of the more consistent characteristics of the English people is their dislike of rigorous abstract argument. When some problem arises, they are very reluctant to puzzle it out from first principles; they would much rather "muddle through", making short-term adjustments to the existing situation on the basis of what they take to be common sense, leaving logic and the ultimate questions to foreigners.[10]

If one follows Derrick and thinks in terms of first principles, then Lewis is rightly understood as having regarded common sense itself as a first principle. For him, in puzzling things out one had best make sure, unless there are absolutely compelling reasons to the contrary, that one's conclusions not undermine the first principle of common sense. Thus in his paper "Jack the Giant Killer," A. D. Nuttall gives the following apt description of Lewis's respect for ordinary people: "We sense [in Lewis] a willingness to engage, if

---

[8] C. S. Lewis, *The Weight of Glory and Other Addresses* (New York: Harper Collins, 2001), 128.
[9] McGrath, *The Intellectual World of C. S. Lewis*, 66–7.
[10] Derrick, *C. S. Lewis and the Church of Rome*, 171–2.

necessary, in fundamental philosophy but that the philosophy Lewis would give us would be one . . . close to the conceptual practice of the ordinary person."[11]

As I discussed in the Introduction, Lewis was a philosopher by nature and in his early adult years studied and tutored others in philosophy at Oxford. *The Problem of Pain*, *The Abolition of Man*, and *Miracles* are arguably his most philosophical books. Beyond these, there is Book One of *Mere Christianity* and various essays and letters in which he expressed his philosophical views on a variety of topics. But while these books and essays are philosophical in nature, none has the purpose of systematically addressing the issue of happiness. Thus, if one wants to systematize Lewis's thought on happiness, one must do a good bit of work taking what he said here and there and putting it together into a coherent position, much like one takes the pieces of a jigsaw puzzle and puts them together to form a whole. The pieces of the puzzle are Lewis's comments about goodness, evilness, and pleasure and pain, and how they fit together into his overall view of happiness. As John Lawlor, who was a student of Lewis's at Oxford in the late 1930s, rightly points out, Lewis's notion of happiness is "a theme perhaps too little touched upon in latter-day assessments of Lewis . . . ."[12]

With an author like Lewis who wrote so much over the span of his life, there is always the worry that his view on a matter changed over time, so that any attempt to state and elaborate upon it inevitably misrepresents one or more of its formulations. However, as others have pointed out, Lewis's views remained remarkably unchanged over the course of his professional life.[13] This is certainly the case with the topics of this chapter. Lewis held the same views about happiness, good, and evil from the beginning to the end.

The nature of happiness, good, and evil

According to David Hume, recalling the ancient Greek philosopher, Epicurus, the problem of evil is as follows: "Is he [God] willing to prevent evil, but

---

[11] A. D. Nuttall, "Jack the Giant Killer," in *Critical Essays on C. S. Lewis*, ed. George Watson (Aldershot: Scolar Press, 1992), 271.
[12] John Lawlor, *C. S. Lewis: Memories and Reflections* (Dallas, TX: Spence Publishing Company, 1998), xiii.
[13] For example, see Victor Reppert's "The Ecumenical Apologist: Understanding C. S. Lewis' Defense of Christianity," and Mona Dunckel's "C. S. Lewis as Allegorist: *The Pilgrim's Regress*," which are both in *C. S. Lewis: Life, Works, and Legacy, Vol. 3, Apologist, Philosopher, and Theologian*, ed. Bruce Edwards (Westport, CN: Praeger, 2007), 1–28 and 29–49 respectively.

not able? Then he is impotent. Is he able, but not willing? Then he is malevolent. Is he both able and willing? Whence then is evil?"[14] Here is Lewis's statement of the problem of evil: "If God were good, He would wish to make His creatures perfectly happy, and if God were almighty, He would be able to do what He wished. But the creatures are not happy. Therefore God lacks either goodness, or power, or both."[15] What is significant for my purposes is that Lewis sees the lack of perfect happiness as the gist of the problem of evil.

To understand perfect happiness we must have a concept of happiness. Here, Lewis believed that we should cast our lot with common sense and the popular or ordinary view of happiness. In preparing his readers for his treatment of the problem of evil, Lewis said that "[t]he possibility of answering it depends on showing that the terms 'good' and 'almighty', and perhaps also the term 'happy' are equivocal: for it must be admitted from the outset that if the popular meanings attached to these words are the best, or the only possible, meanings, then the argument is unanswerable."[16] What is especially interesting is that while Lewis saw the need to clarify the popular meanings of "almighty" and "moral good" ("almighty," he said, does not mean "the power to do anything"—in particular, it does not mean the power to do what is logically impossible—and "good," when used in a moral sense of God, does not mean something entirely different from our idea of human moral good), he saw no need to say anything about the popular meaning of "happy."

The obvious question, then, is what is the popular meaning of "happy" about which Lewis saw no need to comment? The ancient Greek philosopher, Aristotle, in his *Nicomachean Ethics*, said that most people would agree that the highest good attainable by action is happiness: "for both the common run of people and cultivated men call it happiness. . . . But when it comes to defining what happiness is, they disagree, and the account given by the common run differs from that of the philosophers. The former say it is some clear and obvious good, such as pleasure . . . ."[17]

A person of the common run believes that happiness is pleasure. Philosophers disagree. When it comes to happiness, Lewis hangs with the commoners. In his mind, nothing is more commonsensical than our desire to be happy. And just as commonsensical is our belief that the degree of happiness we desire cannot be had in this life. In his engaging biography

---

[14] David Hume, *The Philosophy of David Hume*, ed. V. C. Chappell (New York: The Modern Library, 1963), 567.
[15] C. S. Lewis, *The Problem of Pain* (New York: Macmillan, 1962), 26.
[16] Lewis, *The Problem of Pain*, 26.
[17] Aristotle, *Nicomachean Ethics*, trans. Martin Ostwald (Indianapolis: Bobbs-Merrill, 1962), 1095a17–23.

of C. S. Lewis, Alan Jacobs writes that Lewis believed there was a concerted effort on the part of those in the educational establishment who oppose common sense to convince us that they and others have the power to make heaven on earth and give it to us. As Lewis saw the matter, "[a]lmost our whole education has been directed to silencing this shy, persistent, inner voice"[18] that informs us that our true happiness lies outside and beyond this world. How can we be set free from this evil enchantment? Jacobs writes "Lewis begins his disenchanting spell in this surprising way: by calling us back to our pleasures...."[19]

Some people might find it surprising that a Christian would beckon us to return to our pleasures in the context of thinking about happiness. However, for anyone who has seriously read Lewis, such an appeal will not come at all as a surprise because he embraced the commonsense belief that pleasure is what constitutes happiness. Stated in slightly more philosophical terms, Lewis was a hedonist about happiness. What this means is that he identified happiness with experiences of pleasure and nothing but experiences of pleasure. According to the philosopher Nicholas White, almost all theorists about happiness agree that a hedonistic understanding of happiness has the following advantage over other understandings: "[I]t takes happiness to be constituted by something [pleasure] that . . . everyone finds attractive, or even attractive in the extreme. It's so attractive, in fact, that virtually every philosopher who's not a hedonist [about happiness] has felt obliged to explain why not."[20] Lewis recognized no such obligation because he embraced what is so attractive.

In order to express accurately the common view of happiness as pleasure, it is helpful to explain briefly a couple of the components of the conceptual apparatus of which Lewis made use in expressing his understanding of this view of happiness. The first conceptual component is the idea of an intrinsic property (characteristic) of a subject, entity, or thing. An intrinsic property is one that an object has, and its having that property is not derived from its relationship to anything else. Stated slightly differently, an intrinsic property is one that an object has in and of itself.[21] Lewis invoked the idea of

---

[18] Lewis, *The Weight of Glory*, 31.
[19] Jacobs, *The Narnian*, 189.
[20] Nicholas White, *A Brief History of Happiness* (Oxford: Blackwell, 2006), 53–4.
[21] Lewis thought the best examples of intrinsic properties come from our own selves. For example, he regarded the capacities to experience pleasure and pain as intrinsic properties, as well as the capacity to believe and the power to choose. A self has these characteristics before it interacts with other selves and things in its environment. As I will point out in Chapter 2, Lewis doubted whether we know any intrinsic properties of the material world.

an intrinsic property when he was discussing something that is intrinsically impossible. Thus, he wrote that "[t]he absolutely impossible may also be called the intrinsically impossible because it carries its impossibility within itself, instead of borrowing it from other impossibilities which in their turn depend upon others."[22]

The second conceptual component in Lewis's theoretical apparatus for explicating the common idea of happiness is not surprisingly the idea of the logical opposite of an intrinsic property. It is the idea of an extrinsic property, where such a property is one that is had by an object in virtue of its standing in a relationship to something else. The most prevalent kind of extrinsic property is instrumental in nature, where an instrumental property is one that is had by an object in virtue of that object's production of a property in another object. For example, a certain food might be healthy (have the property of being healthy) because it is instrumental in producing or preserving health in a person who eats it. While strictly speaking being an instrumental property is only one kind of extrinsic property, it will suffice for explaining Lewis's thought to speak of the two as if they were identical. Hence, in what follows I will simply speak in terms of intrinsic and instrumental properties.

With this intrinsic-instrumental conceptual apparatus in place, I begin my exposition of Lewis's understanding of happiness with comments from his book *The Problem of Pain*. Given that it is a book about the problem of evil, one might ask why did Lewis not entitle it *The Problem of Evil*? One answer to this question, which is nonphilosophical in nature, was provided by Lewis himself. In a letter to Miss Tunnicliff about the title *The Problem of Pain*, he wrote "As for the title and subject of my actual book [they] were not of my own independent choice: I had been asked to deal with that subject for a series."[23] But why would he be asked to deal with pain? Here we must turn to another explanation for the title of the book, which is philosophical in nature. This explanation is found in *The Problem of Pain* itself, where Lewis wrote that "Pain is unmasked, unmistakable evil . . . ."[24] Given that Lewis believed pain is evil, it is not at all difficult to see how he agreed to the title *The Problem of Pain*.

In claiming that pain is "unmasked, unmistakable evil," Lewis was asserting that pain is intrinsically evil. It is in and of itself and, therefore, in

---

[22] Lewis, *The Problem of Pain*, 27–8.
[23] Lewis, *The Collected Letters of C. S. Lewis: Volume III*, 146. The series Lewis mentions was the "Christian Challenge" series whose purpose was to introduce the Christian faith to people outside the Church. See Hooper, *C. S. Lewis: Companion and Guide*, 294.
[24] Lewis, *The Problem of Pain*, 92.

every instance, evil. Thus, it differs from things like "meat, or beer, or the cinema,"[25] which might be evil in some contexts but not in others. Lewis said that "[a]n individual Christian may see fit to give up [these] sorts of things for special reasons . . . but the moment he starts saying [these] things are bad in themselves . . . he has taken the wrong turning."[26]

To make clear Lewis's view about the intrinsic evilness of pain, consider what Jerry Root says in his book about Lewis's view of evil: "Things mean nothing in isolation from other things. Though it is possible to say that pain hurts all by itself, I cannot say whether that pain is good or bad all by itself, for it can only be understood in relationship to other things."[27] Now it might be Root's view that an experience of pain cannot be bad (evil) all by itself—independent of its relationship to anything else. But this was not Lewis's view. Here is what Lewis had to say: "I have no doubt at all that . . . pain in itself [is] an evil . . . ."[28] For Lewis, pain is intrinsically evil.[29]

It is important to emphasize that if pain is, as Lewis held, intrinsically evil, its being so is thoroughly compatible with it also being instrumentally good. For example, Lewis believed that pain is instrumentally good insofar as it is used by God to call our attention to Him: "God whispers to us in our pleasures, speaks in our conscience, but shouts in our pains: it is His megaphone to rouse a deaf world. . . . No doubt Pain as God's megaphone is a terrible instrument; it may lead to final and unrepented rebellion. But it gives the only opportunity the bad man can have for amendment."[30]

If Lewis believed pain is intrinsically evil, then it is not at all implausible to think that he regarded pleasure as intrinsically good. Literary evidence shows that fairly early in his academic life he was sympathetic with this view of pleasure. Thus, Lewis recorded in his diary *All My Road Before Me* that one day in 1922, when he was in his early twenties, he sat all morning "in the dining room and worked on my dissertation, trying to prove that no pleasure

---

[25] Lewis, *Mere Christianity*, 79.
[26] Lewis, *Mere Christianity*, 78–9.
[27] Jerry Root, *C. S. Lewis and a Problem of Evil: An Investigation of a Pervasive Theme* (Eugene, OR: Pickwick Publications, 2009), 182.
[28] Lewis, *Christian Reflections*, 21.
[29] Another author who fails to grasp Lewis' view of pain is Joe Puckett, Jr. According to Puckett, "[t]he evil of pain is not the pain itself. . . . Suffering feels so wrong because we know that it hinders us from seeing . . . the good that God has created." (*The Apologetics of Joy: A Case for the Existence of God from C. S. Lewis's Argument from Desire* [Eugene, OR: Wipf and Stock, 2012], 83. Lewis would have agreed that pain is instrumentally evil, if it prevents a person from seeing God's created good. But Lewis would also have insisted that pain itself is intrinsically evil.
[30] Lewis, *The Problem of Pain*, 93, 95.

could be considered bad, considered in itself."[31] And a little over twenty years later he would write that it is the Christian's duty to prepare for the difficulties of life, where this preparation requires that "we must practise in abstaining from pleasures which are not in themselves wicked."[32]

To say that no pleasure is in itself (intrinsically) evil, bad, or wicked, however, is not to say that every pleasure is intrinsically good. For example, all pleasures might be neither intrinsically evil nor intrinsically good. They might have no intrinsic value at all. Lewis, however, believed that all pleasures are intrinsically good. In a letter written on January 18, 1941, to Canon Oliver Chase Quick, who had written to Lewis about *The Problem of Pain*, Lewis said "I think *all* pleasure simply good: what we call bad pleasures are pleasures produced by actions, or inactions, [which] break the moral law, and it is those actions or inactions [which] are bad, not the pleasures."[33] Elsewhere, Lewis was explicit about the intrinsic goodness of pleasure (and the intrinsic evilness of pain) when he wrote "I have no doubt at all that pleasure in itself is a good and pain in itself an evil; if not, then the whole Christian tradition about heaven and hell and the passion of our Lord seems to have no meaning. Pleasure, then, is good; a 'sinful' pleasure means a good offered, and accepted, under conditions which involve a breach of the moral law."[34]

At this point, it is important to draw the distinction between an intrinsic good that is pleasurable and pleasure that is intrinsically good and make clear that Lewis, without denying the former, affirmed the latter. Immediately before Lewis made the statement that I just cited about all pleasure being in itself good, he asked whether he could "find any intrinsic goodness in culture . . . ."[35] He answered that "the most obviously true answer is that

---

[31] C. S. Lewis, *All My Road Before Me* (New York: Harcourt, Inc., 1991), 98. Lewis wrote the following in *De Bono et Malo*, which was penned in 1930 to Owen Barfield as part of their intellectual exchange known as "The Great War": "For if we ask a man why he is hurrying and he replies 'To catch a train': and we ask him again 'Why' and so on: in the end he is bound to answer *either* 'Because this is my duty' *or* 'Because this is my pleasure': that is *either* 'This is the manifestation of universal good demanded by my time and place – in willing this I will as spirit' *or* 'This is my particular good – this is what I as soul regard as my end'. And if you asked him why he ought to do his duty, or why he liked pleasure, he would justly leave you unanswered as a fool. There is no answer to the ultimate [grounding] but our inability to answer (as in the face of an axiom) is not ignorance but knowledge: for we see . . . why there is no answer." *De Bono et Malo*, CSL/MS-34/X, The Marion E. Wade Center, Wheaton College, Wheaton, IL, 8.

In this passage, Lewis invoked pleasure as one of two ultimate explanations for why people act as they do. Given the explanatory role Lewis accorded to pleasure, it is plausible to think that he regarded pleasure as not only not bad but also good.

[32] Lewis, *God in the Dock*, 54.
[33] Lewis, *The Collected Letters of C. S. Lewis: Volume II*, 462–3.
[34] Lewis, *Christian Reflections*, 21.
[35] Lewis, *Christian Reflections*, 21.

it [culture] has given me quite an enormous amount of pleasure."[36] Root comments that Lewis "is not here speaking of moral goodness, but of a goodness that is pleasurable . . . ."[37] Strictly speaking, Lewis is saying that culture is instrumentally good because it provides him with experiences of pleasure. It is true that both culture and the experienced pleasure are nonmoral (not moral, which is not to say immoral) goods. However, it is the pleasure that is the nonmoral intrinsic good.

Two paragraphs back I quoted Lewis's claim that a sinful pleasure is really the illicit taking and enjoying of that which is good in itself. This idea was stressed by Lewis in a different context when he wrote that the expression "bad pleasures" is a kind of shorthand for "'pleasures snatched by unlawful acts.' It is the stealing of the apple that is bad, not the sweetness. The sweetness is still a beam from the glory. That does not palliate the stealing. It makes it worse. There is sacrilege in the theft. We have abused a holy thing . . . [and ignored] the smell of Deity that hangs about it."[38] The smell of deity hangs about pleasure because, as Screwtape reminded his devilish nephew, Wormwood, our experience of it is ultimately from God:

> Never forget that when we are dealing with any pleasure in its healthy and normal and satisfying form, we are, in a sense, on the Enemy's ground. I know we have won many a soul through pleasure. All the same, it is His invention, not ours. He made the pleasures: all our research so far has not enabled us to produce one. All we can do is to encourage the humans to take the pleasures which our Enemy has produced, at times, or in ways, or in degrees, which He has forbidden.[39]

In defense of his view of pleasure's intrinsic goodness, Lewis contrasted pleasure as a simple, intrinsic good with states of the mind that give rise to pleasure. In some cases, the states of mind are themselves intrinsically evil and yet instrumentally good because they give rise to experiences of pleasure that are intrinsically good. Lewis labeled these states of mind *mala mentis gaudia* or bad pleasures of the mind. As examples of these pleasures, Lewis gave resentment or grievance: "Aren't these intrinsically vicious pleasures . . . 'mixed'? . . . [R]esentment is pleasant only as a relief from, or alternative to, humiliation. I still think that those experiences which are pleasures in their own right can all be regarded as I suggest [which is as intrinsically

---

[36] Lewis, *Christian Reflections*, 21.
[37] Root, *C. S. Lewis and a Problem of Evil*, 104.
[38] C. S. Lewis, *Letters to Malcolm: Chiefly on Prayer* (New York: Harcourt, 1992), 89, 90.
[39] Lewis, *The Screwtape Letters*, 41–2.

good]."⁴⁰ What Lewis termed "mixed," the philosopher G. E. Moore, who was a contemporary of Lewis, called an "organic whole."⁴¹ The idea of an organic whole is as follows. With a mental state like resentment, one considers, say, the legitimately achieved success of another person at one's own expense; one then realizes that the other person has experienced pleasure from his or her success; one then experiences anger about that individual's pleasurable success; and finally, one gets pleasure from that anger. This Moorean organic whole is intrinsically evil, because of the way the parts are related (pleasure from anger that is derived from an awareness of someone else's legitimate success). But Lewis maintained that the pleasure one experiences as a part of that whole never ceases to be intrinsically good.

Before proceeding, it is worth pointing out that A. D. Nuttall highlights the similarity of Lewis's view that pleasure is good with that of Moore. After noting this similarity, Nuttall stresses that

> whatever philosophers may say, ordinary people are quite clear that evaluation [of pleasure as good] is one thing and the registration [experience] of pleasure is another. ... Lewis implicitly assents to Moore's contention that "good" is [a] non-natural [property which] ... rests on the fact that it is logically and practically possible for a person to stand back from any object whatsoever and ask, "Is this really good?"⁴²

Again, some comments are warranted. Nuttall is saying that there is the experience of pleasure and the evaluation of the objective goodness of pleasure. Given this distinction, one can ask "Is pleasure good?" And Lewis's answer was "Yes." Indeed, pleasure is intrinsically good. To say, as Moore did, that the goodness of pleasure is non-natural is to say that though the goodness of pleasure is real and known to be so, it is not apprehended by means of one or more of the five senses; it cannot be seen, tasted, smelled, touched, or heard. This is because the goodness of pleasure is immaterial in nature. So "Pleasure is good" is just as true as "The ball is round." The goodness of pleasure is a real property of the pleasure just as the roundness of the ball is a real property of the ball. But they differ in the way that they are known (the roundness of the ball is seen and felt, while the pleasure is

---

⁴⁰ Lewis, *Letters to Malcolm*, 94–5.
⁴¹ G. E. Moore, *Principia Ethica* (Cambridge: Cambridge University Press, 1968), 30–6. In *That Hideous Strength* (New York: Scribner, 2003), 53, the Deputy Director of National Institute of Co-Ordinated Experiments (NICE) says the following: "Everyone in the Institute feels that his own work is not so much a departmental contribution to an end already defined as a moment or grade in the progressive self-definition of an organic whole."
⁴² Nuttall, "Jack the Giant Killer," 273–4, 282.

apprehended introspectively) because one is a material property while the other is not.

Finally, Lewis believed that not only do we know the goodness of pleasure, but that goodness is indefinable because it is a simple property; it is one that is not made up out of any other properties. Here are Moore's words, which, as Nuttall suggests, Lewis could have penned:

> If I am asked "What is good?" my answer is that good is good, and that is the end of the matter. Or if I am asked "How is good to be defined?" my answer is that it cannot be defined, and that is all I have to say about it.... My point is that "good" is a simple notion, just as "yellow" is a simple notion; that, just as you cannot, by any manner of means, explain to any one who does not already know it, what yellow is, so you cannot explain what good is.... It is in this sense that I deny good to be definable. I say that it is not composed of any parts, which we can substitute for it in our minds when we are thinking of it.[43]

Euthyphro and action

In the second section of this chapter, I made the point that Lewis believed that to solve the problem of evil it is necessary to make clear that "almighty" does not mean the power to do just anything. In keeping with his positions about "almightiness" and the intrinsic goodness and evilness of pleasure and pain respectively, Lewis espoused the Platonic position on what in philosophy is known as Euthyphro's Dilemma (named after the character Euthyphro in the Platonic dialogue of that name). The Dilemma as applied to the property

---

[43] Moore, *Principia Ethica*, 6, 7, 8. Lewis expressed the Moorean view of the indefinability of "good" and "yellow" in describing the consumption of fruit in the final installment of the Narnia stories, *The Last Battle* (New York: Harper Collins, 1984), 172: "'Here goes then!' said Eustace. And they all began to eat. What was the fruit like? Unfortunately no one can describe a taste."

It appears that Lewis had an interest in the word "good" at an early age. In an essay entitled "Are Athletes Better than Scholars," which was written in 1913 while he attended Cherbourg School, Lewis wrote "No philosopher, however learned, has ever discovered what we exactly mean by the word 'good'." Lewis's statement is cited by Adam Barkman in his *C. S. Lewis and Philosophy as a Way of Life* (Allentown, PA: Zossima Press, 2009), 24.

While James Patrick believes Lewis did not agree with Moore's view of "good," he does discuss Moore in his treatment of Lewis as a moral philosopher. See James Patrick, "The Heart's Desire and the Landlord's Rules: C. S. Lewis as a Moral Philosopher," in *The Pilgrim's Guide: C. S. Lewis and the Art of Witness*, ed. David Mills (Grand Rapids, MI: Eerdmans, 1998), 70–85. The fact that Patrick sees the need to mention Moore when discussing Lewis should alert us to the fact that Lewis' view of "good" raises the specter of Moore.

of being right asks of some action whether God commands that it be right because it is right, or it is right because God commands that it be so. Lewis answered that

> [w]ith Hooker, and against Dr Johnson, I emphatically embrace the first alternative. The second might lead to the abominable conclusion . . . that charity is good only because God arbitrarily commanded it—that He might equally well have commanded us to hate Him and one another and that hatred would then have been right. . . . God's will is determined by His wisdom which always perceives, and His goodness which always embraces, the intrinsically good.[44]

As I hope to make apparent two sections hence, Lewis believed that morality (principles of morally right and wrong action) is basically about the happiness of others. That is, an action is morally right because it is performed for a reason that is concerned in one way or another with the happiness of another person or persons (e.g., with preserving or increasing that happiness). Given that happiness consists in experiences of pleasure that are intrinsically good, God could not command that hatred be morally right because hatred leads to actions whose purpose is either to decrease pleasure or increase pain in the lives of others. Furthermore, God could not command that pleasure be intrinsically evil or pain intrinsically good.

Just as Lewis was keen on pointing out that because pleasure is intrinsically good it is illicit to attempt to have experiences of it in morally wrong ways, so also he was equally intent on making clear that no one pursues what is intrinsically bad or evil for its own sake. Lewis believed that the idea that someone could pursue what is intrinsically evil for its own sake is conceptually incoherent. In writing about Christ's turning water into wine, Lewis emphasized that the miracle, among other things, made clear that God was not a being who "loves tragedy and tears and fasting *for their own sake* (however He may permit or demand them for special purposes) . . . ."[45] While grieving the loss of his wife Joy Davidman, Lewis wrote "But we are not at all—if we understand ourselves—seeking the aches for their own sake."[46] Lewis noted that we come closest to the idea of someone pursuing the bad

---

[44] Lewis, *The Problem of Pain*, 100. Cf. Lewis, *Christian Reflections*, 79–80; *The Pilgrim's Regress* (Grand Rapids, MI: Eerdmans, 1992), 129–30. In a manuscript now referred to as "Early Prose Joy," which is part of a notebook of Lewis's from late 1930 or early 1931, Lewis wrote "[n]o one could argue more hotly than I that a morality which depended on divine command was no morality at all." "Early Prose Joy": C. S. Lewis's Early Draft of an Autobiographical Manuscript." *Seven* 30 (2013): 37.

[45] Lewis, *Miracles*, 221–2.

[46] C. S. Lewis, *A Grief Observed* (New York: HarperSanFrancisco, 2001), 54.

for its own sake in cases of cruelty. Even here, however, Lewis stressed that those who are cruel are so not for the sake of that which is evil. "[C]ruelty does not come from desiring evil as such,"[47] but from the desire for some good, which is either pleasure or something that leads to pleasure:

> But in reality we have no experience of anyone liking badness just because it is bad. The nearest we can get to it is in cruelty. But in real life people are cruel for one of two reasons—either because they are sadists, that is, because they have a sexual perversion which makes cruelty a cause of sensual pleasure to them, or else for the sake of something they are going to get out of it—money, or power, or safety. But pleasure, money, power, and safety are all, as far as they go, good things. The badness consists in pursuing them by the wrong method, or in the wrong way, or too much. I do not mean, of course, that the people who do this are not desperately wicked. I do mean that wickedness, when you examine it, turns out to be the pursuit of some good in the wrong way. You can be good for the sake of goodness: you cannot be bad for the mere sake of badness. . . . [N]o one ever did a cruel action simply because cruelty is wrong—only because cruelty was pleasant or useful to him. . . . In order to be bad he must have good things to want and then to pursue in the wrong way . . . .[48]

However, not all of our activity is immoral, illicit, or vicious. Some is virtuous (done well) and it, too, can and should be a source of pleasure. The fact that habitual virtuous activity can and should provide pleasure for its agent troubled Lewis. A danger, as he saw it, was that the pleasure from such activity could be particularly absorbing and might become an idol and, thereby, supply a motive that would make the performance of the "virtuous" activity a matter of pride:

> This problem of the pleasure in what Aristotle called an "unimpeded activity" is one that exercises me very much . . . when the work done is a duty, or at least innocent.
> On the one hand, Nature, whether we will or know [not], attaches pleasure to doing as well as we can something we can do fairly well: and as it is a clear duty to practise all virtuous activities until we can do them well—possess the Habit of doing them—it is a sort of duty to increase such pleasures. On the other hand, they are pleasures of a particularly urgent, absorbing sort, very apt to become idols, and very closely allied

---

[47] Lewis, *God in the Dock*, 23.
[48] Lewis, *Mere Christianity*, 43–4.

to Pride. I heard it recently said in a Lenten sermon that even self-denial can become a kind of hobby—and in a way it is true.[49]

In light of Lewis's recognition that pleasure can be attached to virtuous activity, it needs to be emphasized that Lewis believed it is the pleasure that accompanies virtuous activity, and not the virtuous activity itself, that constitutes happiness. That Lewis believed this is evidenced by the fact that he could slide effortlessly from talking about the pleasures contained in the hubbub of everyday life (where that life surely includes virtuous activity) to talking about the happiness that is present in that life. In his discussion of Eros or being in love in his book *The Four Loves*, his belief in the connection between pleasure and happiness is evident in the following statement: "As Venus [the animally sexual element] within Eros does not really aim at [the agent's own] pleasure [within Eros, Venus is about the good of the beloved], so Eros does not aim at [the agent's own] happiness."[50] When Lewis wrote about unliterary readers in *An Experiment in Criticism*, he said that "they like stories which enable them—vicariously, through the characters—to participate in pleasure or happiness."[51] When he described riding a bicycle in *Present Concerns*, he stated that

> [cycling] really is a remarkably pleasant motion. . . . Whether there is, or whether there is not, in this world or in any other, the kind of happiness which one's first experiences of cycling seemed to promise, still, on any view, it is something to have had the idea of it. The value of the thing promised remains even if that particular promise was false—even if all possible promises of it are false.[52]

Lewis also affirmed the link between pleasure and happiness in the life of Paradisal man:

> Now Paradisal man always chose to follow God's will. In following it he also gratified his own desire, both because all the actions demanded of him were, in fact, agreeable to his blameless inclination, and also because the service of God was itself his keenest pleasure, without which

---

[49] Lewis, *The Collected Letters of C. S. Lewis: Volume II*, 188.
[50] C. S. Lewis, *The Four Loves* (New York: Harcourt, 1988), 106. Interestingly, Lewis introduced his treatment of the four loves (affection, friendship, Eros, and charity) with a discussion of two types of pleasures, Need-Pleasures and Pleasures of Appreciation (10–11) and described Eros as "the king of pleasures" (96).
[51] C. S. Lewis, *An Experiment in Criticism* (Cambridge: Cambridge University Press, 1961), 37.
[52] C. S. Lewis, *Present Concerns*, (New York: Harcourt, 1986), 67–8.

as their razor edge all joys would have been insipid to him. The question "Am I doing this for God's sake or only because I happen to like it?" did not then arise, since doing things for God's sake was what he chiefly "happened to like." His God-ward will rode his happiness like a well-managed horse . . . . Pleasure was then an acceptable offering to God because offering was a pleasure.[53]

From these citations, it is clear that Lewis believed happiness is composed of experiences of pleasure.[54] Moreover, he affirmed that pleasure can and should accompany virtuous activity. But while he knew pleasures might become idols and allied with pride, he stressed that they need not suffer this fate. Indeed, he thought that when pleasures are understood correctly they actually point us to God:

> We can't—or I can't—hear the song of a bird simply as a sound. Its meaning or message ("That's a bird") comes with it inevitably—just as one can't see a familiar word in print as a merely visual pattern. The reading is as involuntary as the seeing. . . . In the same way it is possible to "read" as well as "have" a pleasure. Or not even "as well as." The distinction ought to become, and sometimes is, impossible; to receive it and to recognise its divine source are a single experience. This heavenly fruit is instantly redolent of the orchard where it grew. This sweet air whispers of the country from whence it blows. It is a message. We know we are being touched by a finger of that right hand at which there are pleasures for evermore. There need be no question of thanks or praise as a separate event, something done afterwards. To experience the tiny theophany is itself to adore.
>
> Gratitude exclaims, very properly, "How good of God to give me this." Adoration says, "What must be the quality of that Being whose far-off and momentary coruscations are like this!" One's mind runs back up the sunbeam to the sun.[55]

Lewis believed that one kind of human activity that diffuses the sunbeam that is pleasure is intellectual activity. For example, in opposition to "that new Puritanism which has captured so many critics and taught us to object to pleasure in poetry simply because it is pleasure,"[56] Lewis insisted that reading

---

[53] Lewis, *The Problem of Pain*, 98.
[54] And happiness excludes pain: "the happiness was all in the past, and the pain all in the present, each clearly excluding its opposite. . . ." "Early Prose Joy," 15.
[55] Lewis, *Letters to Malcolm*, 89–90.
[56] C. S. Lewis, *Selected Literary Essays*, ed. Walter Hooper (Cambridge: Cambridge University Press, 1969), 200–1.

is a legitimate source of pleasure. Thus, he wrote that he derived pleasure from reading ("I think re-reading old favourites is one of the things we differ on, isn't it, and you do it very rarely. I probably do it too much. It is one of my greatest pleasures: indeed I can't imagine a man really enjoying a book and reading it only once."),[57] and he believed that the experiencing of pleasure is a purpose for which it is perfectly appropriate to read ("Our ancestors were sometimes shamelessly frank about the kind of pleasure they demanded from certain kinds of literature.").[58] Not only did Lewis believe that a reader not uncommonly reads for pleasure, but he also thought that when there is more than one plausible reading of a text, the correct reading is likely the one that brings the reader (the most) pleasure. Thus, when commenting on a particular reading of Chaucer's *Canterbury Tales*, Lewis wrote: "And the pleasure which not a few generations have now had in Chaucer thus read is strong, though not conclusive, evidence that they have read him correctly."[59] Pleasure could serve as a criterion of a correct reading only because an author like Chaucer wrote with the purpose of giving his readers experiences of pleasure. And pleasure was not only for the reader. As Lewis pointed out, he wrote for pleasure. "The truth is that I have a constant temptation to over asperity as soon as I get a pen in my hand, even when there is no subjective anger to prompt me: it comes, I think, simply from the pleasure of using the English language forcibly . . . ."[60]

For the sake of making clear distinctions, we can call the kind of pleasures mentioned in the previous paragraph *mental* pleasures. Lewis also believed that physical activity is a source of pleasure. These *physical* pleasures or "pleasures of the body"[61] include those that come from something as momentary as scratching an itch[62] and as lengthy as a walking tour. The academic philologist, Ransom, in Lewis's science fiction novel *Out of the Silent Planet*, most surely expresses Lewis's reason for walking in the following exchange:

> "How do you come to be in this benighted part of the country?"
> "I'm on a walking-tour, said Ransom . . . ."
> "God!" exclaimed Devine. . . . Do you do it for money, or is it sheer masochism?"
> "Pleasure, of course," said Ransom . . . .[63]

---

[57] Lewis, *The Collected Letters of C. S. Lewis: Volume II*, 54.
[58] Lewis, *Selected Literary Essays*, 173.
[59] Lewis, *Selected Literary Essays*, 54.
[60] Lewis, *The Collected Letters of C. S. Lewis: Volume II*, 187.
[61] Lewis, *Selected Literary Essays*, 113.
[62] Lewis, *Selected Literary Essays*, 300.
[63] Lewis, *Out of the Silent Planet*, 18.

And physical pleasures can be mixed with mental pleasures. For example, in a letter to Mary van Deusen he wrote the following about physical and mixed pleasures:

> I feel strongly, with you, that there was something more than a physical pleasure in those youthful activities. Even now, at my age, do we often have a *purely* physical pleasure? Well, perhaps, a few of the more hopelessly prosaic ones; say, scratching or getting one's shoes off when one's feet are tired. I'm sure my meals are not a purely physical pleasure. All the associations of every other time one has had the same food (every rasher of bacon is now 56 years thick with me) come in: and with things like Bread, Wine, Honey, Apples, there are all the echoes of myth, fairy-tale, poetry, [and] scripture.[64]

The memories of earlier pleasures led Lewis to write on a different occasion that "A pleasure is full grown only when it is remembered."[65]

A treatment of Lewis's view of happiness would be incomplete without mentioning friendship. In his autobiography, *Surprised by Joy*, Lewis wrote that "[f]riendship has been by far the chief source of my happiness . . . ."[66] Friendship is not identical with happiness but is a source of it. And how is this? Lewis tells us in *The Four Loves* that

> [f]riendship arises out of mere Companionship when two or more of the companions discover that they have in common some insight or interest or even taste which the others do not share and which, till that moment, each believed to be his own unique treasure (or burden). The typical expression of opening Friendship would be something like, "What? You too? I thought I was the only one."[67]

Given that Lewis believed pleasure can be derived from both mental and bodily sources, it is fair to conclude that the shared interest of friendship can be either mental (e.g., literature) or bodily (e.g., walking) in nature.

Hedonism

Lewis was well aware that his claim that pleasure is intrinsically good would lead to the charge that he was a hedonist. For example, in the letter to Canon

---

[64] Lewis, *The Collected Letters of C. S. Lewis: Volume III*, 583.
[65] Lewis, *Out of the Silent Planet*, 74.
[66] C. S. Lewis, *Surprised by Joy* (New York: Harcourt, Inc., 1955), 33.
[67] Lewis, *The Four Loves*, 65.

Quick from which I quoted in the Introduction, Lewis said about his book *The Problem of Pain* that "I wasn't writing on the Problem of Pleasure! If I had been you might find my views *too* hedonistic. I [would] say that every pleasure (even the lowest) is a likeness to, even, in its restricted mode, a foretaste of, the end for [which] we exist, the fruition of God."[68] Because Lewis's conception of happiness was hedonistic, he had Screwtape complain about God that "He's a hedonist at heart. . . . He makes no secret of it; . . . He's vulgar . . . . He has a bourgeois mind."[69] What is interesting is that this intellectual attraction to a hedonistic conception of happiness in which happiness is of supreme value appears early in Lewis's life. In a letter to his father in late October 1914, from which I also quoted in the Introduction, Lewis wrote "[l]et us have wisdom by all means, so long as it makes us happy: but as soon as it runs against our peace of mind, let us throw it away and 'carpe diem'."[70]

The matter of hedonism also arose for Lewis in the context of his treatment of literature. In his book *An Experiment in Criticism*, he discussed the goodness of literature and agreed that there is a specific literary good. "Some readers may complain that I have not made clear what this good is. Am I, they may ask, putting forward a hedonistic theory and identifying the literary good with pleasure?"[71] In giving an affirmative answer to the inquiry, Lewis distinguished between a work of literary art as *Logos* (something said) and *Poiema* (something made).[72] The Poiema of a literary work involves its aural beauties and the balance and contrast and unified multiplicity of its successive parts. As such, it is shaped for the purpose of providing satisfaction and "[o]ur experience of the work as Poiema is unquestionably a keen pleasure."[73] Lewis then launched into a lengthy discussion of the pleasure that is proper to a literary work and said that there are many sources of it, including the exercise of mental faculties such as imagination and the order of thoughts prescribed, in the case of poetry, by the poet.[74]

Strictly speaking, hedonism is the philosophical thesis that pleasure is not only intrinsically good but also that it is the *only* intrinsic good, and that happiness is constituted by experiences of pleasure. Thus, if Lewis, though a hedonist about happiness, was not a philosophical hedonist, he must have recognized the existence of some other intrinsic good. And this

---

[68] Lewis, *The Collected Letters of C. S. Lewis: Volume II*, 463.
[69] Lewis, *The Screwtape Letters*, 101.
[70] Lewis, *The Collected Letters of C. S. Lewis: Volume I*, 85.
[71] Lewis, *An Experiment in Criticism*, 130.
[72] Lewis, *An Experiment in Criticism*, 132.
[73] Lewis, *An Experiment in Criticism*, 132.
[74] Lewis, *An Experiment in Criticism*, 133-4.

he did. In "Hedonics" he says that "We have had enough, once and for all, of Hedonism – the gloomy philosophy which says that Pleasure is the only [intrinsic] good."[75] In *The Problem of Pain*, Lewis argued that justice, which is the idea that a person should receive what he is due, is an additional intrinsic good that requires that unrepentant people be denied the happiness for which he believed they were created. Of the unrepentant person, Lewis wrote:

> Supposing he *will* not be converted, what destiny in the eternal world can you regard as proper for him? Can you really desire that such a man, *remaining what he is* (and he must be able to do that if he has free will) should be confirmed forever in his present happiness—should continue, for all eternity, to be perfectly convinced that the laugh is on his side? And if you cannot regard this as tolerable, is it only your wickedness— only spite—that prevents you from doing so? Or do you find that conflict between Justice and Mercy, which has sometimes seemed to you such an outmoded piece of theology, now actually at work in your own mind, and feeling very much as if it came to you from above, not from below? You are moved, not by a desire for the wretched creature's pain as such, but by a truly ethical demand that, soon or late, the right should be asserted, the flag planted in this horribly rebellious soul, even if no fuller and better conquest is to follow.[76]

As I have already pointed out, Lewis believed that our experiences of pleasure are really a likeness to and a foretaste of our enjoyment of God.[77] He maintained that our enjoyment of God is the end for which we exist and that this end is complete or perfect happiness: "God not only understands but *shares* the desire . . . for complete and ecstatic happiness. He made me for no other purpose than to enjoy it."[78] And in *The Great Divorce*, one of the Ghosts says "I wish I'd never been born . . . . What *are* we born for?" To which a Spirit answers, "For infinite happiness."[79] According to Lewis, infinite, complete, or ecstatic happiness is the life of the blessed and we must suppose "the life of

---

[75] Lewis, *Present Concerns*, 54–5.
[76] Lewis, *The Problem of Pain*, 121–2.
[77] Lewis, *The Collected Letters of C. S. Lewis: Volume II*, 463. In commenting on Lewis' *Letters to Malcolm*, Richard J. Mouw writes that "[w]hat Malcolm fails to understand, Lewis claims, is that even the most frivolous sorts of pleasures can function as 'shafts of glory' that awaits [sic] us in the end time. . . . Lewis talks about how ordinary experiences, particularly pleasures, are anticipations of the future glory. . . ." "Surprised by Calvin." *First Things* 191 March (2009): 15.
[78] Lewis, *The Collected Letters of C. S. Lewis: Volume II*, 123.
[79] C. S. Lewis, *The Great Divorce* (New York: Harper San Francisco, 2001), 61.

the blessed to be an end in itself, indeed The End...."[80] Writing at the outset of the Second World War, Lewis made clear that God not only made him for no other purpose than perfect happiness, but He also made others for the same purpose, even members of the Gestapo:

> In fact I provisionally define Agapë as "steadily remembering that inside the Gestapo-man there is a thing [which] says I and Me just as you do, which has just the same grounds (neither more nor less) as your 'Me' for being distinguished from all its sins however numerous, which, like you, was made by God for eternal happiness...."[81]

The relation between happiness and morality

Lewis believed that (i) God created each of us to be perfectly happy; (ii) perfect happiness is comprised of nothing but experiences of pleasure; and (iii) pleasure is intrinsically good. Lewis also believed that because pleasure is intrinsically good, (iv) we desire it (and perfect happiness) for its own sake. But though we are created for perfect happiness and desire it for its own sake, it is not morally (ethically) permissible to pursue it in just any way whatsoever. How, on Lewis's view, is happiness related to morality (ethics)?

According to Lewis, we as ordinary people begin our thought about morality with the following commonsensical idea:

> The ordinary idea which we all have before we become Christians is this. We take as our starting point our ordinary self with its various desires and interests. We then admit that something else—call it "morality" or "decent behaviour"... —has claims on this self: claims which interfere with its own desires. What we mean by "being good" is giving in to those claims. Some of the things the ordinary self wanted to do turn out to be what we call "wrong": well, we must give them up.[82]

Morality involves giving things up; it involves self-restraint and going without. "But," one might ask, "*Why* should I give up those things that will satisfy my desires? What is the object or concern of this 'morality' that calls upon me to temporarily delay or permanently reject the satisfaction of my desires?"

---

[80] Lewis, *Letters to Malcolm*, 92.
[81] Lewis, *The Collected Letters of C. S. Lewis: Volume II*, 409.
[82] Lewis, *Mere Christianity*, 195.

Elsewhere, Lewis pointed out that many think of the purpose of virtue as unselfishness or self-denial. He believed this view is mistaken:

> If you asked twenty good men today what they thought the highest of the virtues, nineteen would reply, Unselfishness. But if you had asked almost any of the great Christians of old, he would have replied, Love. You see what has happened? A negative term has been substituted for a positive, and this is of more than philological importance. The negative idea of Unselfishness carries with it the suggestion not primarily of securing good things for others, but of going without them ourselves, as if our abstinence and not their happiness was the important point. I do not think this is the Christian virtue of Love. The New Testament has lots to say about self-denial, but not about self-denial as an end in itself.[83]

If the purpose of virtue in the form of unselfishness is not self-denial, what is it? In the passage just cited, Lewis gave the following answer: the virtuous or moral person exercises restraint in pursuit of what is good for himself for the sake of the *happiness* of others.[84] In *The Screwtape Letters*, the goal of Screwtape and his cohorts is to get people to think precisely the opposite of what is true: it is to "teach a man to surrender benefits not that others may be happy [which is the right reason for the surrender] but that he may be unselfish in forgoing them [which is the wrong reason for the surrender]."[85] In short, the view that one sacrifices goods that would benefit oneself for the purpose of being unselfish and not for the sake of the happiness of someone else is of the devil.

---

[83] Lewis, *The Weight of Glory*, 25.

[84] In *Mere Christianity*, 72, Lewis made clear that in our ordinary thinking morality is primarily about dealings with others: "Morality, then, seems to be concerned with three things. Firstly, with fair play and harmony between individuals. Secondly, with what might be called tidying up or harmonising the things inside each individual. Thirdly, with the general purpose of human life as a whole: what man was made for: what course the whole fleet ought to be on.... And it is quite natural, when we start thinking about morality, to begin with the first thing, with social relations."

Julia Annas writes that "intuitively ethics is thought to be about the good of others, so that focusing on your own good seems wrong from the start." Julia Annas, "Virtue Ethics and the Charge of Egoism," in *Morality and Self-Interest*, ed. Paul Bloomfield (Oxford: Oxford University Press, 2008), 205, footnote 1. Elsewhere, she makes clear that this other-directedness understanding of morality is the view of most people: "Aristotle in the *Rhetoric* makes it plain that most people tended to see the ... characteristic aim of the virtuous person, as being associated with acting in the interests of others, as opposed to your own." *The Morality of Happiness* (Oxford: Oxford University Press, 1993), 323–4. The "view of most people" is the commonsensical view. Thus, it is not surprising that Lewis espoused it.

[85] Lewis, *The Screwtape Letters*, 121.

Common sense believes that morality requires restraint on the agent's part for the sake of the happiness (the good) of others. Lewis also drew our attention to the happiness of others in his treatment of kindness. In his words, kindness is "the desire to see others than the self happy; not happy in this or in that, but just happy."[86] And what about love? Lewis maintained that it "is not affectionate feeling, but a steady wish for the loved person's ultimate good as far as it can be obtained."[87] And insofar as love of another person is wishing for that person's ultimate good, it is like our love for ourselves, where the expression "love for ourselves" means "we wish our own good."[88]

Because morality is concerned with the happiness of others, being moral can lead to the sacrifice of one's own happiness. In making this point, Lewis recalled an elderly acquaintance of his when he (Lewis) was answering a question about which of the world's religions provides the greatest happiness:

> Which of the religions of the world gives to its followers the greatest happiness? While it lasts, the religion of worshipping oneself is the best.
>
> I have an elderly acquaintance of about eighty, who has lived a life of unbroken selfishness and self-admiration from the earliest years, and is, more or less, I regret to say, one of the happiest men I know. From the moral point of view it is very difficult! I am not approaching the question from that angle. As you perhaps know, I haven't always been a Christian. I didn't go to religion to make me happy. I always knew that a bottle of Port would do that. If you want a religion to make you feel really comfortable, I certainly don't recommend Christianity.[89]

If you want the comfort of happiness *in this life* for yourself, look elsewhere than to Christianity. So Lewis advised. Two points are relevant here. First, those who look for permanent happiness in this life are deceiving themselves (and, by implication, others). In an essay on the thought of William Morris, Lewis pointed out how the political left deceives itself if it thinks that enduring happiness is located in this world:

> The Left agrees with Morris that it is an absolute duty to labour for human happiness in this world. But the Left is deceiving itself if it thinks that any zeal for this object can permanently silence the reflection that every moment of this happiness must be lost as soon as gained, that all who

---

[86] Lewis, *The Problem of Pain*, 40.
[87] Lewis, *God in the Dock*, 49.
[88] Lewis, *Mere Christianity*, 129–30.
[89] Lewis, *God in the Dock*, 58.

enjoy it will die, that the race and the planet themselves must one day follow the individual into a state of being which has no significance—a universe of inorganic homogeneous matter moving at uniform speed in a low temperature. Hitherto the Left has been content, as far as I know, to pretend that this does not matter.[90]

Second, while perfect happiness is only available in another life, there is no reason to deny that some degree of happiness can be had in this life. But Lewis believed that not only would one be better off not thinking about earthbound happiness, but also there is the risk that too much of this happiness could lead one to forget about the ultimate Giver of it:

> How right you are: the great thing is to stop thinking about happiness. Indeed the best thing about happiness itself is that it liberates you from thinking about happiness—as the greatest pleasure that money can give us is to make it unnecessary to think about money. . . .
>
> Here is one of the fruits of unhappiness: that it forces us to think of life as something to go *through*. And out at the other end. If only we could steadfastly do that while we are happy. I suppose we [should] need no misfortunes. It is hard on God really. To how few of us He *dare* send happiness because He knows we will forget Him if He gave us any sort of nice things for the moment . . . .[91]

And what goes for happiness goes for pleasure, which is how it must be if the former is composed of instances of the latter. Thus, while God "shouts in our pain," He "whispers to us in our pleasures."[92]

Given that the experience of happiness and pleasures that compose it can induce forgetfulness of their divine source,[93] some individuals go so far as to claim that the desire for perfect happiness is bad. Lewis categorically disagreed with them:

> If there lurks in most modern minds the notion that to desire our own good and earnestly to hope for the enjoyment of it is a bad thing, I submit that this notion . . . is no part of the Christian faith. Indeed, if we consider the unblushing promises of reward and the staggering nature of the rewards promised in the Gospels, it would seem that Our

---

[90] Lewis, *Selected Literary Essays*, 230.
[91] Lewis, *The Collected Letters of C. S. Lewis: Volume III*, 93.
[92] Lewis, *The Problem of Pain*, 93.
[93] "When you are happy, so happy that you have no sense of needing Him, so happy that you are tempted to feel His claims upon you as an interruption . . . ." Lewis, *A Grief Observed*, 5–6.

Lord finds our desires not too strong, but too weak. We are half-hearted creatures, fooling about with drink and sex and ambition when infinite joy is offered us, like an ignorant child who wants to go on making mud pies in a slum because he cannot imagine what is meant by the offer of a holiday at the sea.[94]

Not only is the desire for perfect happiness not bad, but also Lewis believed that the desire for it is itself evidence for the existence of the afterlife:

[W]e remain conscious of a desire which no natural happiness will satisfy. But is there any reason to suppose that reality offers any satisfaction to it? "Nor does being hungry prove that we have bread." But I think it may be urged that this misses the point. A man's physical hunger does not prove that man will get any bread; he may die of starvation on a raft in the Atlantic. But surely a man's hunger does prove that he comes of a race which repairs its body by eating and inhabits a world where eatable substances exist. In the same way, though I do not believe (I wish I did) that my desire for Paradise proves that I shall enjoy it, I think it a pretty good indication that such a thing exists and that some men will.[95]

Elsewhere, Lewis wrote that a Christian is "one [who] believes that men are going to live forever, [and] that they were created by God and so built that they can find their true and lasting happiness only by being united to God. . . ."[96] And he believed that being united to God was like being at home: "As Dr Johnson said, 'To be happy at home is the end of all human endeavour'. (1st to be happy, to prepare for being happy in our real Home hereafter: 2nd, in the meantime, to be happy in our houses.)."[97]

Lewis believed that the desire for perfect happiness is itself evidence for the existence of the paradisal afterlife. What warrants repeating is that Lewis believed this happiness consists of nothing but experiences of pleasure. Some people who write about Lewis's belief concerning the availability of perfect happiness in the afterlife fail to mention that he was a hedonist about happiness. For example, in his recent book *Surprised by Meaning*, Alister McGrath claims that our heart's desire in this life is for a better world, where this better world is our true home.[98] McGrath goes on to write that Lewis

---

[94] Lewis, *The Weight of Glory*, 26.
[95] Lewis, *The Weight of Glory*, 32–3.
[96] Lewis, *God in the Dock*, 109.
[97] Lewis, *The Collected Letters of C. S. Lewis: Volume III*, 580.
[98] Alister E. McGrath, *Surprised by Meaning* (Louisville, KY: Westminster John Knox Press, 2011), 91.

believed "human longing is primarily concerned with intimating another transcendent world, the inhabitation of which is the ultimate goal of our life. It is only secondarily concerned with the existence of God, even though this transcendent realm is indeed the 'kingdom of God.'"[99] When McGrath provides Lewis's characterization of this transcendent realm, he describes it as an order of existence in which there is no pain and suffering, but only beauty, meaning, and significance.[100]

What needs to be stressed here is how McGrath's description of Lewis's view strangely leaves out any mention of pleasure. One cannot help but wonder how McGrath could have missed Lewis's emphasis on happiness and pleasure. For Lewis, the Kingdom of God is first and foremost a place of perfect happiness that, while it requires the absence of pain and suffering, consists in positive experiences of pleasure. One must remember that the absence of pain and suffering is consistent with the absence of pleasure and happiness (the absence of pain and suffering does not entail the presence of pleasure and happiness). Such a state would be value neutral. It is impossible to avoid the conclusion that Lewis would have regarded McGrath's treatment of his (Lewis's) view of the transcendent realm as seriously deficient.

Surprised by Meaning is one of McGrath's most recent books.[101] Twenty-three years earlier, he wrote *Justification by Faith*. In it, he said the following about hedonism and Lewis:

> The paradox of hedonism—the simple yet stultifying fact that pleasure cannot satisfy—is another instance of [the phenomenon of recognizing that what we are seeking is not located in what we desire but beyond it]. Pleasure, beauty, personal relationships—all seem to promise so much, and yet when we grasp them we find what we were seeking was not located in them, but lies beyond them. The great English literary critic and theologian C. S. Lewis captured this insight perfectly:
>
>> The books or the music in which we thought the beauty was located will betray us if we trust in them; it was not *in* them, it only came *through* them, and what came through them was longing. These things—the beauty, the memory of our own past—are good images

---

[99] McGrath, *Surprised by Meaning*, 95.
[100] McGrath, *Surprised by Meaning*, 91, 94, 98.
[101] In his recent book *The Intellectual World of C.S. Lewis* (139), McGrath says that for Lewis "[t]he real apologetic issue was about the meaning of life...." Nowhere in the book does McGrath talk about the meaning of life as the experience of happiness (pleasure) as a key idea in Lewis's intellectual world.

of what we really desire; but if they are mistaken for the thing itself they turn into dumb idols, breaking the hearts of their worshippers. For they are not the thing itself; they are only the scent of a flower we have not found, the echo of a tune we have not heard, news from a country we have not visited.[102]

As I have already mentioned, Lewis revealed in a letter that were he to have written on the problem of pleasure, one would have thought that he was a hedonist. And he described God as a hedonist. So McGrath's intimation that Lewis would have had problems with a hedonistic view of happiness because pleasure cannot satisfy is simply wrong. As will become evident later in this chapter in the section on Joy or Sehnsucht, Lewis did believe, as McGrath points out, that we are all longing for some object located in another world and of which the objects of this world are like scents and echoes. But these objects function as scents and echoes in their capacity as sources of pleasure. While what they supply is intrinsically good, their transience makes us long for a source of pleasure that is constant and forevermore. Lewis came to believe that only God in another life can provide the unceasing and everlasting pleasure that we so deeply desire because of its goodness.

Lewis was well aware that mention of goodness often immediately turns a person's attention to morality. Given that this is the case, it is easy for an individual to think that goodness itself is strictly moral in nature and that with which the living of life is ultimately concerned. Lewis disagreed and sought to make clear that perfect happiness is what is fundamentally good and lasts forever, while moral goodness is transitory:

> All right, Christianity will do you good—a great deal more good than you ever wanted or expected. And the first bit of good it will do you is to hammer into your head . . . the fact that what you have hitherto called "good"—all that about "leading a decent life" and "being kind"—isn't quite the magnificent and all-important affair you supposed. It will teach you that in fact you can't be "good" (not for twenty-four hours) on your own moral efforts. And then it will teach you that even if you were, you still wouldn't have achieved the purpose for which you were created. Mere *morality* is not the end of life. You were made

---

[102] Alister McGrath, *Justification by Faith* (Grand Rapids, MI: Zondervan, 1988), 111–12. The Lewis citation, which is very slightly inaccurate, comes from *The Weight of Glory*, 30–1.

for something quite different from that. . . . The people who keep on asking if they can't lead a decent life without Christ, don't know what life is about; if they did they would know that a "decent life" is mere machinery compared with the thing we men are really made for. Morality is indispensible: but the Divine Life, which gives itself to us and which calls us to be gods, intends for us something in which morality will be swallowed up.[103]

[The moral realm] exists to be transcended. . . . [It is a] schoolmaster, as St. Paul says, to bring us to Christ. We must expect no more of it than of a schoolmaster; we must allow it no less. I must say my prayers to-day whether I feel devout or not; but that is only as I must learn my grammar if I am ever to read the poets.

But the school-days, please God, are numbered. There is no morality in Heaven. The angels never knew (from within) the meaning of the word *ought*, and the blessed dead have long since gladly forgotten it.[104]

There is more. Not only will morality ultimately be swallowed up by the perfected state of ecstatic happiness, but so also will the freedom of the will, at least as it is expressed in morality:

You may ask, do I then think that moral value will have no place in the state of perfection? Well it sounds a dreadful thing to say, but I'm almost inclined to answer No. It [the state of perfection] is never presented in Scripture in terms of service is it?—always in terms of suggesting fruition—a supper, a marriage, a drink. "I will give him the morning star." May not that be one of the divine jokes—to see people like Marcus Aurelius and [Matthew] Arnold & [John Stuart] Mill at last submitting to the fact that they can give up being *good** and start *receiving* good instead.

*I don't mean, of course, "can begin being bad", but that when the *beata necessitas non peccandi* [the blessed necessity of not sinning] is attained, the will—the perilous bridge by [which] we get home—will cease to be the important thing or to exist, as we now know it, at all. The sword will be beaten into a ploughshare. The supreme volition of self-surrender is thus a *good suicide* of will: we will thus once, in order to will no more.[105]

---

[103] Lewis, *God in the Dock*, 112.
[104] Lewis, *Letters to Malcolm*, 115.
[105] Lewis, *The Collected Letters of C. S. Lewis: Volume II*, 463–4.

Eudaemonism

The literary evidence is clear: Lewis was a hedonist about happiness. He believed that happiness consists of nothing but experiences of pleasure. However, some have claimed otherwise. For example, James Patrick says that Lewis was "a convinced eudaemonist."[106] Unfortunately, Patrick never tells the reader what he means by "eudaemonist." Adam Barkman is a bit more informative. After telling us that Lewis was a eudaemonist about happiness, he goes on to explain that in calling Lewis a eudaemonist he means that Lewis believed virtue (a disposition to act in a certain way) is a part of happiness. For example, he says that "Lewis agreed with Plato (and . . . also with Aristotle) that although virtue is a means to happiness, it is also an essential part of happiness . . . ."[107] Indeed, according to Barkman, "Lewis, borrowing insight from the Christian Boethius, insisted that virtue constitutes not only part of our temporary happiness, but also part of our eternal Happiness—our Happiness in Heaven."[108] To support these claims, Barkman quotes the following passage from Lewis's *Mere Christianity*:

> We might think that the "virtues" were necessary only for this present life—that in the other world we could stop being just because there is nothing to quarrel about and stop being brave because there is no danger. Now it is quite true that there will probably be no occasion for just or courageous acts in the next world, but there will be every occasion for being the sort of people that we can become only as the result of doing such acts here. The point is not that God will refuse you admission to His eternal world if you have not got certain qualities of character: the point is that if people have not got at least the beginnings of those qualities inside them, then no possible external conditions could make a "Heaven" for them—that is, could make them happy with the deep, strong, unshakable kind of happiness God intends for us.[109]

Nowhere in this extended passage did Lewis say that virtue is a *part* of happiness in either this or the heavenly life. At most, he conveyed the idea that virtue is a *necessary condition* of happiness (a condition without which

---

[106] Patrick, *The Magdalen Metaphysicals*, 127. *Eudaemonia* comes from the Greek words *eu* (good) and *daimōn* (spirit). It was roughly the idea of having a good spirit, and this came to mean (again roughly) that personal well-being is the chief end of man. However, the idea of personal well-being cries out for some definition.
[107] Barkman, *C. S. Lewis and Philosophy as a Way of Life*, 395.
[108] Barkman, *C. S. Lewis and Philosophy as a Way of Life*, Cf. 403.
[109] Lewis, *Mere Christianity*, 80–1.

one cannot be happy). However, it does not follow from the fact that one thing is a necessary condition of another that the former is a part of the latter.

David Horner claims Lewis was a eudaemonist who believed that happiness does not consist of experiences of pleasure. In an online article entitled "The Pursuit of Happiness: C. S. Lewis' Eudaimonistic Understanding of Ethics," Horner states that "the 'pursuit of happiness,' for us [as opposed to classical thinkers, among whom Horner counts Lewis], is not a specifically moral pursuit. At best, it is *non*moral, a matter of prudential self-interest.... These days, our English word 'happiness' usually refers to a ... subjective state of pleasure.... But classical thinkers seldom, if ever, conceived of *eudaimonia* in that way."[110]

All the literary evidence I have provided to this point indicates that Lewis was a modern insofar as he believed happiness consists of nothing but nonmoral experiences of pleasure. If we think in terms of moral virtue, then, as I made clear in the previous section, Lewis explicitly maintained that moral activity will have no place in the perfectly happy life of heaven. Thus, the idea that he was a eudaemonist who believed that happiness consists of virtuous activity is hard to square with what he wrote.[111] Again, Lewis's view was not

[110] David Horner, "The Pursuit of Happiness: C. S. Lewis's Eudaimonistic Understanding of Ethics," *In Pursuit of Truth/A Journal of Christian Scholarship*, April 21, 2009. http://www.cslewis.org/journal.

Nicholas Wolterstorff makes the same point about classical thought in response to the question "What Is Eudaimonism?": "The eudaimonist holds that the ultimate and comprehensive goal of each of us is that we live our lives as well as possible, the well-lived life being, by definition, the happy life, the *eudaimōn* life.... It is important to understand what sort of goal happiness is. 'Happiness' is not the name of experience of a certain sort. 'Pleasure' names experiences of a certain sort; 'happiness' does not. The eudaimonist is not saying that one's sole end in itself is or should be bringing about experiences of a certain sort, everything else being a means.... [T]he ancient eudaimonists insisted that *eudaimonia* is activity. Happiness does not consist in what happens to one but in what one makes of what happens to one." *Justice: Rights and Wrongs* (Princeton: Princeton University Press, 2008), 150, 151, 152.

[111] In a published exchange that I have had with Horner (Stewart Goetz, "C. S. Lewis on Pleasure and Happiness," *Christian Scholar's Review* 40 (2011): 283–302; and David A. Horner, "C. S. Lewis is a Eudaimonist," *Christian Scholar's Review* 40 (2011): 303–10), he points out that I erroneously understood him to be claiming that Lewis was a eudaimonist in the Aristotelian sense that happiness is synonymous with (or just is) doing or living well, or consists in living a moral or virtuous life. *Mea culpa*. But if Lewis was not an Aristotelian eudaemonist, what kind of a eudaemonist was he? According to Horner, Lewis affirmed the classical idea that to desire one's own good and earnestly hope for the enjoyment of it is a good thing and central to what morality is all about. Thus, Lewis disagreed with the modern orientation toward morality, which maintains that all considerations of the agent's happiness are irrelevant to, or even incompatible with, the demands of morality.

Lewis did believe that agents desire and hope for their happiness. But it does not follow from this that he also was a eudaemonist in the sense that he believed the happiness of agents is central to what morality is all about. It is thoroughly consistent to hold, as

that there will be no morally virtuous individuals in the heavenly realm. Given the existence of community in that life, it is required that its members be of such a nature that they make each other happy "with the deep, strong, unshakable kind of happiness God intends for us."[112] But Lewis believed that because the virtuous in heaven will "spontaneously and delightfully"[113] do what they do from the resources of a fixed character, what they do will have no moral value:

> Kant thought that no action had moral value unless it were done out of pure reverence for the moral law, that is, without inclination . . . . All popular opinion is, indeed, on Kant's side. The people never admire a man for doing something he likes: the very words "But he *likes* it" imply the corollary "And therefore it has no merit." Yet against Kant stands the obvious truth, noted by Aristotle, that the more virtuous a man becomes the more he enjoys virtuous actions. . . .
>
> We therefore agree with Aristotle that what is intrinsically right may well be agreeable, and that the better a man is the more he will like it; but we agree with Kant so far as to say that there is one right act—that of self surrender—which cannot be willed to the height by fallen creatures unless it is unpleasant.[114]

Lewis did, that agents desire their happiness while believing that morality is primarily concerned with the good of others. Moreover, considerations of an agent's happiness can ultimately be relevant to and compatible with the demands of morality, as Lewis believed, in the following non-eudaemonist way: being moral guarantees being perfectly happy in the end because God gives the morally upright the happiness for which they so deeply yearn. As Nicholas White points out, there are two ways in which to avoid an ultimate conflict between morality and one's own happiness: "either because happiness, being all-inclusive, therefore includes being moral or morally upright [which is the standard understanding of eudaemonism], or because being morally upright guarantees being happy (perhaps through divine agency) . . . ." White, *A Brief History of Happiness*, 119. Lewis affirmed the latter alternative, without ever embracing the former.

In the end, Horner maintains that Lewis believed happiness consists neither of experiences of pleasure ("The Pursuit of Happiness") nor in living or doing well or moral or virtuous action ("C. S. Lewis is a Eudaimonist"). In what, then, did Lewis believe happiness consists? What about intellectual virtue—actively contemplating truth or God? Lewis obviously believed happiness did not consist of this in the present life and, as I will discuss in Chapter 4, he believed it did not consist of this in the afterlife.

[112] Lewis, *Mere Christianity*, 81.
[113] Lewis, *Letters to Malcolm*, 115.
[114] Lewis, *The Problem of Pain*, 99–100, 101. Lewis was a Kantian about ethics long before he wrote *The Problem of Pain* in 1940. For example, he wrote the following in his correspondence with his friend Owen Barfield in 1930: "Whenever an act is done an attempt is made for certain motives to bring about a certain result, and certain consequences follow. Whether these consequences coincide with the result intended or not is morally irrelevant. Nor can they ever do so. For the consequences continue as long as time, but the intended result is definite. The moral quality of the act depends solely on the intention and motive. Thus A gives to B a drug intending to save him, because

Philosophers distinguish between events with respect to which persons are passive (the events happen to them; such events are passions) and those with respect to which they are active (the events are done by them; they are actions). Now an experience of pleasure is an event with respect to which a person is essentially *passive* and over which he lacks ultimate control. In light of Lewis's belief that happiness is composed of experiences of pleasure, the natural conclusions to draw are that he also believed the happiness available in this life is subject to a significant degree of luck and, therefore, that he rejected eudaemonism. Not so, according to Horner. In his mind, Lewis, like classical eudaemonists, believed that happiness in this life is not a matter of luck.[115] Here is what Lewis had to say about the matter of happiness and luck:

> I went away [from a discussion] thinking about the concept of a "right to happiness".
> At first this sounds to me as odd as a right to good luck. For I believe—whatever one school of moralists may say—that we depend for a very great deal of our happiness . . . on circumstances outside all human control. A right to happiness doesn't, for me, make much more sense than a right to be six feet tall, or to have a millionaire for your father, or to get good weather whenever you want to have a picnic.[116]

In making his case that Lewis was a eudaemonist, Horner says that "All too often, the pursuit of happiness represents to us something actually *im*moral: 'because I want to be happy' is probably the most common reason we hear— or give—for justifying morally wrong behavior. . . . But Lewis disagrees."[117] But Lewis did not disagree. Indeed, it is evident from the just-completed survey of his thought about pleasure and happiness that he believed the desire for pleasure and happiness is what leads people to act immorally. People are cruel because they want to experience the intrinsic goodness of pleasure and cannot achieve their goal through permissible means. No one,

---

B living is of use to him, and actually (because the bottle was wrongly labelled) kills him. A gives B a drug intending to save him, through charity, and actually kills him. A gives B a drug intending to kill him, because B stands between him and an end and actually saves him. A gives B a drug intending to kill him, because that is the only way to rid the world of a tyrant, and actually saves him. It will be seen that in all these cases the consequences made no difference (morally), but that every change in the intention and motive creates a new moral situation." *De Bono et Malo*. Even earlier in 1928, Lewis wrote: "a sound theory of ethics, such as was propounded by Kant . . . ." See his *Summa Metaphysices contra Anthroposophos*, CSL/MS-29/X, The Marion E. Wade Center, Wheaton College, Wheaton, IL, Part II, Section V.

[115] Horner, "The Pursuit of Happiness."
[116] Lewis, *God in the Dock*, 318.
[117] Horner, "The Pursuit of Happiness."

Lewis said, acts badly for the sake of acting badly. They act badly to get the pleasure that they desire and rightly believe constitutes their happiness. And they desire this pleasure and happiness because, as he emphasized, pleasure is intrinsically good.

The fact that Lewis believed pleasure is intrinsically good helps to clarify in one other way why he was not a eudaemonist. Nicholas Wolterstorff writes that "[e]udaimonism thinks of non-instrumental [intrinsic] goods as . . . activities; hence we get its understanding of well-being as the well-lived life. . . . All eudaimonists agreed that actions of living well are the only non-instrumental goods."[118] Lewis believed it is false that all intrinsic goods are actions. The primary intrinsic good is pleasure, a passion, and well-being consists of experiences of it, not the actions that produce it.

In considering whether Lewis was a eudaemonist about happiness, I have to this point focused on specific things Lewis said about happiness and pleasure that support the case that he was not. However, there is a more general consideration that works against his being a eudaemonist. This is the fact that Lewis was a believer in common sense and eudaemonism is anything but commonsensical in nature. Julia Annas reminds us of this important point about eudaemonism:

> [A]ncient [eudaemonistic] theories are all more or less revisionary, and some of them are highly counterintuitive. They give an account of happiness which, if baldly presented to a non-philosopher without any of the supporting arguments, sounds wrong, even absurd. . . . [A]ncient theories greatly expand and modify the ordinary non-philosophical understanding of happiness, opening themselves up to criticism from non-philosophers on this score.
>
> It is in fact common ground to the ancient theories that, on the one hand, we are all right to assume that our final end is happiness of some kind, and to try to achieve happiness in reflecting systematically on our final end; but that, on the other hand, we are very far astray in our initial assumptions about what happiness is. . . . So we should not be surprised that ancient theories have counter-intuitive consequences about happiness. . . . The conception of happiness that we start with could not possibly be unaltered at the end of the process of reflection and conscious adoption of an ethical theory.
>
> A modern response at this point might well be that, given this situation, ancient theories should just have abandoned the idea of giving an account of happiness. What they said about virtue, nature and the

---

[118] Wolterstorff, *Justice: Rights and Wrongs*, 176, 219.

interests of others is compelling; they only spoil things by casting their theories in terms of happiness, condemning themselves to failure by persisting in an unsuitable framework.[119]

Lewis, though steeped in classical and medieval literature, considered himself a modern when it came to happiness, but only because modernity stood with common sense about the nature of happiness. For Lewis, there was no question of being a modern just for the sake of being a modern. Indeed, he considered himself a dinosaur.[120] What was important was common sense and if modernity stood by it, while antiquity did not, then so much the worse for antiquity. Annas emphasizes in her book that Aristotle was a eudaemonist about happiness. As far as Lewis was concerned, then, Aristotle advocated a revisionary conception of happiness that was at odds with the commonsensical notion of happiness as consisting of nothing but experiences of pleasure.[121] And Lewis could find no reason to jettison common sense about this issue.

---

[119] Annas, *The Morality of Happiness*, 331. In light of Annas' distinction between the ordinary, nonphilosophical person's conception of happiness and that of the eudaemonist, one should always be circumspect when one reads a comment like the following from Wolterstorff: "Before the modern period, almost no one thought of the good life as the experientially satisfying life. Eudaimonism, the ethical framework of the ancients, conceived of the good life as the well-lived life, not as the experientially satisfying life." (*Justice: Rights and Wrongs*, 148) Three pages later, Wolterstorff quotes the passage from Aristotle that I cited earlier in which Aristotle points out that the common run of people, as opposed to those who are cultivated, think of happiness as pleasure (*Nicomachean Ethics*, 1095a17-23). So when Wolterstorff says almost no one before the modern period thought of happiness as the experientially satisfying life, he probably means no *philosopher* thought of it in this way. Ordinary people did, as Aristotle knew well.

[120] See his deservedly famous essay "*De Descriptione Temporum*," in *Selected Literary Essays*, edited by Walter Hooper (Cambridge: Cambridge University Press, 1969), 1-14. Lewis ends the essay with these words: "Speaking not only for myself but for all other Old Western men whom you may meet, I would say, use your specimens while you can. There are not going to be many more dinosaurs."

[121] According to Annas, eudaemonists believe that an individual's entry point for ethical reflection is *his own* final good or happiness. (*The Morality of Happiness*, Chapter 1) She points out that an objection which is often raised against eudaemonism is that it excludes a proper place for the agent to be concerned about the good of others. In response, she says that the validity of the objection turns on how one conceives of a person's happiness. If one believes ethics starts with the role that the virtues play in the agent's happiness (happiness consists, at least in part, of virtuous activity), then "[t]here is no reason, *prima facie*, why the good of others [as the object of virtuous activity] cannot matter to me independently of my own interests, just because it is introduced as something required for my own good." (*The Morality of Happiness*, 127) However, if one conceives of an agent's happiness hedonistically, then there is a problem for finding a proper role for a concern for the good of others within a eudaemonist framework. "Thus, whether there is a conflict between aiming at one's own good and aiming at the good of others depends on what content is given to one's own good. For theories which specify this as

Possible objections to Lewis's understanding of happiness

With Lewis's non-eudaemonist, hedonistic view of happiness before us, I take up in this section various objections that might be raised against his position and respond to them as I believe he might well have done.

Those suspicious of a view of pleasure like Lewis's sometimes point out (and rightly so) that the claim that pleasure is intrinsically good and pain is intrinsically evil means that the goodness of pleasure is not explained by pleasure's relationship to anything else and the evilness of pain is not explained by pain's relationship to anything else. This implies that pleasure is good and pain is evil, regardless of what God says about the matter. Surely this undermines God's omnipotence or all-powerfulness. After all, if God were to say that pleasure is intrinsically evil and pain is intrinsically good, then that would be the case. Hence, Lewis was just wrong when he said that pleasure is intrinsically good.

Lewis would likely have responded that these objectors are absurdly stringing words together when they say that pleasure might not be intrinsically good but in and of itself evil, and pain might not be intrinsically evil but in and of itself good. Lewis wrote that "[God's] omnipotence means power to do all that is intrinsically possible, not to do the intrinsically impossible."[122] Because pleasure is intrinsically good, it is impossible that it ever be in and of itself evil. To claim that pleasure might be intrinsically evil is nonsense. "[M]eaningless combinations of words do not suddenly acquire meaning simply because we prefix to them the two other words 'God can,'" and "nonsense remains nonsense even when we talk it about God."[123] If this were not the case, then God could make Himself exist and not exist at the same time or make Himself simultaneously perfectly morally good and perfectly

---

pleasure there is a problem, since there are obvious ways in which aiming at the good of others comes into conflict with achieving one's own good." (*The Morality of Happiness*, 128, footnote 258).

· As a hedonist about happiness, Lewis believed that one's entry point for ethics is reflection about the good (happiness) *of others*, where recognition of that good leads to the belief that there are moral limits to the pursuit of one's own good (which consists of experiences of pleasure). Lewis was well aware that in this life the pursuit of one's own good, where this is commonsensically conceived hedonistically, can conflict with the good of others. However, he believed the solution to this problem was not to revise, as eudaemonists do, our commonsense conception of happiness so that it includes the performance of virtuous behavior, but to stick with common sense and trust that God will grant perfect happiness in the afterlife to those who do not seek it at any price in this life.

[122] Lewis, *The Problem of Pain*, 28.
[123] Lewis, *The Problem of Pain*, 28.

morally evil. Lewis was blunt about speaking nonsense concerning God: "I think we must attack wherever we meet it the nonsensical idea that mutually exclusive propositions about God can both be true."[124]

Suspicion among Christians concerning a view like Lewis's about pleasure and happiness arises on another front. There are some who believe that to maintain that pleasure is intrinsically good threatens or poses a problem for God's goodness. Lewis would most surely have responded that this belief is false. In thinking about the concepts of good and evil, one must always be careful to distinguish between different kinds of good and evil. When we say that pleasure is good, we mean that it is good in a nonmoral sense. To say that the intrinsic goodness of pleasure is nonmoral in nature is to say that its value is *not moral* in character. It is not to say that it is *immoral* or bad in nature, as when one says that a person is immoral. In contrast, when one says that God is good, one does mean that God is good in a *moral* sense.

In spite of the distinction between nonmoral and moral goodness, some Christians insist that God is intrinsically good. Lewis would probably have answered that these individuals are confused (or, as he says in a quote cited below in response to an objection about the goodness of sexual pleasure, "muddleheaded") about the distinction between the concept of being intrinsically good and that of not being able to act immorally, which is that of being necessarily morally good. The latter is a moral value concept, while the former is a nonmoral one.

Along a slightly different line, many Christians (and many non-Christians) are reluctant to affirm without qualification that pleasure is intrinsically good. When discussing matters of value, they typically think of pleasure as first and foremost an accompaniment of action, where the nature of the action affects the quality of the pleasure. Thus, when an action is virtuous, the pleasure that goes with that action perfects and completes it. When an action is vicious, pleasure's perfective quality is lost. For example, Aristotle held that "[t]he pleasure proper to a morally good activity is good, the pleasure proper to a bad activity evil. . . . So we see that differences in activities make for corresponding differences in pleasures."[125]

To illustrate their point, advocates of this Aristotelian view sometimes use the example of sex. Chad Walsh recounts a time that Lewis shared a conversation he had with some psychology-minded friends: "They had spent the entire evening discussing sex in the language of the clinic—'release for tensions,' etc. Suddenly Lewis burst out, 'If a visitor from Mars had overheard them he would never have suspected that sex has any connection with

---

[124] Lewis, *God in the Dock*, 102.
[125] Aristotle, *Nicomachean Ethics*, 284; 1175b27.

pleasure!'"[126] According to those who are opposed to the idea that pleasure is intrinsically good, the purpose of sex between a man and a woman is not that they experience pleasure but that they procreate (an action). They say that the purpose of sex cannot be that the man and woman experience the pleasure that accompanies the act of sexual intercourse, because that pleasure often leads to illicit sexual activity, single parent families, poverty, and abortion. The distinction between moral (virtuous) and immoral (vicious) action must serve as the basis for distinguishing between good and bad (evil) pleasures.

In answer to this objection, Lewis would probably have emphasized that it is necessary to keep clear in one's mind the distinction between one's ultimate purpose (which, in his view, is that one experience nothing except pleasure, which is perfect happiness) and the purpose of the human reproductive system (which is the generation of offspring). Because pleasure accompanies the sexual act, one and the same act of sex can be the means to accomplishing both purposes. On some occasions, however, accomplishing justly (in a just way) one of these purposes (that one experience pleasure) may not be possible because a necessary condition for justly accomplishing the other (that one generate offspring) is lacking. For example, while one can obtain pleasure from sexual intercourse outside marriage, the mutual long-term commitment that is necessary to nurture and raise a child that might be conceived is absent. Therefore, one is morally obligated to refrain from sexual intercourse outside marriage and delay for at least the time being the experience of pleasure that accompanies the sexual act, even though the pleasure experienced from such intercourse is intrinsically good. "The Christian attitude does not mean that there is anything wrong about sexual pleasure . . . . It means that you must not isolate that pleasure and try to get it by itself . . . ."[127] As I have already pointed out, Lewis held that the expression "bad pleasures" is a loose and popular way of saying "'pleasures snatched by unlawful acts.' It is the stealing of the apple that is bad, not the sweetness. The sweetness is still a beam from the glory. That does not palliate the stealing. It makes it worse. There is sacrilege in the theft. We have abused a holy thing . . . [and ignored] the smell of Deity that hangs about it."[128] In the case of illicit sex, one is stealing pleasure, which is itself good, from an act that is proper only within the bonds of the marital commitment:

---

[126] Chad Walsh, *C. S. Lewis: Apostle to the Skeptics* (New York: Macmillan, 1949), 13.
[127] Lewis, *Mere Christianity*, 105.
[128] Lewis, *Letters to Malcolm*, 89, 90.

The biological purpose of sex is children . . . . But if a healthy young man indulged his sexual appetite whenever he felt inclined, and if each act produced a baby, then in ten years he might easily populate a small village. This appetite is in ludicrous and preposterous excess of its function. . . . Modern people are always saying, "Sex is nothing to be ashamed of." They may mean two things. They may mean "There is nothing to be ashamed of in the fact that the human race reproduces itself in a certain way, nor in the fact that it gives pleasure." If they mean that, they are right. Christianity says the same. It is not the thing, nor the pleasure, that is the trouble. The old Christian teachers said that if man had never fallen, sexual pleasure, instead of being less than it is now, would actually have been greater. I know some muddle-headed Christians have talked as if Christianity thought that sex, or the body, or pleasure, were bad in themselves. But they were wrong.[129]

Again, to reiterate what Lewis said elsewhere, "I think *all* pleasure simply good: what we call bad pleasures are pleasures produced by action, or inactions, which break the moral law, and it is those actions or inactions which are bad, not the pleasures."[130] "So we must practise in abstaining from pleasures which are not in themselves wicked."[131]

To elucidate Lewis's position on happiness, it is helpful to consider the philosopher Robert Nozick's idea of an experience machine.[132] Nozick asks his readers to imagine a machine, the programming of which will provide them with uninterrupted pleasure for as long as they wish (which readers, upon reflection, come to realize is for eternity), if they connect to it. As Nozick points out, a person who is connected to the experience machine does not have to *do* anything. An individual never has to *act*; he simply *passively* experiences pleasure. What Nozick wants to know is whether a reasonable person should accept an offer to be connected to the experience machine. Readers typically wrestle with the idea of accepting the offer. On the one hand, they understandably find the thought of experiencing nothing but pleasure extremely attractive. On the other hand, the severance of pleasure from action puzzles them because the connection between pleasure and action is so pervasive in their own lives.

What would Lewis have said about the experience machine and the framework it presupposes? There is good reason to think he recognized our

---

[129] Lewis, *Mere Christianity*, 95–6, 98.
[130] Lewis, *The Collected Letters of C. S. Lewis: Volume II*, 462–3.
[131] Lewis, *God in the Dock*, 54.
[132] Robert Nozick, *Anarchy, State, and Utopia* (New York: Basic Books, 1974), 42–5.

essential passivity with respect to experiences of pleasure. Gilbert Meilaender nicely brings this out in some of his comments about Lewis's science fiction story entitled *Perelandra*[133]:

> What Lewis provides in *Perelandra* . . . is his picture of the appropriate attitude toward created things. What we are to remember—and what is so easy to forget—is that they are . . . gifts of the Creator meant to be received. This is the key to understanding the picture Lewis paints. The proper posture for the creature is one of receptivity. In *Perelandra* we see several ways in which this posture could be corrupted or destroyed. First it is always possible to seek ways to assure ourselves of repeating the pleasure. This is what makes money so suspect in Lewis' eyes—it is a means by which we assure ourselves that we can have the pleasure whenever we want it. It provides a measure of independence. One no longer has to throw oneself into the wave. . . .
>
> This theme comes out most clearly in *Perelandra* in the symbolism of the Fixed Land. Perelandra is largely a world of floating islands, but it also has a Fixed Land. The Lady (and the King) are permitted to go onto the Fixed Land but not to dwell there or sleep there. . . . This sort of trust [of living on the floating islands] involves a willingness to receive what is given . . . as well as a willingness to let it go again without grasping after repetition of the pleasure. Always, one must throw oneself into the wave.[134]

The proper attitude toward pleasure is to recognize that it is a gift and to receive it as such. In the deepest sense, one is a patient with respect to the experience of pleasure. One should ultimately choose to trust one's Creator for future experiences of it and not choose to hold on to those experiences of it that one has without any regard for morality. One should choose to do one's moral duty, which is to trust God for the pleasure (happiness) for which one so deeply yearns. The experience of this pleasure is rightly bestowed upon and received by those who choose the moral way of life vis-à-vis pleasure. In *The Weight of Glory*, Lewis stressed that the proper rewards of moral activity are not merely tacked on to the activity but are the activity in its consummation.[135] Thus, it is plausible to think he would have maintained that the example of the experience machine seductively breaks the consummative link between morally right action and pleasure that the

---

[133] C. S. Lewis, *Perelandra* (New York: Scribner, 2003).
[134] Meilaender, *The Taste for the Other*, 17–19.
[135] Lewis, *The Weight of Glory*, 26–7.

concepts of fittingness and justice forge. Because pleasure is such a great good, and perfect happiness is the greatest good, it is fitting or just that only those who are virtuous experience it.

In other words, Lewis would have insisted that while it is possible conceptually by means of a thought experiment like the experience machine to pull apart passivity (experiencing pleasure) and activity (the pursuit of pleasure) and recognize that the former is possible without the latter, what is fitting and just is an attractive conceptual force that necessarily draws them back together so that only virtuous people ultimately justly experience pleasure in the form of perfect happiness. But the reality of this attractive force in no way transforms virtuous activity itself into a constituent of happiness. And while heaven might conceptually be the ultimate experience machine (an existence in which God constantly infuses the once-virtuous with nothing but pleasure without any further activity on their part), there is no reason to think that it must or will be like this. It is conceptually coherent to think that pleasure will always remain attached to the nonmoral (not immoral) activity of the blessed in the afterlife, activity of which they will never grow weary and from which they will never need rest.

Natural law

Broadly speaking, the idea of natural law is the idea of moral principles that ought to govern actions and which arise out of the nature of the individuals who are the objects and performers of those actions. Given Lewis's view of pleasure's intrinsic goodness and pain's intrinsic evilness, was he in any sense a natural law theorist when it comes to morality? Lewis said that if by "natural law" one means no more than "the doctrine of objective value, the belief that certain attitudes are really true, and others really false, to the kind of thing the universe is and the kind of things that we are,"[136] what he called "the *Tao*,"[137] then, yes, he was a natural law theorist. Here are his words: "This thing which I have called for convenience the *Tao*, and which others may call Natural Law or Traditional Morality or The First Principles of Practical Reason or the First Platitudes, is not one among a series of possible systems of value."[138]

However, if one thinks of natural law in more specific terms than this, then Lewis himself disavowed being a natural law theorist. For example, in

---

[136] C. S. Lewis, *The Abolition of Man* (New York: HarperSanFrancisco, 2001), 18.
[137] Lewis, *The Abolition of Man*, 18.
[138] Lewis, *The Abolition of Man*, 43.

his essay "On Ethics," he disclaims "trying to reintroduce in its full Stoical or medieval rigour the doctrine of Natural Law."[139]

What might explain this disclaimer? Lewis's position on the intrinsic goodness of pleasure and the intrinsic evilness of pain helps provide an answer to this question. Consider the Stoics, who maintained that the pleasures and pains of ordinary life are not really good and evil respectively.[140] In their view, experiences of pleasure and pain do not matter and they recommended indifference toward them in living life. Theirs was the view of the person who supposedly understood his or her place in the overall scheme of things. With the right attitude toward pleasure and pain, an individual would accept what is going to happen as an inevitable/determined outcome of the way the universe is.[141]

Clearly Lewis could not have reintroduced the Stoic view of natural law in its details, given his understanding of pleasure and pain. A right attitude toward them would affirm their respective intrinsic goodness and evilness. Given their intrinsic values, experiences of them do matter. Indeed, ultimately nothing matters more. Indifference toward them is not a rational possibility.

According to Lewis, the fundamental locus of value is nonmoral in nature in the form of experiences of pleasure and pain. Yet, when he argued for the existence of the *Tao*, Lewis maintained that the first principles of practical reason, the principles of action that comprise natural law or traditional morality, are *simply seen* to be true (are self-evident) and are not derived from propositions about facts that have no trace of value.[142] After all, to be a *first* principle just is to be a principle that is not derived from other principles. And according to Lewis, "Natural Law or Traditional Morality or the First Principles of Practical Reason ... is the sole source of all value judgements."[143] It might appear, then, that Lewis believed that the first principles of action that comprise natural law do not depend on the value judgments about the intrinsic goodness of pleasure and the intrinsic evilness of pain, which serve as the basis of our conception of perfect happiness and its intrinsic goodness.

If we read Lewis carefully, however, a plausible case can be made for the view that he believed the first principles of practical reason, principles which

---

[139] Lewis, *Christian Reflections*, 55.
[140] White, *A Brief History of Happiness*, 93.
[141] White, *A Brief History of Happiness*, 96.
[142] Lewis, *The Abolition of Man*, 20, 39, 40.
[143] Lewis, *The Abolition of Man*, 43.

are just seen to be true, arise out of the nonmoral good of the happiness of others. For example, in *Miracles* Lewis said the following:

> I myself ... believe that the primary moral principles on which all others depend are rationally perceived. We "just see" that there is no reason why my neighbour's happiness should be sacrificed to my own, as we "just see" that things which are equal to the same thing are equal to one another. If we cannot prove either axiom, that is not because they are irrational but because they are self-evident and all proofs depend on them. Their intrinsic reasonableness shines by its own light. It is because all morality is based on such self-evident principles that we say to a man, when we would call him to right conduct, "Be reasonable."[144]

It seems, then, that Lewis's understanding of the *Tao* as it relates to the first principles of morality that are just seen to be true is as follows: The first principles of moral action that comprise the natural law are based on the nonactional and nonmoral concept of a person's happiness, which refers to a subjective state of that individual that consists of nothing but experiences of pleasure. Given this concept and the fact that my neighbor is equal to me in the sense that his happiness, all other things being equal, should not be sacrificed to mine, I *just see* that certain actions are impermissible for me in my pursuit of my happiness. The *Analects of Confucius* captures this with "Never do to others what you would not like them to do to you."[145] For Lewis, the *Tao* fundamentally consists of the moral principles that describe these impermissible actions. And all of this is a matter of rational insight into nonmoral and moral good and the relationship between them.

Joy or *Sehnsucht*

No philosophical tour of Lewis's views of pleasure and happiness would be complete without mention of what Lewis called "Joy," where this is understood as a special kind of desire, longing, or homesickness that has links to the idea of *Sehnsucht* in the literature of Romanticism. In the words of Corbin Scott Carnell, *Sehnsucht* involves "a sense of separation [estrangement] from what is desired, a ceaseless longing which points always beyond."[146] Throughout

---

[144] Lewis, *Miracles*, 54.
[145] Lewis quotes this principle as an illustration of the *Tao* in *The Abolition of Man*, 85.
[146] Corbin Scott Carnell, *Bright Shadow of Reality: Spiritual Longing in C. S. Lewis* (Grand Rapids, MI: Eerdmans, 1999), 27.

his book, Carnell reminds readers that the concept of *Sehnsucht* defies final definition or analysis. Nevertheless, *Sehnsucht* as ceaseless longing or desire and its linkage as such with Joy in Lewis's mind indicates that the idea of Joy warrants treatment here because of its own bearing on the topics of pleasure and happiness.

In his autobiographical work entitled *Surprised by Joy*, Lewis described Joy in the following ways:

> [It] is that of an unsatisfied desire which is itself more desirable than any other satisfaction. I call it Joy, which is here a technical term and must be sharply distinguished both from Happiness and from Pleasure. Joy (in my sense) has indeed one characteristic, and one only, in common with them; the fact that anyone who has experienced it will want it again. Apart from that, and considered only in its quality, it might almost equally be called a particular kind of unhappiness or grief. But then it is a kind we want. I doubt whether anyone who has tasted it would ever, if both were in his power, exchange it for all the pleasures in the world. But then Joy is never in our power and pleasure often is.[147]

> All Joy reminds. It is never a possession, always a desire for something longer ago or further away or still "about to be."[148]

> Joy is distinct not only from pleasure in general but even from aesthetic pleasure. It must have the stab, the pang, the inconsolable longing.[149]

> I came to know by experience that [Joy] is not a disguise of sexual desire. Those who think that if adolescents were all provided with suitable mistresses we should soon hear no more of "immortal longings" are certainly wrong. I learned this mistake to be a mistake by the simple, if discreditable, process of repeatedly making it. From the Northernness one could not easily have slid into erotic fantasies without noticing the difference; but when the world of Morris became the frequent medium of Joy, this transition became possible. It was quite easy to think that one desired those forests for the sake of their female inhabitants, the garden of Hesperus for the sake of his daughters, Hylas' river for the river nymphs. I repeatedly followed that path—to the end. And at the end one found pleasure; which immediately resulted in the discovery that pleasure (whether that pleasure or any other) was not what you had been looking for. . . . Joy is not a substitute for sex; sex is very often

---

[147] Lewis, *Surprised by Joy*, 17–18.
[148] Lewis, *Surprised by Joy*, 78.
[149] Lewis, *Surprised by Joy*, 72.

a substitute for Joy. I sometimes wonder whether all pleasures are not substitutes for Joy.[150]

Lewis, then, held that Joy is a *desire*. As Stephen Logan points out, Lewis did not say that "the unsatisfied desire is more satisfying [than any other satisfied desire], but that it is more *desirable* [than any other satisfaction]."[151] According to Lewis, "considered only in its quality, [Joy] might almost equally be called a particular kind of unhappiness . . . ."[152] This implies that Joy might itself be simultaneously both extrinsically evil (its present failure to be satisfied is painful) and extrinsically good (the idea of some day possessing that at which Joy is directed produces pleasure in the present). Though Joy might be pleasurable in this way, it is not identical with pleasure (and, therefore, also not identical with happiness). Beyond not being identical with pleasure, Joy differs from pleasure by not being even indirectly subject to the will (choice). One can choose a multitude of activities that will produce pleasure, but not so with Joy: "Thence arose the fatal determination to recover the old thrill [Joy], and at last the moment when I was compelled to realize that all such efforts were failures. I had no lure to which the birds would come."[153] Lewis claimed that the source of the error of thinking that Joy is obtainable by an act of will is the deeper error of thinking that the object of Joy is a *state of mind*:

> The first [blunder] was made at the very moment when I formulated the complaint that the "old thrill" was becoming rarer and rarer. For by that complaint I smuggled in the assumption that what I wanted was a "thrill," a state of my own mind. And there lies the deadly error. Only when your whole attention and desire are fixed on something else . . . does the "thrill" arise. It is a by-product. Its very existence presupposes that you desire not it but something other and outer. If by any perverse askesis [training] or the use of any drug it could be produced from within, it would at once be seen to be of no value. For take away the object, and what, after all, would be left? . . . And the second error is, having thus falsely made a state of mind your aim, to attempt to produce it. From the fading of the Northernness I ought to have drawn the conclusion that the Object, the Desirable, was further away, more external, less subjective, than even such a comparatively public and external thing as a system of mythology—had, in fact, only shone through that system. . . . But far

---

[150] Lewis, *Surprised by Joy*, 169–70.
[151] Stephen Logan, "Literary Theorist," in *The Cambridge Companion to C. S. Lewis*, eds. Robert MacSwain and Michael Ward (Cambridge: Cambridge University Press, 2010), 37.
[152] Lewis, *Surprised by Joy*, 18.
[153] Lewis, *Surprised by Joy*, 166.

more often I frightened [Joy] away by my greedy impatience to snare it, and, even when it came, instantly destroyed it by introspection, and at all times vulgarized it by my false assumption about its nature.[154]

Joy itself, considered simply as an event in my own mind, turned out to be of no value at all. All the value lay in that of which Joy was the desiring. And that object, quite clearly, was no state of my own mind or body at all. In a way, I had proved this by elimination. I had tried everything in my own mind and body; as it were, asking myself, "Is it this you want? Is it this?" Last of all I had asked if Joy itself was what I wanted; and, labeling it "aesthetic experience," had pretended I could answer Yes. But that answer too had broken down. Inexorably Joy proclaimed, "You want—I myself am your want of—something other, outside, not you nor any state of you."[155]

So Joy is a desire whose object is not a state of mind. There is much evidence in support of the view that Lewis thought of the direct object of Joy as a *place*. In *The Pilgrim's Regress*, which was written in 1933 not long after his conversion to Christianity, Lewis described the object of an intense longing (what he came to refer to as "Joy") as a mysterious distant island: "[T]here came to him [John, the pilgrim and main character] from beyond the wood a sweetness and a pang so piercing . . . . It seemed to him that a mist which hung at the far end of the wood had parted for a moment, and through the rift he had seen a calm sea, and in the sea an island, where the smooth turf sloped down unbroken to the bays . . . ."[156] As McGrath says, "Although 'the Landlord' – God – features prominently in [*The Pilgrim's Regress*], it is quite clear that the sense of longing experienced by John, the pilgrim, concerns this island. Desire is not associated primarily with finding the Landlord; it is the island that John seeks, believing it to be the source of his heart's desire."[157] Almost a decade after writing *The Pilgrim's Regress*, we still find Lewis referring to Joy's object as a place, as "our own far-off country,"[158] "Heaven,"[159] and "another world."[160]

---

[154] Lewis, *Surprised by Joy*, 168–9.
[155] Lewis, *Surprised by Joy*, 220–1.
[156] Lewis, *The Pilgrim's Regress*, 8.
[157] McGrath, *The Intellectual World of C. S. Lewis*, 115.
[158] Lewis, *The Weight of Glory*, 29.
[159] Lewis, *The Weight of Glory*, 33.
[160] Lewis, *Mere Christianity*, 137. In "Early Prose Joy," Lewis discussed the influence of the plays of W. B. Yeats and the poems of William Morris on his idea of Joy. He explicitly noted that they thought of the object of this special desire as a place: "These plays and poems were all really written on the same theme: they told of men crazed with the desire for something out of reach, something here generally envisaged as a *place* . . . beyond the world." "Early Prose Joy," 19.

In an afterword to the third edition of *The Pilgrim's Regress* in 1943, Lewis wrote that "if a man diligently followed this desire, pursuing the false objects until their falsity appeared and then resolutely abandoning them, he must come out at last into the clear knowledge that the human soul was made to enjoy some object that is never fully given—nay, cannot even be imagined as given—in our present mode of subjective and spatio-temporal existence."[161] And speaking of *Sehnsucht* in the works of Edmund Spenser, Lewis wrote that it would not be regarded by a Christian Platonist "as a horrible form of spiritual dram-drinking," but "would logically appear as among the sanest and most fruitful experiences we have," because the longed-for object "really exists and really draws us to itself."[162] But in the end, slightly more than two decades after his conversion to Christianity and *The Pilgrim's Regress*, Lewis lost his interest in Joy. In *Surprised by Joy* he wrote the following: "But what, in conclusion, of Joy? . . . To tell you the truth, the subject has lost nearly all interest for me since I became a Christian. . . . I now know that the experience, considered as a state of my own mind, had never had the kind of importance I once gave it. It was valuable only as a pointer to something other and outer."[163]

Two questions loom large. First, where does God fit into Lewis's account of Joy? Is God the "object" the soul was made to enjoy? McGrath provides a thoroughly reasonable answer: "Lewis clearly assumes that 'heaven' entails God, so that an argument for the existence of heaven is an indirect argument for the existence of God. Yet the primary focus of the approach [through Joy] remains focused on a place, rather than a person."[164]

Second, where do pleasure and happiness fit into Lewis's account of Joy? Could someone as thoughtful as Lewis, who claimed that "We know we are being touched by a finger of that right hand at which there are pleasures for evermore"[165] and that "God not only understands but *shares* the desire . . . for complete and ecstatic happiness . . . [and] made me for no other purpose than to enjoy it,"[166] also claim that Joy is directly aimed at a place and indirectly at a person, but has nothing to do with pleasure and happiness? Any charitable reader must answer "No." Surely Lewis believed that the pleasures that are for evermore and comprise complete and ecstatic happiness are to be had if and only if one makes peace with and finds one's rest in God in heaven. In short,

---

[161] Lewis, *The Pilgrim's Regress*, 204–5.
[162] C. S. Lewis, *Poetry and Prose in the Sixteenth Century* (Oxford: Clarendon Press, 2002), 357.
[163] Lewis, *Surprised by Joy*, 238.
[164] McGrath, *The Intellectual World of C. S. Lewis*, 117.
[165] Lewis, *Letters to Malcolm*, 90.
[166] Lewis, *The Collected Letters of C. S. Lewis: Volume II*, 123.

the object of Joy is not a state of mind but an idyllic place (heaven) where one can experience a state of mind (perfect happiness) through a personal relationship with the being (God) who provides that happiness.

In other words, Lewis held that God made all people for perfect happiness and that experiences of pleasure in this life are an early taste of what is in store for believers in their far-off heavenly country in God's presence. Joy is a desire for a paradisal place with its God, who, when He is thanked, praised, and served, provides the pleasure that constitutes ecstatic happiness:

> [B]ut the mind and, still more, the body receives life from Him at a thousand removes—through our ancestors, through our food, through the elements. The faint, far-off results of those energies which God's creative rapture implanted in matter when He made the worlds are what we now call physical pleasures; and even thus filtered, they are too much for our present management. What would it be to taste at the fountainhead of that stream of which even these lower reaches prove so intoxicating? Yet that, I believe, is what lies before us. The whole man is to drink joy from the fountain of joy. As St. Augustine said, the rapture of the saved soul will "flow over" into the glorified body. In the light of our present specialized and depraved appetites, we cannot imagine this *torrens voluptatis* [torrent of pleasure] . . . .[167]

> The Scotch catechism says that man's chief end is "to glorify God and enjoy Him forever". But we shall then know that these are the same thing. Fully to enjoy is to glorify. In commanding us to glorify Him, God is inviting us to enjoy Him.[168]

> [The Christian] believes . . . that [men] were created by God and so built that they can find their true and lasting happiness only by being united to God . . . .[169]

In summary, rather than Joy being at odds with the idea of perfect happiness as nothing but experiences of pleasure, the existence of Joy or Sehnsucht is, as Peter Kreeft says, a strong clue "that infinite happiness exists and that you are designed to enjoy it."[170] John Beversluis puts it this way: "As a Christian Romantic, Lewis was convinced that all men desire God, since all men desire happiness and true happiness can be found in God alone."[171] Ultimately, then,

---

[167] Lewis, *The Weight of Glory*, 44.
[168] C. S. Lewis, *Reflections on the Psalms* (New York: Harcourt, 1986), 96–7.
[169] Lewis, *God in the Dock*, 109.
[170] Peter Kreeft, "C. S. Lewis's Argument from Desire," in *G. K. Chesterton and C. S. Lewis: The Riddle of Joy*, eds. Michael H. Macdonald and Andrew A. Tadie (Grand Rapids, MI: Eerdmans, 1989), 254.
[171] John Beversluis, *C. S. Lewis and the Search for Rational Religion* (Grand Rapids, MI: Eerdmans, 1985), 27.

the explanation for why Joy, as an unsatisfied desire, is more desirable than any satisfaction of another desire is because its satisfaction, when it occurs, will be a thoroughly pleasurable state of mind that never ends and to which the pleasures of satisfied desire in this world are but pointers.

Can we really understand the nature of perfect happiness?

If I am right, Lewis believed that perfect or ecstatic happiness consists of nothing but experiences of pleasure. But would Lewis have presumed to have insight into such a matter? Would he not have thought such presumption the height of foolish arrogance? One might try to support an affirmative answer to this question in the following way.

In discussing the New Creation, which is the world that is breaking in with the Incarnation and Resurrection of Christ, Lewis considered events like the Transfiguration of Christ. This was, in his words, "an anticipatory glimpse of something to come."[172] We do not know to what the luminosity or shining whiteness of Christ's transformed human form points. "We are therefore compelled to believe that nearly all we are told about the New Creation is metaphorical."[173] But Lewis believed that we should not be surprised by our limited understanding of this matter because metaphor is very often necessary when we are talking about something that is not perceptible by the five senses. With metaphor, we use what is perceptible by one or more of the five senses to refer to what is not so perceptible: "When a man says that he grasps an argument he is using a verb (*grasp*) which literally means to take something in the hands, but he is certainly not thinking that his mind has hands or that an argument can be seized like a gun."[174] Similarly, when Scripture says that Christ is seated at the right hand of God, we must understand this metaphorically because God is a being who has no hands because He has no body.[175] Even Christ's coming down from heaven is metaphor, but perfectly understandable metaphor, given that simple-minded people see the sky as a huge dome that is sensuously most like infinity.[176] Given our need for metaphor in understanding the world to come, is it not plausible to think that Lewis believed experiencing nothing but pleasure is a metaphor for perfect happiness, which is beatitude or the vision of God?

---

[172] Lewis, *Miracles*, 249.
[173] Lewis, *Miracles*, 250.
[174] Lewis, *Miracles*, 114.
[175] Lewis, *Miracles*, 253.
[176] Lewis, *Miracles*, 116, 258.

The answer is "No," and for the following reason. An experience of pleasure is itself something that is not perceptible by any of the five senses. Hence, it cannot be a metaphor for something like perfect happiness (beatitude) that is also not perceptible in this way. It itself is this happiness. What Lewis believed was distinctive about the Christian understanding of perfect happiness is not that it consists of pleasure but that it includes the body as a source of it. "By teaching the resurrection of the body [Christianity] teaches that Heaven is not merely a state of the spirit but a state of the body as well . . . ."[177]

In making this point about the bodily nature of our heavenly existence, Lewis found it necessary to address what he thought would be on most people's minds, namely, that heavenly bliss, given that it is bodily in nature, must involve sexual intercourse, because "the sexual act [is] the highest bodily pleasure."[178] Here, he believed we are like a small boy, who on being told that sexual intercourse is the highest source of pleasure, immediately asks whether one eats chocolates at the same time. When he is told "No," he might regard the absence of chocolates as the chief feature of sex. "In vain would you tell him that the reason why lovers in their carnal raptures don't bother about chocolates is that they have something better to think of."[179] Lewis says we are in the same position vis-à-vis heaven. We know about sexual intercourse, but not about the bodily life in heaven that will provide us with pleasure without the sexual act. The nature of perfect happiness (beatitude) as experiences of pleasure is not in question at this point.[180] What is in question is the nature of the bodily life that, without sexual intercourse, will provide us with those experiences of pleasure.

Can a convincing argument be put together for the view that Lewis did not hold a hedonistic view of happiness from the fact that he used terms like "beatitude"[181] and "the vision of God"[182] in describing our heavenly existence? Once again, I believe the answer must be "No." Unlike some today,[183] Lewis

---

[177] Lewis, *Miracles*, 263.
[178] Lewis, *Miracles*, 260.
[179] Lewis, *Miracles*, 261.
[180] It is interesting to note that Clyde S. Kilby, when discussing Lewis's answers to five objections to eternal punishment, considers the fourth objection and says that it "is that there can be no pleasure in heaven to those who know there is a single soul in hell." *The Christian World of C. S. Lewis* (Grand Rapids, MI: Eerdmans, 1964), 69. In formulating the fourth objection in *The Problem of Pain*, Lewis himself did not state it in terms of pleasure in heaven. But anyone who has seriously read and digested Lewis's thought will agree with Kilby that Lewis thought of heaven as a fundamentally pleasurable existence.
[181] Lewis, *Miracles*, 256.
[182] Lewis, *The Weight of Glory*, 28.
[183] I especially have in mind the New Testament scholar N. T. Wright. See N. T. Wright, *Surprised by Hope: Rethinking Heaven, the Resurrection, and the Mission of the Church* (New York: HarperOne, 2008).

was not at all cautious about using the term "heaven" to refer to the Christian view of the afterlife,[184] even though he knew it conjured up in the minds of many the idea of a Platonic bodiless existence. Rather than abandon use of the word, Lewis preferred to clarify the nature of that to which it refers. And as I have just highlighted, Lewis believed heaven involves bodily sources of pleasure. But it also involves more than that. In reflecting on the concept of heavenly glory, Lewis concluded that it consisted (at least in part) in one being praised by God for a job well done. "I suddenly remembered that no one can enter heaven except as a child; and nothing is so obvious in a child—not in a conceited child, but in a good child—as its great and undisguised pleasure in being praised."[185] Once again, what is at the center of the heavenly life is the pleasure that constitutes happiness, this time the pleasure that comes from the praise of the source of all pleasure, bodily and non-bodily alike, God. Of this heavenly life Lewis asked "What would it be to taste at the fountainhead that stream [of pleasures] of which even these [physical pleasures] prove so intoxicating? Yet that, I believe, is what lies before us. The whole man is to drink from the fountain of joy."[186] It is because God is the fountain of the *torrens voluptatis* that Lewis unhesitatingly spoke of God, beatitude, or the vision of Him as our proper end or purpose.

---

[184] Lewis, *The Weight of Glory*, 28–9.
[185] Lewis, *The Weight of Glory*, 36–7.
[186] Lewis, *The Weight of Glory*, 44.

2

Supernatural Persons

> *The superiority of the Scientific description clearly consists in giving for the coldness of the night a precise quantitative estimate which can be tested by an instrument. The test ends all disputes. . . . On the other hand it does not, of itself, give us any information about the quality of a cold night, does not tell us what we shall be feeling if we go out of doors.*[1]

The body and happiness

From the topics covered in the preceding chapter, it is evident that Lewis thought long and hard about happiness, pleasure, and pain and their respective values as intrinsically good and intrinsically evil. If the number of places in which Lewis mentioned his views about the soul and body is any indication of their importance in his philosophical reflections, then it is hard to avoid the conclusion that they took a back seat to his interest in happiness and related issues.

Indeed, Lewis's interest in the soul-body question might even have arisen out of his thoughts about happiness. For example, in *Mere Christianity* we find Lewis discoursing on pleasure and sex and then moving to the body as a source of happiness in the resurrection life: "Christianity is almost the only one of the great religions which thoroughly approves of the body—which believes that matter is good, that God Himself once took on a human body, that some kind of body is going to be given to us even in Heaven and is going to be an essential part of our happiness . . . ."[2]

It is not too much of a stretch to hold that Lewis believed it was the idea of the resurrection body as a source of a significant part of our happiness that to some extent led early Christians to emphasize the bodily nature of the afterlife, without their ever denying the existence of the soul and its survival: "The earliest Christian documents give a casual and unemphatic assent to the belief that the supernatural part of a man [the soul] survives the death of

---

[1] Lewis, *Christian Reflections*, 130.
[2] Lewis, *Mere Christianity*, 98.

the natural organism. But they are very little interested in the matter. What they are intensely interested in is the restoration or 'resurrection' of the whole composite creature by a miraculous divine act . . . ."[3]

Lewis's view of the body

As an adherent of mere Christianity, Lewis affirmed the resurrection of the dead and the life of the world to come. But in conversations with Roman Catholics, he came to realize that the idea of the resurrection of the body could generate some serious disagreement. For example, Lewis found himself at odds with Catholic members of the Inklings[4] about the practice of cremation. His Roman Catholic friends disagreed with the practice because of what they believed were its pernicious effects on belief in the Christian doctrine of the resurrection of the dead:

> At our Thursday meeting we had a furious argument about cremation. I had never realised the violence of the Papist dislike of the practice, which they forbid. Neither Tolkien nor Havard, to my mind, produced a real argument against it, but only said "you'd find in fact" that it was always supported by atheists; and that a human corpse was the temple of the Holy Ghost. I said "but a vacated temple" and said it [would] be reasonable to blow up a Church to prevent it being defiled by Communists. They denied this, and said if you destroyed a chalice to prevent it being used for Black Mass [a sacrilegious parody of the Roman Catholic Mass] you [would] be mortally guilty: for it was *your* business to reverence it and what the magicians did to it afterwards was theirs. I was surprised at the degree of passion the subject awoke in us all.[5]

The topic of cremation was on Lewis's mind again in a letter to Sheldon Vanauken from February 1955:

> [A Roman Catholic] tells me that they in general forbid cremation because, [though] it by no means logically implies, yet in uneducated minds it tends to *go with*, disbelief in the resurrection of the body.

---

[3] Lewis, *Miracles*, 44.
[4] The Inklings was a group composed of Lewis and several of his male friends. According to Humphrey Carpenter, "[t]hey generally met on Thursday evenings during the University term and sometimes in vacation." They also met regularly on Tuesdays, "Tuesday being the day on which the Inklings had taken to gathering at lunch time . . . ." *The Inklings: C. S. Lewis, J. R. R. Tolkien, Charles Williams, and Their Friends* (London: HarperCollins, 1997), 115, 122.
[5] Lewis, *The Collected Letters of C. S. Lewis: Volume II*, 358.

But they allow it when there is any special reason—e.g. a plague. I don't think, myself, it matters one way or the other.[6]

At the time when Lewis made reference to cremation in these letters, the Roman Catholic Church opposed it because it supposedly implied a denial of the resurrection of the body. Since then, the Church has changed its view: "The Church permits cremation, provided that it does not demonstrate a denial of faith in the resurrection of the body."[7] But the idea of the resurrection of the body was also of interest to Lewis for a reason made vivid by cremation: when a human body is cremated its parts are dispersed into the vast receptacle that is the material world with the possibility of being incorporated into the body of another human being. As I will discuss in Chapter 4, the decomposition of the human body raised questions in the minds of people like Augustine and Aquinas about the nature of the resurrection body. In particular, it led them to wonder whether a person's resurrection body would contain the same parts that composed his or her mortal human body in this life. Given his philosophical mind, Lewis on occasion took the opportunity to weigh in on the issue of the identity of the resurrection body. For example, he came down against the idea that to be raised from the dead is to have the same parts of one's earthly body, which during life have been organically integrated into a whole and "[a]t death . . . [fall] back gradually into the inorganic,"[8] reassembled:

> I agree . . . that the old picture of the soul re-assuming the corpse—perhaps blown to bits or long since usefully dissipated through nature—is absurd. Nor is it what St. Paul's words imply.[9]

> We must, indeed, believe the risen body to be extremely different from the mortal body . . . . It is presumably a foolish fancy (not justified by the words of Scripture) that each spirit should recover those particular units of matter which he ruled before. For one thing, they would not be enough to go round: we all live in second-hand suits and there are doubtless atoms in my chin which have served many another man, many a dog, many an eel, many a dinosaur. Nor does the unity of our bodies, even in this present life, consist in retaining the same particles. My form remains one, though the matter in it changes continually. I am, in that respect, like a curve in a waterfall.[10]

---

[6] Lewis, *The Collected Letters of C. S. Lewis: Volume III*, 566.
[7] *Catechism of the Catholic Church* (New York: Doubleday, 1995), Section 2301.
[8] Lewis, *God in the Dock*, 33.
[9] Lewis, *Letters to Malcolm*, 121.
[10] Lewis, *Miracles*, 244, 246–7.

So Lewis believed that the resurrection body will not be made up of the same parts that it had in this life. He thought that the idea of the resurrected body implies "matter of some kind rushing towards organism as now we see it rushing away."[11] But he wondered if the kind of "matter" need be material in the sense of being different from what is psychological, mental, or ideational in nature. Thus, he speculated in the spirit of idealism (the view that what is "material" is nothing more than ideas or sensations in the soul) that the resurrection body will be "inside the soul": "[a]t present we tend to think of the soul as somehow 'inside' the body. But the glorified body of the resurrection as I conceive it—the sensuous life raised from its death—will be inside the soul."[12] In terms of an instrumental good discussed in the last chapter, Lewis said that "in this life matter would be nothing to us if it were not the source of sensations."[13] It is sensations that Lewis believed are ultimately important to us and, hence, "[w]e are not, in this doctrine [of the resurrection of the body], concerned with matter as such at all; with waves and atoms and all that. What the soul cries out for is the resurrection of the senses."[14] This is because in our present life, matter, as depicted by physics (in largely mathematical terms), lacks those properties that are of ultimate concern to us:

> You know ... that the "real world" of our present experience (coloured, resonant, soft or hard, cool or warm, all corseted by perspective) has no place in the world described by physics or even by physiology. Matter enters our experience only by becoming sensation (when we perceive it) or conception (when we understand it). That is, by becoming soul. That element in the soul which it becomes will, in my view, be raised and glorified; the hills and valleys of Heaven will be to those you now experience not as a copy is to an original, nor as a substitute is to the genuine article, but as the flower to the root, or the diamond to the coal. It will be eternally true that they originated with matter; let us therefore bless matter. But in entering our soul as alone it can enter—that is, by being perceived and known—matter has turned into soul ....[15]

---

[11] Lewis, *God in the Dock*, 33.
[12] Lewis, *Letters to Malcolm*, 122.
[13] Lewis, *Letters to Malcolm*, 121.
[14] Lewis, *Letters to Malcolm*, 121.
[15] Lewis, *Letters to Malcolm*, 123. In saying matter enters experience only by becoming sensation, Lewis probably meant that all we know about the nature of material objects is how they appear to us in sensation, which is to say that we really do not know anything about the intrinsic nature of matter (what matter is like independent of its relationship to our perception of it).

But Lewis was not done. In thinking of the resurrection of the body and the world it inhabits, he creatively suggested that perhaps we should be thinking of a power of the soul to imaginatively create a public sensuous life at will. Such a life "need no longer be private to the soul in which it occurs. I can now communicate to you the fields of my boyhood . . . only imperfectly, by words. Perhaps the day is coming when I can take you for a walk through them."[16]

From the foregoing comments of Lewis about the resurrection body, it is clear he believed not only that a person's body in the resurrection will not include the parts had by his or her body in this life, but also that the *nature* of the resurrection body will be different from that of the human body (the resurrection body will be a different kind of body).[17] Moreover, Lewis thought that the *value* of having a body of any kind was instrumental in nature: the body is good insofar as it is a source of good sensations. Sensations, however, are had by a soul or spirit,[18] and it, as opposed to its body, remains the same entity or thing throughout life and survives death. The view that there is a soul-body composite is known among philosophers and theologians as "soul-body dualism," "substance dualism," or simply "dualism." Lewis was a soul-body dualist who at times tended toward idealism.

---

[16] Lewis, *Letters to Malcolm*, 122.
[17] In written correspondence, Jerry Walls has expressed uneasiness with my claim that Lewis believed the resurrection body of a person will not contain any of the matter that composed the earthly body of that individual. According to Walls, the resurrection body "will be physical, can be touched, can eat, can be recognized with distinguishing marks like scars, etc." Here, Walls seems to have in mind Jesus's resurrection body and the fact that he was able to eat with his disciples and show them the wounds in his body from being crucified (Lk. 24. 36-43; Jn 20. 19-29).

Lewis recognized these facts about Jesus's resurrection body and acknowledged that "references to the risen *body* make us uneasy: they raise awkward questions." Lewis went on to claim that "[t]he body which lives in that new mode is like, and yet unlike, the body His friends knew before the execution. It is differently related to space and probably to time, but by no means cut off from all relation to them. It can perform the animal act of eating. It is so related to matter, as we know it, that it can be touched . . . . [T]he [Gospel] records say that the glorified, but still in some sense corporeal, Christ withdrew into some different mode of being about six weeks after the Crucifixion . . . ." (Lewis, *Miracles*, 240, 241, 254).

In sum, Lewis' view of the resurrection body of Jesus was that it was corporeal in some sense that made it both like and unlike his corporeal body before the resurrection. Beyond this, we are left with awkward questions that we really do not know how to answer. As best as I can ascertain, Lewis never held a view of the resurrection body other than that it was a different kind of corporeal body that did not include the material contents of the pre-resurrection body.

[18] Lewis used these terms "soul" and "spirit" interchangeably: for example he points out that "'Spiritual' is often used to mean simply the opposite of 'bodily' or 'material'" and he adds that "a good word for ['Spirit'] . . . would be 'soul' . . . ." See *Miracles*, 278, 280.

Mental-to-mental causation

In his journal entry for January 18, 1931, Lewis's brother, Warren, after reading the letters of the poet John Keats and coming across something Keats said about the soul, wrote the following: "I wish though, he wasn't interested in such [a] subject as 'The Soul': an infallibly yawn raising topic, though J [Jack, i.e., C. S.] disagreed with me when I said so on our evening walk . . . ."[19] Warren did not spell out why his brother believed the topic of the soul was not a yawner. Rather than speculate further about why Lewis thought it interesting (I suggested in the opening section of this chapter that Lewis's interest in the soul and body might have grown out of his interest in happiness), I turn to what he had to say about the soul.

To begin, Lewis believed that the existence of the human soul in its body is "but a faint image of the Divine Incarnation itself—the same thing in a minor key."[20] Our embodiment is properly viewed as an image of the Incarnation because God is an "eternal self-existent Spirit"[21] who becomes embodied in Jesus of Nazareth. Because we too are souls (spirits), to live with other human beings is to live with other divine beings:

> It is a serious thing to live in a society of possible gods and goddesses, to remember that the dullest and most uninteresting person you can talk to may one day be a creature which, if you saw it now, you would be strongly tempted to worship, or else a horror and a corruption such as you now meet, if at all, only in a nightmare. All day long we are, in some degree, helping each other to one or other of these destinations. It is in the light of these overwhelming possibilities, it is with the awe and the circumspection proper to them, that we should conduct all our dealings with one another, all friendships, all loves, all play, all politics. There are no *ordinary* people. You have never talked to a mere mortal. Nations, cultures, arts, civilizations—these are mortal, and their life is to ours as the life of a gnat. But it is immortals whom we joke with, work with, marry, snub, and exploit—immortal horrors or everlasting splendours.[22]

---

[19] Warren Lewis, *Brothers and Friends*, 77.
[20] Lewis, *Miracles*, 178.
[21] Lewis, *Miracles*, 176.
[22] Lewis, *The Weight of Glory*, 45-6. Lewis also contrasted the mortality of the state with the immortality of the individual in *Mere Christianity*, 74-5 "If individuals live only seventy years, then a state, or a nation, or a civilisation, which may last for a thousand years, is more important than an individual. But if Christianity is true, then the individual is not only more important but incomparably more important, for he is everlasting and the life of a state or a civilisation, compared with his, is only a moment." And why does the state exist at all? Not surprisingly, Lewis thought that "[t]he State exists simply to promote and to protect the ordinary happiness of human beings in this life." Lewis, *Mere Christianity*, 199.

One way Lewis used to make clear that there is a difference between a soul and its body was to highlight the distinction between the first- and third-person points of view and to stress that there is no way of getting to the former by remaining at all times in the latter. He began with a story:

> I was standing today in the dark toolshed. The sun was shining outside and through the crack at the top of the door there came a sunbeam. From where I stood that beam of light, with the specks of dust floating in it, was the most striking thing in the place. Everything else was almost pitch-black. I was seeing the beam, not seeing things by it.
> Then I moved, so that the beam fell on my eyes. Instantly the whole previous picture vanished. I saw no toolshed, and (above all) no beam. Instead I saw, framed in the irregular cranny at the top of the door, green leaves moving on the branches of a tree outside and beyond that, 90 odd million miles away, the sun. Looking along the beam, and looking at the beam are very different experiences.[23]

With the distinction between looking along and looking at drawn, Lewis turned to the experience of pain:

> A physiologist . . . can study pain and find out that it "is" (whatever *is* means) such and such neural events. But the word *pain* would have no meaning for him unless he had "been inside" by actually suffering. If he had never looked *along* pain he simply wouldn't know what he was looking *at*. The very subject for his inquiries from outside exists for him only because he has, at least once, been inside.[24]

So the physiologist can study neural events and know that they are correlated but not identical with pain only because he has experienced pain, where the experience of pain occurs in the physiologist's soul. Lewis made the same point about correlation and nonidentity with regard to neural events and thoughts:

> The cerebral physiologist may say, if he chooses, that the mathematician's thought is "only" tiny physical movements of the grey matter. But then what about the cerebral physiologist's own thought at that very moment? A second physiologist, looking at it, could pronounce it also to be only tiny physical movements in the first physiologist's skull. Where is the rot to end?

---

[23] Lewis, *God in the Dock*, 212.
[24] Lewis, *God in the Dock*, 214.

The answer is that we must never allow the rot to begin. We must, on pain of idiocy, deny from the very outset the idea that looking *at* is, by its own nature, intrinsically truer or better than looking *along*.[25]

So by looking along thought, as we look along pain, we realize that thought is not identical with a physical event or events. Lewis's view here is thoroughly Cartesian (after the seventeenth-century French philosopher and mathematician René Descartes) in nature. That is, as far as he was concerned, there is an obvious fundamental ontological distinction between a soul's psychological life and what goes on in its material body. There is a clear and basic line of demarcation that separates what goes on in us and what happens in the material world around us. Indeed, Lewis was not in the least bit deterred from characterizing what goes on in a soul in terms of what is often today referred to derogatorily as the "Cartesian theater"[26]:

> All sorts of things are, in fact, doing just what the actor does when he comes through the wings. Photons or waves (or whatever it is) come towards us from the sun through space. They are, in a scientific sense, "light". But as they enter the air they become "light" in a different sense: what ordinary people call *sunlight* or *day*, the bubble of blue or grey or greenish luminosity in which we walk about and see. Day is thus a kind of stage set.
>
> Other waves (this time, of air) reach my eardrum and travel up a nerve and tickle my brain. All this is behind the scenes; as soundless as the whitewashed passages are undramatic. Then somehow (I've never seen it explained) they step on the stage (no one can tell me *where* this stage is) and become, say, a friend's voice or the *Ninth Symphony*. Or, of course, my neighbor's wireless—the actor may come on stage to play a drivelling part in a bad play. But there is always the transformation.
>
> Biological needs, producing, or stimulated by, temporary physiological states, climb into a young man's brain, pass on to the mysterious stage and appear as "Love" . . . .[27]

---

[25] Lewis, *God in the Dock*, 215.
[26] For example, see Daniel Dennett, *Consciousness Explained* (Boston: Little, Brown, 1991).
[27] Lewis, *God in the Dock*, 247–8. Here, with his usual sagacity, Lewis foresaw a version of what in contemporary philosophy is known as the "hard problem" or "explanatory gap," which is the inability to explain how what is material in nature either causes or constitutes what is qualitative in nature (e.g., experiences of pleasure, pain, color, sound, taste). See David Chalmers, *The Conscious Mind: In Search of a Fundamental Theory* (Oxford: Oxford University Press, 1996) and Joseph Levine, *Purple Haze: The Puzzle of Consciousness* (Oxford: Oxford University Press, 2001).

So there is a sequence of material events and then there is the occurrence of an immaterial psychological event, whether it be the seeing of color, the hearing of a sound, or the experience of pain or love. Lewis was a Cartesian dualist. Materialism (physicalism), the philosophical view that *everything that exists is material (physical) in nature*, is false.

But while Lewis believed one could readily see the falsity of materialism by means of considerations like those described in the immediately preceding paragraphs, his favorite argument against materialism made use of the soul's ability to reason (think). To understand this argument, Lewis had us first consider another philosophical view know as *naturalism*, which among the educated elite was (and remains to this day) closely associated with materialism. In concise terms, naturalism is the view that *whatever* happens in the world can only be explained in terms of what is material and not mental in nature. In Lewis's own words, "*Nature* means to him [a naturalist] merely 'everything' or 'the whole show' or 'whatever there is,'"[28] and with nature being the whole show, whatever happens is "an inevitable result of the [material] character of the whole system."[29] Naturalists, then, are materialists when it comes to providing explanations and also, typically, in maintaining that everything that exists is material in nature. As I noted in the previous paragraph, Lewis argued that the process of reasoning, which is "a more than natural activity" in a "more than natural agent [a soul],"[30] provides a decisive refutation of naturalism. While his "argument from reason" has been examined and discussed in multiple places, it warrants attention here because it is an extremely important part of the explanation for why he believed in the existence of the soul.

Lewis's most extended treatment of the argument from reason is found in his book *Miracles*. There are two editions of the book because Lewis, in light of a critique of his argument by the Cambridge philosopher Elizabeth Anscombe, saw the need to restate his presentation of it. Though much has been written about whether Lewis lost faith in the argument, the simple fact is that he would not have revised *Miracles* in the way that he did had he ceased to believe in the soundness of the argument.[31]

---

[28] Lewis, *Miracles*, 6.
[29] Lewis, *Miracles*, 15.
[30] Lewis, *Miracles*, 177.
[31] Victor Reppert rightly says the following: "I should note that Lewis not only revised his chapter [in] *Miracles* [in response to Anscombe's critique], but he also expanded the chapter. Now if you really thought that someone had proved you wrong, why in the world would you expand the very chapter that one's opponent had refuted?" "The Ecumenical Apologist," 5.

What, then, is the argument? As I indicated a moment ago, Lewis believed that the problem for naturalism is that if it is true then we do not reason. Naturalism "is really a theory that there is no reasoning,"[32] where by "reasoning" Lewis meant "the practice of inference."[33] If naturalism is true, "what we thought to be our inferences"[34] are not. How does this follow from naturalism?

According to Lewis, reasoning is essentially a *mental* process. While he never explicitly addressed the issue of what it is to be mental, it is clear that Lewis believed an event is "mental" in nature if and only if it is *about* something.[35] "Acts of thinking are no doubt events; but they are a very special sort of events. They are 'about' something other than themselves . . . ."[36] Events of thinking are typically about things other than those acts of thinking (things like cars, ice-cream cones, the thinking subject, or the argument from reason) by means of their *contents* that take us to those things, where content is the object of a propositional attitude like a belief, a desire, or a thought. For example, I can believe that my car is not a lemon, I can hope that my car is not a lemon; I can think that my car is not a lemon; I can believe that the argument from reason is not sound; I can hope that the argument from reason is not sound; and I can think that the argument from reason is not sound. The content here is "the argument from reason is not sound," and the propositional attitude is about the argument from reason by means of this content. Lewis added elsewhere that "to talk of one bit of matter as being true about another bit of matter seems to me to be nonsense."[37] Hence, in his mind the fact that a thought is about something is sufficient to establish the immaterial nature of that thought: "[P]hysical events, as such, cannot in any intelligible sense be said to be 'about' or to 'refer to' anything."[38] And we should never forget that we are as familiar with thought as we are anything else. We know what it is. We begin with it. Indeed, we are more familiar with thought than we are with what it is to be material. What is material in nature is the mystery:

> In saying that thinking is not matter I am not suggesting that there is anything mysterious about it. In one sense, thinking is the simplest

[32] Lewis, *Miracles*, 27.
[33] Lewis, *Miracles*, 29.
[34] Lewis, *Miracles*, 32.
[35] The *locus classicus* of the aboutness of the mental as that which distinguishes it from the material is Franz Brentano, *Psychology from an Empirical Standpoint*, trans. Antos C. Rancurello, D. B. Tyrrell, and Linda L. McAlister (New York: Routledge, 1995), Book One, Chapter 1.
[36] Lewis, *Miracles*, 25.
[37] Lewis, *Christian Reflections*, 64.
[38] C. S. Lewis, *The Discarded Image: An Introduction to Medieval and Renaissance Literature* (Cambridge: Cambridge University Press, 1964), 166.

thing in the world. We do it all day long. We know what it is like far better than we know what matter is like. Thought is what we start from: the simple, intimate, immediate *datum*. Matter is the inferred thing, the mystery.[39]

In addition to mental events having contents and, thereby, being immaterial, events in our mental lives are of two ultimate and irreducibly distinct kinds, namely, actions and passions, which is a distinction that explains or grounds the difference between our being agents and patients. A belief (or, more strictly, the coming to have a belief) is a mental passion, not an action, and, therefore, it is something with respect to which one is directly a patient and not an agent. A choice (strictly speaking, the making of a choice) is a mental action and something with respect to which one is directly an agent. When one makes a choice, one is actively doing something. One's nature as an agent and patient can be intertwined. For example, one can choose to turn on the radio and listen to the morning news and come to learn that one's favorite sports team lost the night before. Or one can choose to investigate naturalism and come to believe in its truth or falsity. In these cases, even though one chooses an action (to turn on the radio or to look into naturalism), the belief that is formed as a result of that chosen action is caused and something with respect to which one is a patient.

Mental events like believings that result from reasoning are caused events with content and with respect to which the believer is a patient. Content, however, is not only believed. It is also said by Lewis to be seen, apprehended, grasped, or known,[40] and sometimes when it is apprehended it becomes part of a reasoning (inferential) process, where what goes on is something like the following.[41]

Consider one of the most important logical inference rules taught in any logic course, *modus ponens*: If A then B; A; therefore B. If one apprehends "If A then B" and also apprehends A, then one cannot help believing that B follows from the contents of these two apprehensions. When believing is the result of an inference like this, the believing is causally explained by the

---

[39] Lewis, *Christian Reflections*, 64. The similarity here with Descartes's view is striking: "Thus . . . this ego, this soul, by which I am what I am, is entirely distinct from the body and is easier to know than the latter. . . . [A]ll the other things of which [certain persons] might think themselves more certain, such as their having a body, or the existence of the stars and of an earth, and other such things, are less certain." René Descartes, *Discourse on Method*, trans. Laurence J. LaFleur (Upper Saddle River, NJ: Prentice-Hall, 1956), 21, 24.
[40] "If you distrust the sensory metaphor in *seen*, you may substitute *apprehended* or *grasped* or simply *known*." Lewis, *Miracles*, 25.
[41] Here I draw upon Stewart Goetz and Charles Taliaferro's *Naturalism* (Grand Rapids, MI: Eerdmans, 2008), 117–22.

mental events of apprehending, grasping, or being aware of mental contents and the logical relationships between them.[42] When this apprehending of mental contents occurs, it causally produces believings.

For example, if one becomes aware that "If Jones accepts the job offer, then he will have to pay more in taxes" ("If A, then B") and aware that "Jones accepts the job offer" (A), then one cannot help but believe that "Jones will have to pay more in taxes" (B) follows from what one has apprehended.

Now consider *modus ponens* again. However, this time assume that besides believing *modus ponens* and apprehending A, one also believes A. In this case, one cannot help also believing B (which is different from being causally determined to believe that B follows from "If A then B" and A, upon apprehending them). In terms of Jones, if one believes Jones accepted the job offer, then one will come to believe that Jones will have to pay more in taxes.

Lewis was convinced that in examples like these we have instances of mental-to-mental causation involving apprehensions and believings. We have genuine instances of reasoning (making inferences) and we *know* that we reason. Here are Lewis's words: "'But', it will be said, 'it is incontestable that we do in fact reach truths by inferences'. Certainly. The Naturalist and I both admit this. We could not discuss anything unless we did."[43]

Given that we know that we reason, Lewis concluded that naturalism must be false. It must be false because reasoning makes clear to us that nature is not the whole show in the sense that not everything that happens is explicable in terms of nonmental, material causes. In contemporary philosophical terms, reasoning violates what is known as the principle of the causal closure of the material world.[44] According to this principle, the world is closed (not open) to mental explanations in the sense that no event can ultimately be explained in terms of something other than what is material (nonmental). Thus, the explanation of a mental event can include nothing other than what is material in nature and there cannot be instances of mental-to-mental causation of any kind, including the kind just illustrated by the examples involving Jones. But if naturalism is itself a philosophical position that is arrived at on the basis of reasoning, as naturalists concede it is, then the game is up. Naturalism ends

---

[42] Lewis, *Miracles*, 23–5.
[43] Lewis, *Miracles*, 31.
[44] For more on the causal closure principle, see Goetz and Taliaferro, *Naturalism*, Chapter 2; Stewart Goetz, "Making Things Happen: Souls in Action," in *The Soul Hypothesis*, eds. Mark Baker and Stewart Goetz (London: Continuum Press, 2011), 99–117; and Stewart Goetz, "Purposeful Explanation and Causal Gaps." *European Journal for Philosophy of Religion* 5 (2012): 141–56.

up being self-defeating because those who espouse it arrive at it on the basis of making inferences. In Lewis's own words:

> Any thing which professes to explain our reasoning fully without introducing an act of knowing thus solely determined by what is known, is really a theory that there is no reasoning.
>
> But this, as it seems to me, is what Naturalism is bound to do. It offers what professes to be a full account of our mental behaviour; but this account, on inspection, leaves no room for the acts of knowing or insight on which the whole value of our thinking, as a means to truth, depends.[45]
>
> It follows that no account of the universe can be true unless that account leaves it possible for our thinking to be a real insight. A theory which explained everything else in the whole universe but which made it impossible to believe that our thinking was valid, would be utterly out of court. For that theory would itself have been reached by thinking, and if thinking is not valid that theory would, of course, be itself demolished. It would have destroyed its own credentials. It would be an argument which proved that no argument was sound—a proof that there are no such things as proofs—which is nonsense.[46]

For those who are not familiar with naturalism and its implications for mental explanation, there might be some skepticism about whether anyone advocates the position Lewis attacked. Does anyone really hold the view that everything that occurs and has an explanation can be given a complete explanation (one that leaves nothing unaccounted for) in thoroughly material terms? Well, a little more than fifty years after the second edition of *Miracles* was published, the philosopher Barry Stroud declared that "'Naturalism' seems to me ... rather like 'World Peace.' Almost everyone swears allegiance to it, and is willing to march under its banner."[47] To make clear that Lewis was not attacking a straw man, consider the following comments by three diehard naturalists.

First, there is David Papineau. He believes naturalism is a commitment to the completeness of physics, where physics is complete in the sense that a purely physical specification of the world, plus physical laws, will always suffice to explain what happens. He is aware that the concepts of physics

---

[45] Lewis, *Miracles*, 27.
[46] Lewis, *Miracles*, 21–2.
[47] Barry Stroud, "The Charm of Naturalism," in *Naturalism in Question*, eds. Mario De Caro and David Macarthur (Cambridge: Harvard University Press, 2004), 22.

change over time. What categories, therefore, will qualify as "physical" in the ultimate or final physics? We cannot, says Papineau, presently answer this question with any certitude. At best, we can specify one category that will not qualify for inclusion, namely, the mental:

> We may not know enough about physics to know exactly what a complete "physics" might include. But as long as we are confident that, whatever it includes, it will have no ineliminable need for any distinctively mental categorizations, we can be confident that mental properties must be identical with (or realized by) certain non-mentally identifiable properties.[48]

So physics in its ideal form will not include mental terms that refer to mental (psychological) properties. For any property or characteristic of the world that is referred to by means of a mental category (term), that category will be replaceable by one that is nonmental in nature, because the property to which it will refer will itself be something nonmental in nature. What about explanations in an ideal physics? Here is what Papineau has to say:

> When I say that a complete physics excludes psychology, and that psychological antecedents are therefore never needed to explain physical effects, the emphasis here is on "needed". I am quite happy to allow that psychological categories *can* be used to explain physical effects, as when I tell you that my arm rose because I wanted to lift it. My claim is only that in all such cases an alternative specification of a sufficient antecedent, which does not mention psychological categories, will also be available.[49]

So, says Papineau, in a complete physics an explanation of events will always be available that does not mention mental (psychological) categories in the sufficient antecedent.

David Armstrong is a second philosopher who advocates naturalism by proposing that an ideal physics has an ultimately privileged explanatory role (no other explanations will supersede those in physics). According to Armstrong, naturalism is "the doctrine that reality consists of nothing but a single all-embracing spatio-temporal system."[50] Contemporary materialism is a form of naturalism and maintains that the single all-embracing temporal

---

[48] David Papineau, *Thinking about Consciousness* (Oxford: Clarendon Press, 2002), 41.
[49] David Papineau, *Philosophical Naturalism* (Oxford: Blackwell, 1993), 31, footnote 26.
[50] David Armstrong, "Naturalism, Materialism, and First Philosophy," *Philosophia* 8 (1978): 261.

system contains nothing but the entities recognized by the most mature physics. Irreducible mental categories have no place in this (or any other) spatio-temporal system as an ultimate or basic explanatory principle, because such a principle entails the characteristic of irreducible intentionality (aboutness, as Lewis thought of it), and intentionality implies the falsity of naturalism. Thus, Armstrong says that "if the principles involved [in analyzing the single, all-embracing spatio-temporal system] were completely different from the current principles of physics, in particular if they involve appeal to mental entities . . . we might then count the analysis as a falsification of Naturalism."[51]

Finally, consider Georges Rey. According to him, the goal of naturalism is to take the beliefs, desires, preferences, choices, and so on that appear to make up our conscious, intelligent, psychological life and explain them in terms that are non-conscious, nonmental, and nonpsychological. Rey insists that any proper explanation of the mental must be in terms that are nonmental. Otherwise, there will be no explanation.

> Any ultimate explanation of mental phenomena will have to be in *non*-mental terms, or else it won't be an *explanation* of it. There might be an explanation of some mental phenomena in terms of others— perhaps *hope* in terms of *belief* and *desire*—but if we are to provide an explanation of all mental phenomena, we would in turn have to explain such mentalistic explainers until finally we reached entirely non-mental terms.[52]

To sum up, naturalism purports to be an account of the universe in the sense that it is "a prime specimen of that towering speculation" that yields "general views of 'reality'."[53] Most remarkably, however, it is a reasoned-to view of reality that makes reasoning impossible. Hence, Lewis concluded it is doomed. Indeed, he believed that for the sake of all involved it had better be doomed because science, which naturalists believe is the discipline upon which all others should be modeled, itself presupposes our ability to reason. It is a discipline whose very existence depends upon the making of inferences. "We infer Evolution from fossils . . . . Unless human reasoning is valid no science can be true."[54] But naturalism entails that humans do not reason. Hence, if naturalism is true, there is no such thing as science. In presenting his argument from reason, Lewis was fond of quoting the following words

---

[51] Armstrong, "Naturalism, Materialism, and First Philosophy," 262.
[52] Georges Rey, *Contemporary Philosophy of Mind* (Oxford: Blackwell, 1997), 21.
[53] Lewis, *Miracles*, 33.
[54] Lewis, *Miracles*, 21.

of J. B. S. Haldane: "If my mental processes are determined wholly by the motions of atoms in my brain, I have no reason to suppose that my beliefs are true . . . and hence I have no reason for supposing my brain to be composed of atoms."[55]

Mental-to-physical causation

According to Lewis, then, the fact that we reason refutes naturalism, because reasoning consists in apprehensions and believings being causally explained by other apprehensions and believings. Reasoning consists of *mental-to-mental causation*. Reasoning is nonnatural or above nature. It is *supernatural*. Lewis recognized that to call what goes on when we reason "'supernatural', is some violence to our ordinary linguistic usage."[56] In terms of the discussion of the previous section, it follows from the fact that reasoning is supernatural that it "won't fit in"[57] to the chain of materialistic causes. But this is no small point. In essence, Lewis believed that what is above nature (the supernatural) gets its foot in the door on any occasion that reasoning takes place, which is countless times each day. And if the supernatural gets its foot in the door on all these occasions, we will need an argument for why it cannot push the door wide open with events like a resurrection from the dead.

In addition to believing that reasoning falsifies naturalism because it consists of mental-to-mental causation, Lewis also believed that it falsifies naturalism because it leads to *mental-to-physical causation*. When he was discussing what the world might have been like before the Fall of Adam, Lewis conceived of that world as one where the soul's (spirit's) power over its body was complete and unresisted. In that situation, "spirit's permanent triumph over natural forces . . . would involve a continued miracle," but it would involve "only the same sort of miracle which occurs [now] every day—for whenever we think rationally we are, by direct spiritual power, forcing certain atoms in our brain . . . to do what they would never have done if left to Nature."[58] And again, "If we are in fact spirits, not Nature's offspring, then there must be some point (probably the brain) at which created spirit even now can produce effects on matter not by manipulation or technics but simply by the wish to do so. If that is what you mean by Magic then Magic is a reality manifested every time you move your hand

---

[55] Lewis, *Miracles*, 22. The quote comes from J. B. S. Haldane, *Possible Worlds* (New York: Harper and Brothers, 1928), 220.
[56] Lewis, *Miracles*, 35.
[57] Lewis, *Miracles*, 35.
[58] Lewis, *Miracles*, 205.

or think a thought."[59] Because such mental-to-physical causation as occurs now does not undermine the integrity of the brain ("The brain does not become less a brain by being used for rational thought"),[60] we should not be surprised if "other parts of Nature might some day obey us as our cortex now does."[61] Such a possibility "would be fantastic only if the present frontier-situation between spirit and Nature in each human being were so intelligible and self-explanatory that we just 'saw' it to be the only one that could ever have existed. But is it [so intelligible and self-explanatory]?"[62] Obviously, thought Lewis, it is not.

Lewis maintained that while the brain can be used for rational thought, being used for rational thought is not the same as being identical with rational thought. And it is worth repeating that he wholeheartedly believed that a thought is not a movement or movements in the brain:

> We are certain that, in this life at any rate, thought is intimately connected with the brain. The theory that thought therefore is merely a movement in the brain is, in my opinion, nonsense, for if so, that theory itself would be merely a movement, an event among atoms, which may have speed and direction, but of which it would be meaningless to use the words "true" or "false."[63]

Lewis held that because reasoning itself involves mental-to-mental causation in a subject that is able to be engaged in mental-to-physical causation, that subject itself is a supernatural object. In other words, instances of these two kinds of causation are sufficient to establish the truth of substance dualism. However, beyond having to recognize mental-to-physical (and physical-to-mental)[64]

---

[59] Lewis, *Miracles*, 245. Lewis said that created spirit "probably" affects matter directly, without making use of any intervening mechanism ("technics"), in the brain. In personal correspondence with Mrs Robert Manly in February 1960, Lewis wrote: "I take it [that] the point at which Rational Soul has purchase on the body—the starting platform from which she controls the whole engine—is the brain." Lewis, *The Collected Letters of C. S. Lewis: Volume III*, 1136.
[60] Lewis, *Miracles*, 205–6.
[61] Lewis, *Miracles*, 250.
[62] Lewis, *Miracles*, 205.
[63] Lewis, *The Weight of Glory*, 103. Lewis was convinced the Incarnation is believable because we already know our thought is not matter in motion: "The discrepancy between a movement of atoms in an astronomer's cortex and his understanding that there must be a still unobserved planet beyond Uranus, is already so immense that the Incarnation of God is, in one sense, scarcely more startling." *Miracles*, 177–8.
[64] It is helpful here to cite again what I quoted in the previous section: "[W]aves . . . of air . . . reach my eardrum and travel up a nerve and tickle my brain. All this is behind the scenes . . . . Then somehow (I've never seen it explained) they step on to the stage [the soul] (no one can tell me *where* this stage is) and become, say, a friend's voice or the *Ninth Symphony*." Lewis, *God in the Dock*, 247–8.

causation, Lewis thought the soul-body relation was shrouded in mystery: "We cannot conceive how the [soul] . . . of any man . . . dwells within his natural organism."[65] Lewis's comment echoed a response of Descartes's to a query from Princess Elizabeth of Bohemia about how it is that a soul moves its body. In a letter to her, Descartes said that concerning the "soul and body [operating] together we have no notion save that of their union."[66] And Descartes wrote in a letter to the philosopher Arnauld:

> [T]hough we are not in a position to understand, either by reasoning or by any comparison drawn from other things, how the mind, which is incorporeal, can move the body, none the less we cannot doubt that it can, since experiences the most certain and the most evident make us at all times immediately aware of its doing so. This is one of those things which are known in and by themselves and which we obscure if we seek to explain them by way of other things.[67]

Given the agreements in views that we have seen in this and the previous section between Lewis and Descartes, it is no surprise that Lionel Adey writes that Lewis in the late 1920s expounded in his "Great War" with his lifelong friend Owen Barfield "the Cartesian dualism he always maintained."[68]

Cartesian dualism is a kind of substance dualism. So far as I know, Lewis never in print addressed the possibility that the subject of mental-to-mental and mental-to-physical causation is a material entity that has two kinds of (dual) properties, material and mental, where use of the latter in reasoning is able causally to affect the material world. In philosophy, this kind of view is commonly referred to as property dualism (or sometimes as the dual-aspect theory).[69] On this view, the reasoning that falsifies naturalism does not occur in a soul, but instead takes place in a human being by virtue of the fact that its brain has mental properties, and events involving those properties causally

---

[65] Lewis, *Miracles*, 178. Also see the "somehow (I've never seen it explained)" in the previous footnote.
[66] René Descartes, *Descartes' Philosophical Writings*, trans. Norman Kemp Smith (New York: The Modern Library, 1958), 252.
[67] Descartes, *Descartes' Philosophical Writings*, 262.
[68] Lionel Adey, *C. S. Lewis' "Great War" with Owen Barfield* (Great Britain: Ink Books, 2002), 54.
[69] While one might be a property dualist/dual-aspect theorist and affirm naturalism because the world is closed to explanation of material events in terms of anything other than material causes, I will assume for the sake of discussion that a property dualist/dual-aspect theorist denies naturalism. For such an individual to affirm naturalism seems to result in the philosophical view known as *epiphenomenalism*, which maintains mental properties are not reducible to material properties but nevertheless cannot explain anything that happens in the material world. They are explanatorily impotent. To say the least, epiphenomenalism is a hard pill to swallow.

produce material effects. According to property dualism, human beings are not a dual soul-body composite but a single entity with a supernatural aspect in the form of mental properties.

If I have read Lewis correctly, I believe he simply assumed the dual-aspect theory is not a viable option. Instead of thinking that he owed an explanation of why it is wrong, he would have wanted to know from anyone who recognized the reality of mental-to-mental and mental-to-physical causation why it is more plausible to think reasoning occurs in a physical entity with two kinds of properties and not in a soul. What possible explanation could such an individual have for thinking that the dual-aspect view is rationally preferable to substance dualism?

In order to render plausible my characterization of Lewis's reasoning at this point, I believe we must once again remind ourselves of the commonsensical nature of Lewis's philosophical thought. He believed that the fact that common sense speaks on behalf of a certain view is a strong consideration in favor of that view. Common sense speaks in favor of soul-body, and not property, dualism. For example, the experimental cognitive scientist Jesse Bering has recently argued that human beings are believers in soul-body (sometimes called "mind-body") substance dualism.[70] As Bering sees things, Darwinian natural selection produced a cognitive system that gave rise to belief in commonsense soul-body dualism. Similarly, the psychologist Nicholas Humphrey, in his recent book *Soul Dust*, recognizes the human inclination to believe in substance dualism. Toward the end of his book, Humphrey points out that other scholars also acknowledge this ordinary belief in substance dualism:

> Thus, development psychologist Paul Bloom aptly describes human beings as "natural-born dualists." Anthropologist Alfred Gell writes: "It seems that ordinary human beings are 'natural dualists,' inclined more or less from day one, to believe in some kind of 'ghost in the machine'. . . ." Neuropsychologist Paul Broks writes: "The separateness of body and mind is a primordial intuition. . . . Human beings are natural born soul makers, adept at extracting unobservable minds from the behaviour of observable bodies, including their own."[71]

To be clear, while Bering, Humphrey, Bloom, Gell, and Broks maintain that human beings naturally believe in substance dualism, they all insist that this belief in substance dualism is false and rests on an illusion. That is, while they

---

[70] Bering, "The Folk Psychology of Souls," 453–98.
[71] Humphrey, *Soul Dust*, 195.

admit it seems to us that we are souls, they claim that, in this case at least, things are not the way they seem. Lewis was well aware of this movement to disenchant the world:

> At the outset the universe appears packed with will, intelligence, life and positive qualities; every tree is a nymph and every planet a god. Man himself is akin to the gods. The advance of knowledge gradually empties this rich and genial universe: first of the gods, then of its colours, smells, sounds and tastes, finally of solidity itself as solidity was originally imagined. As these items are taken from the world, they are transferred to the subjective side of the account: classified as our sensations, thoughts, images or emotions. The Subject becomes gorged, inflated, at the expense of the Object. But the matter does not rest there. The same method which has emptied the world now proceeds to empty ourselves. The masters of the method soon announce that we were just as mistaken (and mistaken in much the same way) when we attributed "souls", or "selves" or "minds" to human organisms, as when we attributed Dryads to the trees. Animism, apparently, begins at home. We, who have personified all other things, turn out to be ourselves mere personifications. Man is indeed akin to the gods: that is, he is no less phantasmal than they.[72]

Lewis thought the final result ridiculous. Why would anyone advocate such a silly view? Not surprisingly, he suggested that one plausible answer has to do with pleasure: "This philosophy [nihilism about the soul's existence], like every other, has its pleasures."[73] There is pleasure to be had in devising arguments that conclude with a denial of the obvious. Moreover, Lewis believed we should never forget that the masters' method to which he referred in the above quote is naturalism. The ultimate absurdity of naturalism is that it ends up devouring the masters themselves. If naturalism is true, the masters no longer exist to think up naturalism.

As I indicated in the Introduction, there has in recent years been a concerted effort to argue that soul-body dualism is a nonbiblical idea imported into the Judeo-Christian view of the world. The introduction of dualism was supposedly a result of the influence of Greek philosophy (especially that of Plato) on the thought of the early church. For example, the highly acclaimed New Testament scholar, N. T. Wright, in discussing Jesus's

---

[72] Lewis, *Present Concerns*, 81–2.
[73] Lewis, *Present Concerns*, 83.

question in the Sermon on the Mount, "What shall it profit for you to gain the whole world and forfeit your soul (*psyche*)," says:

> More particularly, Jesus in the Sermon on the Mount challenges his hearers not to worry about their *psyche*, what they shall eat or drink, or about their *soma* [body], what they shall wear. This distinction is clear, and has nothing whatever to do with Platonic or quasi-Platonic dualism. The body is the outward thing that needs clothing; the *psyche* is [not a soul but] the ongoing life which needs food and drink.[74]

Elsewhere in the same essay, Wright says that the word "'dualism' . . . is one of those terms that I wish we could put out to grass for a long time."[75]

Lewis, I think, would have responded that Wright's rejection of dualism should be put out to pasture, because it was clear to him (Lewis) that the Jews (and Jesus was a Jew) believed in substance dualism:

> From the earliest times the Jews, like many other nations, had believed that man possessed a "soul" or *Nephesh* separable from the body, which went at death into the shadowy world called *Sheol*: a land of forgetfulness and imbecility where none called upon Jehovah any more, a land half unreal and melancholy like the Hades of the Greeks or the Niflheim of the Norsemen. From it shades could return and appear to the living, as Samuel's shade had done at the command of the Witch of Endor.[76]

Moreover, Lewis would not let us forget that the early Christians also believed in ghost survival: "they believed in it so firmly that, on more than one occasion, Christ had had to assure them that He was *not* a ghost."[77] And as Lewis well understood, belief in ghost survival is a belief in a form of substance dualism.

Overall, Lewis held that substance dualism, properly understood, refers to no more, but also to no less, than an ontological distinction between the soul and its body. He thought that, correctly understood, substance dualism is no more a Greek idea than it is a Jewish, Hindu, Buddhist, or Native American idea. Hence, Lewis would have emphasized the distinction between a commonsense, generic dualism and the dualism of those like Plato who philosophized about this ordinary, generic dualism. He would have insisted that what people like Wright fail to grasp is that Plato did not invent

---

[74] Wright, http://www.ntwrightpage.com/Wright_SCP_MindSpiritSoulBody.htm
[75] Wright, http://www.ntwrightpage.com/Wright_SCP_MindSpiritSoulBody.htm
[76] Lewis, *Miracles*, 237.
[77] Lewis, *God in the Dock*, 159.

soul-body dualism, and, therefore, the early church did not buy into such an invention. Given the commonsense notion of soul-body dualism, Lewis would have made clear that one can be a substance dualist and deny both that the soul is naturally immortal (as Plato seems to have thought) and that it is better to be disembodied (again, as Plato seems to have thought) than embodied.

The soul is the person

Gilbert Meilaender, who has written about the social and ethical thought of Lewis,[78] is, like Wright, apparently uneasy with soul-body dualism. In his article entitled "Broken Bodies Redeemed,"[79] he raises what he takes to be the troublesome issue of the union of body and soul in the context of thinking about bioethics. Meilaender claims that we are accustomed, wrongly from his perspective, to saying that the human person (here, I think he means human *being*) "is the union of body and soul," where this view assumes that there are two substances "that are in principle separable, that are temporarily glued together in this life, that will, by God's grace, be separated in such a way that the person continues to live even after the body has died [in the intermediate state], and that will one day have these two parts reunited."[80]

In his effort to call into question soul-body dualism, Meilaender invokes Lewis to support his understanding of a human person. He draws upon Lewis's suggestion in *Miracles* that we should think of a human being as similar to a knight mounted on a horse, where the knight and horse are so wholly one that "the two together make rather a Centaur than a mounted knight."[81] Given this oneness, Meilaender continues, "you can't shoot the horse out from under and have the knight survive unscathed. And you can't imagine the living horse apart from the knight, as if it were 'just' an animal."[82]

What Meilaender does not tell the reader is that Lewis used this image of a centaur twice, once to depict what a human being was like *before* the fall, and a second time to describe a human being in the new creation *after* the

---

[78] For example, see his *The Taste for the Other*.
[79] Gilbert Meilaender, "Broken Bodies Redeemed," www.touchstonemag.com/archives/issue.php?id=126. My response to Meilaender, which follows above, comes from Stewart Goetz, "Mere Dualism?" *Touchstone* April (2007): 9.
[80] Meilaender, "Broken Bodies Redeemed".
[81] Meilaender, "Broken Bodies Redeemed," www.touchstonemag.com/archives/issue.php?id=26.
[82] Meilaender, "Broken Bodies Redeemed," www.touchstonemag.com/archives/issue.php?id=26.

resurrection.[83] Lewis was careful to make clear that the centaur image does not apply to a human being *in* his fallen condition. In this condition, soul and body, spirit and nature, are estranged such that each is at times at odds with the other and the soul's power over its body is disrupted. But most importantly, Lewis used his image of a centaur to support the idea of a working harmony between soul and body, not to suggest that there are not two entities.[84]

Meilaender believes that we should be careful not to think of a *person* as a soul in and of itself, but as a soul united with its body. Lewis would have demurred and insisted that it is right both to think of a *human being* as a soul united with its body and to think of a person as a soul. If we accept that we are persons, which surely seems reasonable, then persons are souls, if we are souls. And Lewis believed that we are souls. In *The Abolition of Man*, he wrote "our souls, that is, ourselves."[85] And in a letter dated February 7, 1950, which was a response to an apparent query from Mrs Frank L. Jones about the nature of a soul, Lewis wrote: "*What is a soul*? I am. (This is the only possible answer: or expanded, 'A soul is that which can say I am')."[86] In *That Hideous Strength*, Lewis described a thoroughgoing materialist named "Frost" who affirmed that his body projected "the illusion of [him] being a soul."[87] While it is true that Lewis recognized that a human being can also say "I" and "Me,"[88] he believed a human being can say this because a soul can say it first.

Lewis sometimes teased out the significance of being able to use "I" in terms of consciousness and its difference from mere sentience.

Suppose that three sensations follow one another—first A, then B, then C. When this happens to you, you have the experience of passing

---

[83] Lewis, *Miracles*, 204–5, 262.
[84] What about the nature of the soul's existence and its relationship to a body between death and the resurrection? While Lewis did not say much about this topic, he was not opposed to the idea that the soul might exist disembodied and unconscious for some time after death before receiving a resurrection body: "I don't say the resurrection of this body will happen at once. It may well be that this part of us sleeps in death, and the intellectual soul is sent to Lenten lands where she fasts in naked spirituality—a ghost-like and imperfectly human condition.... Yet from that fast my hope is that we shall return and re-assume the wealth we have laid down." *Letters to Malcolm*, 123–4. The wealth the soul will have laid down is the color, sound, taste, smell, and feel that we presently know of as the material world.
[85] Lewis, *The Abolition of Man*, 72.
[86] Here we should remember what Lewis said about the Gestapo-man: "inside [him] there is a thing [which] says I and me ...." Lewis, *The Collected Letters of C. S. Lewis: Volume II*, 409.
[87] Lewis, *That Hideous Strength*, 355.
[88] "[I]n every human being a more than natural activity (the act of reasoning) and therefore presumably a more than natural agent is thus united with a part of Nature: so united that the composite creature calls itself 'I' and 'Me'". *Miracles*, 177.

through the process ABC. But note what this implies. It implies that there is something in you which stands sufficiently outside B to notice B now beginning and coming to fill the place which A has vacated; and something which recognizes itself as the same through the transition from A to B and B to C, so it can say "I have had the experience of ABC". Now this something is what I call Consciousness or Soul.... The simplest experience of ABC as a succession demands a soul which is not itself a mere succession of states, but rather a permanent bed along which these different portions of the stream of sensation roll, and which recognizes itself as the same beneath them all.[89]

As I indicated a few paragraphs back, Lewis suggested how a soul's relationship to its physical body might be different in its fallen and pre- and post-fall conditions. Lewis also conceded that while we cannot conceive how a soul dwells in its body, "our own composite existence is not the sheer anomaly it might seem to be, but a faint image of the Divine Incarnation itself—the same theme in a very minor key."[90] However, because he was a thoroughgoing substance dualist, Lewis not only believed that the human soul could and would have a different type of body in the resurrection life, but also believed that while Christ took on a human body to redeem us, he might also have become incarnate in other kinds of bodies in other worlds. For example, in writing to a mother about her son's concern that he (the son) loved the lion, Aslan, of the Narnia stories more than Jesus, Lewis pointed out that "there is one thing Aslan has that Jesus has not—I mean, the body of a lion. (But remember, if there are other worlds and they need to be saved and Christ were to save them as He would—He may really have taken all sorts of bodies in them which we don't know about.)"[91]

It is clear, then, that Lewis never wavered from the view that a human being is a "composite being," one that is composed of a soul and a body. He was a soul-body dualist. Moreover, he maintained both that ordinary people believe in substance dualism and that the Christian message should not call into question this belief. Indeed, it is precisely because Buddhism denied the Atman (soul) that Lewis expressed to Leo Baker in a letter from

---

[89] Lewis, *The Problem of Pain*, 131–2.
[90] Lewis, *Miracles*, 178.
[91] Lewis, *The Collected Letters of C. S. Lewis, Volume III*, 603. In *The Problem of Pain*, 142–3, Lewis speculated that if a lion "is a rudimentary Leonine self," then in the new creation or resurrection life God could give to it "a 'body' as it pleases Him—a body no longer living by the destruction of the lamb, yet richly Leonine in the sense that it also expresses whatever energy and splendour and exulting power dwelled within the visible lion on this earth."

July, 1921 that it (Buddhism) was inferior to Christianity as "a creed for ordinary men."[92]

It is the commonsensical nature of soul-body dualism and the fact that Lewis was an adherent of common sense that supports the conclusion that Lewis would have strongly disagreed with Meilaender's claim that the soul-body dualist understanding of man is a "Disastrous Picture." On the contrary, Lewis would have vigorously contested that claim. Indeed, far from the substance dualist understanding of man being disastrous, in Lewis's mind it served as the basis for a refutation of naturalism and for a belief in the existence of the Absolute Soul, God:

> We must go back to a much earlier view. We must simply accept it that we are spirits . . . at present inhabiting an irrational universe, and must draw the conclusion that we are *not derived from it*. We are strangers here. We come from somewhere else. Nature is not the only thing that exists. There is "another world", and that is where we come from. And that explains why we do not feel at home here.[93]

> When we are considering Man as evidence for the fact that this spatio-temporal Nature is not the only thing in existence, the important distinction is between that part of Man which belongs to this spatio-temporal Nature and that part which does not: or, if you prefer, between those phenomena of humanity which are rigidly interlocked with all other events in this space and time and those which have a certain independence. These two parts of a man may rightly be called Natural and Supernatural: in calling the second "Super-natural" we mean that it is something which invades, or is added to, the great interlocked event in space and time, instead of merely arising from it. On the other hand this "Supernatural" part is itself a created being—a thing called into existence by the Absolute Being . . . .[94]

> In a pond whose surface was completely covered with scum and floating vegetation, there might be a few water-lilies. And you might of course be interested in them for their beauty. But you might also be interested in them because from their structure you could deduce that they had stalks underneath which went down to roots in the bottom. The Naturalist thinks that the pond (Nature—the great event in space and time) is of an indefinite depth—that there is nothing but water however far you go down. My claim is that some of the things on the surface (i.e. in our

---

[92] Lewis, *The Collected Letters of C. S. Lewis: Volume I*, 567.
[93] Lewis, *Present Concerns*, 78.
[94] Lewis, *Miracles*, 275–6.

experience) show the contrary. These things (rational minds [souls]) reveal, on inspection, that they at least are not floating but attached by stalks to the bottom. Therefore the pond has a bottom. It is not pond, pond for ever. Go deep enough and you will come to something that is not pond—to mud and earth and then to rock and finally the whole bulk of Earth and the subterranean fire.[95]

In sum, Lewis believed the soul's awareness of itself *here and now* reveals the falsity of naturalism and the dependent nature of its own existence. Because of the reality of mental-to-mental causation, this awareness by the soul of its contingent existence causes a belief in the existence *here and now* of the Being on which it *here and now* depends for its existence. This Being, thought Lewis, is God: "I presume that only God's attention keeps me (or anything else) in existence at all."[96]

Once more on common sense

Lewis was an advocate for the ordinary person and common sense. He was committed to defending the integrity of beliefs arising out of self-awareness, sense perception, memory, and reason, unless or until there was reason to doubt such beliefs. It is not at all difficult to imagine that Lewis, as an Oxford academic, often heard derisive comments about the naïveté of such an approach when thinking seriously about life and the nature of the world in which we live. Indeed, it is not implausible to describe the academic discipline of philosophy that he knew so well as a profession that seeks to discredit common sense. A tactic often employed by those in or from the academy, who view with scorn the beliefs of others, is to liken the latter's positions to belief in a flat earth. For example, President Barak Obama rebuked opponents of his policy to curb "carbon pollution" with the line "We don't have time for a meeting of the flat-earth society."[97] The President's reference to belief in the flat earth implicitly assumes that only ignoramuses could hold a belief about an environmental issue that enlightened individuals long ago dismissed as poppycock.

Lewis was well aware of attempts to discredit certain beliefs by likening them to a belief in a flat earth. He thought we should doubt the soundness of such an argument because he doubted the existence of a commonsensical

---

[95] Lewis, *Miracles*, 45.
[96] Lewis, *Letters to Malcolm*, 20.
[97] Keith Johnson, Tom Fowler, and Cassandra Sweet, "President Details Sweeping Climate Policies," *The Wall Street Journal*, June 26, 2013, sec. A.

belief that the earth was flat. In *The Discarded Image*, we find him presenting the medieval model of the universe with its celestial mobile spheres and in passing making the following comment: "There was no doubt a level below the influence of the Model. There were ditchers and alewives who had not heard of the *Primum Mobile* and did not know that the earth was spherical; not because they thought it was flat but because they did not think about it at all."[98] Lewis's point here was that common sense does not deliver a belief that the earth is flat. Not because it delivers a belief that the earth has a different shape but because it delivers no belief at all about the topic of the earth's shape.

But how could this be? I think we can plausibly regard Lewis as having reasoned as follows: It is true that as a matter of common sense, ordinary people believe the earth is flat *relative to* the steps that they take and as far as their unaided eyes can see. But beyond these distances, ordinary people believe nothing about the earth's shape. They do not because they have no need in daily life that requires a belief about the matter. They can move and live and have their being without ever turning their attention to it. However, if these individuals, for example, were to take to the sea for a living and see ships disappear on the horizon, they might then contemplate the issue. Moreover, Lewis reminded us that when the ancients did consider the shape of our planet, they concluded that the "Earth is (of course) spherical."[99]

An amusing illustration of Lewis's position about what common sense leaves out comes from the pen of Sir Arthur Conan Doyle. We know from Lewis's letters that his father owned Doyle's work on Sherlock Holmes[100] and it seems that Lewis read it.[101] Here is what Holmes' friend Dr Watson said about Holmes upon first meeting him:

> His ignorance was as remarkable as his knowledge. . . . My surprise reached a climax, however, when I found incidentally that he was ignorant of the Copernican Theory . . . . That any civilized human being

---

[98] Lewis, *The Discarded Image*, 20. The *Primum Mobile* or First Movable was the outermost sphere in the Ptolemaic universe whose "existence was inferred to account for the motions of all the [other spheres]." Lewis, *The Discarded Image*, 96.

[99] Lewis, *The Discarded Image*, 28. See also 140. For a fine contemporary treatment of the invention of belief in the flat earth, see Jeffrey Burton Russell, *Inventing the Flat Earth* (New York: Praeger, 1991).

[100] Lewis wrote to his friend Arthur Greeves in January 1932, that "what makes detective stories appeal to you is that they were one of your first loves in the days when you used to come round and borrow *Sherlock Holmes* from my father . . . ." *The Collected Letters of C. S. Lewis: Volume II*, 34.

[101] In a letter to his father in February 1914, Lewis wrote that "[t]here must be a lot of talk at home about the Greeves affair. What was the dinner like? When you write be sure and tell me all the latest developments. 'The case', as Sherlock Holmes would say, 'is not devoid of interest.'" *The Collected Letters of C. S. Lewis: Volume I*, 48.

in this nineteenth century should not be aware that the earth travelled round the sun appeared to me to be such an extraordinary fact that I could hardly realize it.... "But the Solar System!" I protested. "What the deuce is it to me?" he interrupted impatiently: "you say that we go round the sun. If we went round the moon it would not make a pennyworth of difference to me or to my work."[102]

Sherlock Holmes is fictional, an imaginary character who supposedly never thought about celestial motions because neither his ordinary life nor his work required that he do so. In his case, common sense was idle. An example of how Lewis believed common sense works is found in his treatment of the early Christians' belief that the Son of God sat down at the right hand of the Father:

> What did the early Christians believe? Did they believe that God really has a material palace in the sky and that He received His Son in a decorated state chair placed a little to the right of His own?—or did they not? The answer is that the alternative we are offering them was probably never present to their minds at all. As soon as it was present, we know quite well which side of the fence they came down. As soon as the issue of Anthropomorphism was explicitly before the Church in, I think, the second century, Anthropomorphism was condemned. The Church knew the answer (that God has no body and therefore couldn't sit in a chair) as soon as it knew the question. But till the question was raised, of course, people believed neither the one answer nor the other. There is no more tiresome error in the history of thought than to try to sort our ancestors on to this or that side of a distinction which was not in their minds at all. You are asking a question to which no answer exists....
>
> The earliest Christians were not so much like a man who mistakes the shell for the kernel as like a man carrying a nut which he hasn't yet cracked. The moment it is cracked, he knows which part to throw away. Till then he holds on to the nut, not because he is a fool but because he isn't.[103]

In another context, Lewis sought to answer those who claimed that primitive peoples could not conceive pure spirit (souls distinct from their material bodies):

> We are often told that primitive man could not conceive pure spirit; but then neither could he conceive mere matter. A throne and a local

---

[102] Sir Arthur Conan Doyle, *The Complete Sherlock Holmes* (New York: Doubleday, 1939), 21.
[103] Lewis, *The Weight of Glory*, 131-2, 133.

habitation are attributed to God only at that stage when it is still impossible to regard the throne, or palace even of an earthly king as merely physical objects. In earthly thrones and palaces it was the spiritual significance—as we should say, the "atmosphere"—that mattered to the ancient mind. As soon as the contrast of "spiritual" and "material" was before their minds, they knew God to be "spiritual" and realised that their religion had implied this all along. But at an earlier stage that contrast was not there. To regard that earlier stage as unspiritual because we find there no clear assertion of unembodied spirit, is a real misunderstanding. . . . [I]t is quite erroneous to think that man started with a "material" God or "Heaven" and gradually spiritualised them. He could not have started with something "material" for the "material", as we understand it, comes to be realised only by contrast to the "immaterial", and the two sides of the contrast grow at the same speed. He started with something which was neither and both. As long as we are trying to read back into that ancient unity either the one or the other of the two opposites which have since been analysed out of it, we shall misread all early literature and ignore many states of consciousness which we ourselves still from time to time experience. The point is crucial . . . for . . . any sound . . . philosophy.[104]

Lewis was convinced that, just as the early Christians as ordinary people had no belief about whether God the Father had a throne room that contained chairs for His Son and Him, and ancient peoples initially made no distinction between material and immaterial forms of being until issues they encountered led them to extract these distinctions from a mixed whole, so also ordinary people more generally drew no distinction between a flat and spherical earth until it was demanded of them. And when it was demanded, they unequivocally came down on the side of the sphere. Overall, Lewis believed we moderns too often erroneously ascribe a view to ordinary people about which their common sense never delivered a verdict because they never thought about the matter.

But if Lewis is right and ancient peoples initially made no distinction between material and immaterial forms of being, how could he (and others) be right in claiming that people of common sense affirm a distinction between soul and body? How could it be that dualism is a matter of common sense? As I discussed earlier in this chapter, Lewis believed that ancient peoples, including the Israelites and Christians, distinguished between the soul and body (the ancients were dualists), while thinking of the soul as a ghostly

[104] Lewis, *Miracles*, 122–4.

entity.[105] Initially, this did not translate into a distinction between something that is immaterial and something that is material. The soul was, in Lewis's language, neither and both. It was only upon reflecting about whether the ghostly entity had the same nature as its material body that the immaterial-material distinction came to the fore. Lewis's view was that people knew the answer (that the soul is immaterial) as soon as they knew the question. But until the question was raised, they believed neither the one answer nor the other.

The pleasure of the soul

According to Lewis, experiences of pleasure are intrinsically good and the smell of deity hovers over them. Experiences of pleasure are had by souls and, hence, are through and through spiritual in nature. They are supernatural. Naturalists argue otherwise. For them, pleasures are not supernatural but natural. They are material occurrences in the brain without any intrinsic nature, let alone any good intrinsic nature. Pleasures among philosophers are commonly dubbed *qualia* (plural for the Latin *quale* or quality). Lewis believed that by de-spiritualizing pleasure and denying its intrinsic goodness the naturalist covers over the qualitative divine footsteps on the planet earth. But naturalism is orthodoxy in the professional philosophical world. The naturalist Jaegewon Kim reminds us of just how opposed to common sense the naturalist view of the world is:

> For most of us, there is no need to belabor the centrality of consciousness to our conception of ourselves as creatures with minds. But I want to point to the ambivalent, almost paradoxical, attitude that philosophers [read "naturalists"] have displayed toward consciousness. . . . [C]onsciousness had been virtually banished from the philosophical and scientific scene for much of the last century, and consciousness-bashing still goes on in some quarters, with some reputable philosophers arguing that phenomenal consciousness, or "qualia," is a fiction of bad philosophy. And there are philosophers . . . who, while they recognize phenomenal consciousness as something real, do not believe that a complete science of human behavior, including cognitive psychology and neuroscience, has a place for consciousness . . . in an explanatory/predictive theory of cognition and behavior [read "there is no place for mental-to-physical explanation"]. . . .

---

[105] See Lewis' *Miracles*, 237; *Reflections on the Psalms*, 36–7; and *God in the Dock*, 159.

Contrast this lowly status of consciousness in science and metaphysics with its lofty standing in moral philosophy and value theory. When philosophers discuss the nature of the intrinsic good, or what is worthy of our desire and volition for its own sake, the most prominently mentioned candidates are things like pleasure, absence of pain, enjoyment, and happiness . . . . To most of us, a fulfilling life, a life worth living, is one that is rich and full in qualitative consciousness. We would regard life as impoverished and not fully satisfying if it never included experiences of things like the smell of the sea in a cool morning breeze, the lambent play of sunlight on brilliant autumn foliage, the fragrance of a field of lavender in bloom, and the vibrant, layered soundscape projected by a string quartet. . . . It is an ironic fact that the felt qualities of conscious experience, perhaps the only things that ultimately matter to us, are often relegated in the rest of philosophy to the status of "secondary qualities," in the shadowy zone between the real and the unreal, or even jettisoned outright as artifacts of confused minds.[106]

According to the naturalist, confusion about pleasure entails confusion about the supernatural. Believe what Lewis believed about pleasure and you end up believing in things like souls, happiness, God, and anything else that genuinely makes life worth living. The smell of deity hangs about pleasure.

---

[106] Jaegwon Kim, *Physicalism, Or Something Near Enough* (Princeton, NJ: Princeton University Press, 2005), 10, 11, 12.

Part Two

3

Privation and Goodness

Neither [Milton nor Aristotle] would dispute that the purpose of education is to produce the good man and the good citizen, though it must be remembered that we are not here using the word "good" in any narrowly ethical sense. The "good man" here means the man of good taste and good feeling, the interesting and interested man, and almost the happy man.[1]

Augustine, Aquinas, and Lewis

C. S. Lewis had philosophical views about happiness, pleasure, and pain that he accurately identified as hedonistic. Interestingly, several writers claim that Lewis's philosophical thought was profoundly influenced by that of St Augustine. For example, Adam Barkman says "it is possible to see Augustine as Lewis's pre-eminent philosopher during Lewis's Christian phase . . . because the Saint's golden touch is evident on nearly every branch of Lewis's thought . . . ."[2] There are at least three ways that people believe the writings of Augustine influenced Lewis.

First, Peter Kreeft maintains that Lewis's concept of Joy was rooted in Augustine's assertion that our hearts are restless until they find their rest in God.[3] Second, Gilbert Meilaender believes that Lewis's depiction of the conflict between the cities of St Anne's and Belbury in Lewis's *That Hideous Strength* follows Augustine's idea of the city of God and the earthly city.[4] Third, and most important for this chapter, Douglas Groothuis, after commenting briefly on Augustine's view of evil, says that "[t]he Augustinian view . . .

---

[1] C. S. Lewis, *Rehabilitations and Other Essays* (Oxford: Oxford University Press, 1939), 81.
[2] Barkman, *C. S. Lewis and Philosophy as a Way of Life*, 54.
[3] Peter Kreeft, *C. S. Lewis: A Critical Essay* (Grand Rapids, MI: Eerdmans, 1969), 7. Cf. Meilaender, *The Taste for the Other*, 15, 93; and McGrath, *The Intellectual World of C.S. Lewis*, 107. Augustine's statement is from his *Confessions* trans. William Watts (Cambridge, MA: Harvard University Press, 1995), I, 1.
[4] Meilaender, *The Taste for the Other*, 102–5. Augustine develops his idea of the two cities in his *The City of God*, trans. Marcus Dods (New York: The Modern Library, 1993).

has been defended by . . . [C. S.] Lewis in *Mere Christianity* . . . ."[5] Along with Groothuis, Brian Horne says that Lewis looked favorably on Charles Williams' theology of evil, which "can be traced back to classical Christian sources—through Thomas Aquinas to Augustine of Hippo . . . ."[6]

Now Horne is right about this much: Aquinas took his understanding of evil from Augustine. What is highly dubious is Horne's and Groothuis's belief that Lewis's view of evil, at least at its philosophical core, is traceable to that of Aquinas and Augustine. There are very good reasons to think that Lewis's position on evil was at odds in a most basic and important way with that of Augustine and, thereby, Aquinas. There are equally good reasons to hold that Lewis's view of the value of pleasure was at odds with Aquinas's.

A fair warning to readers: some of the material on Aquinas's understanding of happiness, pleasure, and goodness might need to be read several times. I have worked hard at making what is difficult accessible.[7] Moreover I have liberally quoted from Aquinas, just as I liberally quoted from Lewis, for the purpose of making clear that I am not inventing differences between them.

Augustine's understanding of evil

According to Augustine, God is the supreme good, and as the supreme good He alone is unchangeable. Anything else that exists derives its being from Him. All that God has created is good, but given that He alone is unchangeable, the good things He has created are changeable goods.[8] Now everything that God creates is good insofar as it possesses measure, form, and order: "All things are good: better in proportion as they are better measured, formed and ordered, less good where there is less of measure, form, and order. These three things, measure, form, and order . . . are as it

---

[5] Douglas Groothuis, "Review of *God Forsaken: Bad Things Happen. Is There a God Who Cares? Yes. Here's Proof*," by Dinesh D'Souza, *Christianity Today* (March 2012): 48.
[6] Brian Horne, "A Peculiar Debt: The Influence of Charles Williams on C. S. Lewis," in *Rumours of Heaven: Essays in Celebration of C. S. Lewis*, eds. Andrew Walker and James Patrick (Surrey: Eagle, 1998), 91.
[7] Dorothy L. Sayers, who was a friend of Lewis's, wrote the following about reading Aquinas: "Aquinas (taken in bulk), [is] almost unreadable unless one is accustomed to the scholastic jargon; and even then one could scarcely, I think, read him 'kiver to kiver'. One needs a guide to the important passages." *The Letters of Dorothy L. Sayers: Volume Three: 1944–1950; A Noble Daring*, ed. Barbara Reynolds (Great Britain: The Dorothy L. Sayers Society, 1998), 383.
[8] St Augustine, *The Nature of the Good*, trans. John H. S. Burleigh (Philadelphia: The Westminster Press, 1953), Section I.

were generic good things to be found in all that God has created, whether spirit or body."[9] By "measure, form, and order" Augustine seems to have meant the structure and proportion that is definitive of or proper to an object as a member of its kind. For example, the human body is one that should be symmetrical with respect to the contralateral positioning of its legs, arms, eyes, etc. As properly situated and functioning, these organs contribute to the measure, form, and order of the human organism and, therefore, increase its good. Augustine believed the created order of the universe is a gradation of mutable entities, with spiritual beings occupying a higher place in the order of being than material entities. Measure, form, and order go downward in a hierarchical scale of gradations among kinds of beings, yet members of all types of created objects, because they possess some degree of proper structure and proportionality, are good.

Given this conceptual framework of being and goodness, what, then, is evil? According to Augustine, evil is a disruption or privation of good as measure, form, and order. To the extent that evil is a disruption of this kind, it is disorder and corruption. Wherever there is less measure, form, and order than there ought to be, there evil exists. But whatever is disrupted in this way retains some good to the extent that it maintains some degree of proper structure and proportionality.

Evil, then, is not a thing in itself but a privation or lack of the structure and order that ought to be present in a created object. Augustine stated his view in the following way:

> For what else is that which we call evil but a removal of good? In the bodies of animals, to be afflicted with diseases and wounds is nothing other than to be deprived of health: the aim of treatment is not to make the evils which were in the body, such as diseases and wounds, move from where they were to somewhere else, but rather that they should cease to exist, since a wound or a disease is not in itself a substance but a defect in the substance of flesh. The flesh itself is the substance, a good thing to which those evil things, those removals of the good, known as health, occur. In the same way all evils that affect the mind are removals of natural goods: when they are cured they are not moved to somewhere else, but when they are no longer in the mind once it has been restored to health, they will be nowhere.[10]

---

[9] Augustine, *The Nature of the Good*, Section III.
[10] St Augustine, *The Enchiridion of Faith, Hope, and Love*, trans. Bruce Harbert (Hyde Park, NY: New City Press, 1999), XI, 41.

The renowned scholar of medieval philosophy, Etienne Gilson, summarizes Augustine's understanding of the nature of evil as follows:

> [E]vil can only be the corruption of one or other of these perfections in the nature possessing them. An evil nature is one in which measure, form or order is vitiated, and it is only evil in exact proportion to the degree in which they are vitiated. If the nature were not vitiated, it would be all order, form and measure, i.e. it would be good; even when vitiated, as nature it is still good, and evil only in so far as it is vitiated.[11]

It is important to make clear that on the Augustinian privationist view of evil, nothing—no entity—can be completely evil. Evil as privation is parasitic on good in the sense that it requires for its presence some degree of measure, form, and order. To the degree that this proper structure and proportionality is present, there goodness is present. To the degree that this proper structure and proportionality is absent, there evil is present. But it must be stressed that though evil is a privative parasite, it is not a thing. It is not an entity in its own right. Its status as a privative parasite consists in its being a lack of measure, form, and order.

Equally important for Augustine's view of evil is the idea that evil is not privation or lack *per se*. For example, it is not evil that a stone cannot see. The stone's lack of sight is not evil because it was never intended that a stone should possess the structure and order that facilitates sight. Blindness is only evil in an entity that was supposed to be able to see. Similarly, it is not evil that a tree cannot hear. It was never intended that a tree should be able to hear. Hence, the lack in a tree of the measure, form, and order that facilitates hearing is not evil. A human being, however, should have the requisite structures that promote sight and hearing. Hence, damage to an eye or an ear that results in blindness or deafness in a person is a real evil.

In conclusion, on the Augustinian view of evil, evil cannot exist in and of itself but only as a parasite on what is good. Should all measure, form, and order cease to be, evil would cease to be. All creation is good, some parts containing more structure and order than others. But wherever there is a lack of measure, form, and order that should be present, there is evil.

---

[11] Etienne Gilson, *The Christian Philosophy of Saint Augustine*, trans. L. E. M. Lynch (New York: Random House, 1960), 144.

Aquinas's understanding of evil

Aquinas reiterated the thought of Augustine when it came to the nature of evil. According to Aquinas, "evil cannot signify a certain existing being, or a . . . positive kind of thing. Consequently it signifies a certain absence of a good."[12] Writing approvingly of Augustine's view of evil, Aquinas said "St Augustine writes that evil is not except in good."[13] And again, "by reason of the deprivation that it denotes, evil is said to destroy good, for the decay and privation of good is what indeed it is."[14] Evil is "a defection from good" and as such "is found in things just as decay is, which itself is a sort of evil."[15] And like Augustine, Aquinas made clear that not every absence of good is evil:

> The mere negation of a good does not have the force of evil, otherwise it would follow that wholly non-existents were bad, also that a thing was bad because it did not possess the quality of something else, a man, for instance, who was not swift as a mountain-goat and strong as a lion. The absence of good taken deprivatively is what we call evil, thus blindness is the privation of sight.[16]

In other words, it is not simply the lack of a good that is evil. Evil is the corruption of a thing's nature—what it is that a thing is supposed to be and do. Because a man's nature does not include the property of being able to run like a mountain-goat, the fact that a man is unable to run in that way is not an evil. However, because a man's nature does include being able to see (here, it is appropriate to think of 20-20 vision), the inability to see as he is supposed to see is a real privation and, hence, a real evil. The ultimate subject of the blindness (to whatever degree) is not the eyesight itself but the man.[17] It is the man and not the eyesight that is supposed to be able to see. The following two quotes nicely capture the essentials of Aquinas's understanding of evil:

> Since . . . evil is privative of good and not purely negative, not every absence of good is an evil, but only of that which a thing by nature can have and is expected to have. The lack of sight is an evil in an animal, but

---

[12] St Thomas Aquinas, *Summa Theologiae: Volume 8 (Ia. 44-49), Creation, Variety, and Evil*, trans. Thomas Gilby, O.P. (New York: McGraw-Hill, 1967), Ia. 48, 1 ad.
[13] Aquinas, *Summa Theologiae: Volume 8 (Ia. 44-49), Creation, Variety, and Evil*, Ia. 48, 3 ad.
[14] Aquinas, *Summa Theologiae: Volume 8 (Ia. 44-49), Creation, Variety, and Evil*, Ia. 48, 1 ad 4.
[15] Aquinas, *Summa Theologiae: Volume 8 (Ia. 44-49), Creation, Variety, and Evil*, Ia. 48, 2 ad.
[16] Aquinas, *Summa Theologiae: Volume 8 (Ia. 44-49), Creation, Variety, and Evil*, Ia. 48, 3 ad.
[17] Aquinas, *Summa Theologiae: Volume 8 (Ia. 44-49), Creation, Variety, and Evil*, Ia. 48, 3 ad 3.

not in a stone which is not made to see. Likewise it is not according to the nature of a creature that it should be self-preserving in being.... Hence it is no evil for a creature to be unable to keep itself in existence.[18]

Now, evil is in a substance because something which it was originally to have, and which it ought to have, is lacking in it. Thus, if a man has no wings, that is not an evil for him, because he was not born to have them; even if a man does not have blond hair, that is not an evil, for, though he may have such hair, it is not something that is necessarily due him. But it is an evil if he has no hands, for these he is born to, and should, have—if he is to be perfect. Yet this defect is not an evil for a bird.[19]

In keeping with the privationist understanding of evil, Thomas thought of immoral or vicious action as a privation of how an agent is supposed to choose or will. Thus, he said that "[n]othing that exists is called bad because it exists, but rather because it fails to exist in some way; thus a man is called bad when he fails to be virtuous, and an eye bad when its vision fails."[20] So as agents with choices to make, human beings are rightly thought of as entities which can and are expected to preserve a moral order. When they choose morally or virtuously, they preserve that order. When they choose immorally or viciously, they undermine that order. Thus, "a privation of order, or due harmony, in action is an evil for action. And because there is some due order and harmony for every action, such privation in an action must stand as evil in the unqualified sense."[21] The important point here is that even in the realm of action, as in the realm of nonaction, "evil is lack of some sort of existence."[22]

Is pain evil?

On the privationist account of evil espoused by Augustine and Aquinas, "evil" is a contextually dependent term. In the words of the Thomist scholar Herbert McCabe, "whether or not some state of affairs is to be called evil will depend on where, or in what subject, this state of affairs occurs."[23] That is, the

---

[18] Aquinas, *Summa Theologiae: Volume 8 (Ia. 44-49), Creation, Variety, and Evil*, Ia. 48, 5 ad 1.
[19] St Thomas Aquinas, *Summa Contra Gentiles: Book Three*, trans. Vernon J. Bourke (Notre Dame, IN: University of Notre Dame Press, 1975), 6: 1.
[20] St Thomas Aquinas, *Summa Theologiae: Volume 2 (Ia. 2-11), Existence and Nature of God*, trans. Timothy McDermott, O. P. (New York: McGraw-Hill, 1964), Ia. 5, 3 ad 2.
[21] Aquinas, *Summa Contra Gentiles: Book Three*, 6: 3.
[22] Aquinas, *Summa Theologiae: Volume 2 (Ia. 2-11), Existence and Nature of God*, Ia. 5, 2 ad 3.
[23] Herbert McCabe, *God and Evil in the Theology of St Thomas Aquinas*, ed. Brian Davies (London: Continiuum, 2010), 65.

lack of sight *per se* is not evil. It is the lack of sight in the context of an entity that is supposed to be able to see that is evil. Evil is a privation or deprivation in the sense that it is a lack of the properties that a thing should have. Once again, I can do no better at this point than quote McCabe: "Since evil is a deprivation of good, in order to understand what an evil is we need to know of what good it is the deprivation; and this means that we must know the nature of the thing that is said to be evil. From this it follows that whatever is evil must at least have a nature.... There cannot be anything that is evil without being in some respect good...."[24]

Given the privative understanding of evil, what did Aquinas think about an experience of pain? Is it intrinsically evil? Because Thomas thought evil is privation, he maintained "no essence is evil in itself."[25] Hence, pain, which in its essence is that which hurts, cannot be evil in itself. Aquinas held that "[t]o the extent that [a thing] possesses being, it has something good...."[26] So, pain, insofar as it has being, is good, and in its essence is not evil. As Rudi A. Te Velde says in commenting on Aquinas's view of evil, "[o]ne cannot speak of things as being in themselves [intrinsically] and essentially evil."[27] To say "Pain is intrinsically evil" is to say that pain in its essence is evil and, thus, evil no matter where or when it occurs. As intrinsically evil, pain is evil independent of its relationship to anything else. If pain is intrinsically evil, evilness is natural to it. But because Thomas held that evil is essentially privative in nature and cannot be natural to any subject, pain cannot be intrinsically evil. His position is clear: "it is of the very definition of evil that it be a privation of that which is to be in a subject by virtue of its natural origin, and which should be in it. So, evil cannot be natural to any subject, since it is a privation of what is natural."[28]

Lewis was at odds with Aquinas about the value status of pain insofar as he affirmed the intrinsic evilness of pain. Though I am not aware of any place where Lewis addresses the matter of why experiences of pain fail to satisfy the privative account of evil, his commonsensical approach to philosophical matters would surely have led him to affirm that pain seems to be anything but a lack or absence of some kind. In itself, it is something positive in nature whose essence is evil. "Pain hurts. That is what the word means."[29] And because pain positively hurts, it "insists upon being attended to. God...

---

[24] McCabe, *God and Evil in the Theology of St Thomas Aquinas*, 66.
[25] Aquinas, *Summa Contra Gentiles: Book Three*, 7: 1.
[26] Aquinas, *Summa Contra Gentiles: Book Three*, 7: 3.
[27] Rudi A. Te Velde, "Evil, Sin, and Death: Thomas Aquinas on Original Sin," in *The Theology of Thomas Aquinas* eds. Rik van Nieuwenhove and Joseph Wawrykow (Notre Dame, IN: University of Notre Dame Press, 2005), 145.
[28] Aquinas, *Summa Contra Gentiles: Book Three*, 7: 6.
[29] Lewis, *The Problem of Pain*, 105.

shouts in our pains: it is His megaphone to rouse a deaf world."[30] Deafness is the lack of an ability to hear sound. Pain is something that positively breaks through silence with its intrinsic evilness.

Lewis believed pain is intrinsically evil and as such not a privation. Did he, however, completely dismiss the Thomist (and Augustinian) conception of evil as privation? No. To explain why, consider the following thoughts of John Randolph Willis about Lewis's concept of evil. The quote is lengthy, but well worth serious consideration:

> [I]n the space trilogy Ransom has difficulty explaining the concept of evil to one of the rational beings on Malacandra. He finally hits on the idea of bentness. The silent planet (earth) has become very bent; the people there are held prey by a bent Oyarsa who rules from his own world (hell).
>
> This is an interesting explanation of the meaning of evil, one which Lewis may have taken from Pseudo-Dionysius. It is a felicitous choice for at least two reasons: something that is bent out of shape is obviously distorted, is not normal, does not conform to the usual pattern, represents a lack of some object (person, relationship) of a quality that should be present; by the same token, the bentness is also a nothingness. It never exists by itself; it can only exist in something good. It is a nothing, a lack rather than a something. Hence, nothing is totally evil, since evil can only exist in a good. The devil is not totally evil inasmuch as he is a being, and every being by the fact that it exists is good. Omne ens ist bonum [every being is good], as the philosopher says.
>
> This idea, however, is more compelling logically than psychologically. We somehow feel evil is more than lack, distortion, bentness, nothing. For all of its nonbeing, it can sometimes feel very effective. And it is difficult to think of some of Lewis's fictional characters as merely bent. The witches in *The Chronicles of Narnia* are malevolent figures seeking to work positive harm. So is Screwtape and so are Frost, Winter, and Fairy Hardcastle in *That Hideous Strength*. Thus for Lewis to say that evil is merely a privation of good is not altogether convincing in the face of some of the evil he has depicted for us.[31]

But Lewis did not say that evil is *merely* a privation of good. Here it is helpful to remember that he wrote about the problem of evil under the title *The*

---

[30] Lewis, *The Problem of Pain*, 93.
[31] John Randolph Willis, S.J., *Pleasures Forevermore: The Theology of C. S. Lewis* (Chicago: Loyola University Press, 1983), 56–7.

Problem of Pain. And he did so because he believed pain is a positive (non-privative) reality that is intrinsically evil. Lewis believed, in Willis' words, that "evil is more than lack, distortion, bentness, nothing." It is more than this because it is intrinsically evil and, thus, evil whenever and wherever it is found.

However, there is also instrumental evil, and so far as I know Lewis never denied that instrumental evil is rightly understood as the privation of good. And for good reason. To understand why, consider blindness. Blindness is evil in Lewis's view because it is the absence of sight that should be present. Similarly, immoral action is rightly understood as a deprivation or privation insofar as an agent's choice fails to measure up to the morally required choice that should have been made. But for Lewis, such privations are evil because ultimately they are related to the lack of an intrinsic good or the presence of an intrinsic evil, where the latter is not a privation. Thus, blindness is instrumentally evil because it deprives an individual of a source of pleasure (sight) that he should have. Blindness can also be instrumentally evil if it causes pain in its subject. And an immoral choice to produce bodily harm is not only instrumentally evil insofar as it fails to measure up to the moral standard but can also be instrumentally evil insofar as it produces a privation in the victim's body (for example, a wound), which is itself instrumentally evil because it either produces pain that is intrinsically evil or prohibits experiences of pleasure that are intrinsically good.

In Lewis's view, bodily privations like the loss of sight or hearing are evil only insofar as they are ultimately tied to potential and actual experiences of intrinsically good pleasure and intrinsically evil pain. Thus, the witches in *The Chronicles of Narnia* can seek to work positive harm only because pain is intrinsically evil. The idea of moral evil is accurately captured by the idea of bentness, because that form of evil is a failure to conform to a pattern (Willis' expression) or a failure to measure up to a standard, where that standard is moral duty in the form of choosing rightly. But the idea of moral duty makes sense in Lewis's view only if pain is positively intrinsically evil and undermines the happiness of the person who experiences it.

In sum, contrary to Willis' characterization of Lewis's view of evil, Lewis did not say that evil is merely a privation of good. The idea that all evil is bentness is the view of Aquinas and Augustine. It is not the view of Lewis. And contrary to what people like Groothuis and Horne would have us think, Lewis believed the view of evil held by these distinguished medieval thinkers was inadequate when applied to experiences of pain. Lewis assented to a view of evil that helps explain his adherence to a hedonistic view of happiness, where perfect happiness is nothing but experiences of pleasure that are intrinsically good. This happiness cannot include experiences of pain because pain is intrinsically evil.

I close this section with a point of clarification. While Lewis denied that the evilness of pain is nothing more than a privation of good, he did affirm that moral evil is parasitic on the possibility of experiencing the intrinsic goodness of pleasure, and it is important not to confuse the concept of privation with that of being parasitic. For example, in challenging the cosmological idea "that there are two equal and independent powers at the back of everything, one of them [morally] good and the other [morally] bad, and that this universe is the battlefield in which they fight out an endless war,"[32] Lewis insisted that "[moral] evil is a parasite, not an original thing."[33] To illustrate his point, Lewis stressed that in the context of the Christian account of the creation and Fall, nothing was originally just evil (bad). Thus, even "the devil is a fallen angel"[34] (a good being gone bad) and "pleasure, money, power, and safety are all . . . good things."[35] The devil as a fallen angel is an instance of the truth that no one is ever evil for the sake of being evil. No one ever pursues evil for its own sake. Because the performance of an evil action is parasitic on the possible experience of some good, the former would never occur without the possibility of the latter: "Wickedness, when you examine it, turns out to be the pursuit of some good in the wrong way. You can be good for the mere sake of goodness: you cannot be bad for the mere sake of badness. . . . Goodness is, so to speak, itself: badness is only spoiled goodness. And there must be something good first before it can be spoiled."[36]

Ultimately, in Lewis's view, good beings can go bad morally only because God, the single, thoroughgoing morally "Good Power,"[37] created them to enjoy what is good. "All the things which enable a bad man to be effectively [morally] bad are in themselves good . . . ."[38] In this way, evil in its moral form is parasitic for its occurrence on what is nonmorally intrinsically good (pleasure). But a morally evil choice, while it is parasitic on what is good, is also a privation insofar as it is a failure to measure up to the standard of

---

[32] Lewis, *Mere Christianity*, 42.
[33] Lewis, *Mere Christianity*, 45.
[34] Lewis, *Mere Christianity*, 45.
[35] Lewis, *Mere Christianity*, 44.
[36] Lewis, *Mere Christianity*, 44.
[37] Lewis, *Mere Christianity*, 44.
[38] Lewis, *Mere Christianity*, 45.

choice that should have been met.³⁹ Moreover, the experience of pain that is caused by a morally evil choice is a non-privative, positive reality. And the experience of this positive, evil reality is parasitic on what is good in the sense that no one would take the risk of causing it in others or himself unless there were the intrinsic good of experiencing pleasure to be had and enjoyed.⁴⁰

---

[39] One might view the standard itself as a good thing, but in Lewis' view it would have to be viewed as a derivatively good thing, because it presupposes the possibility of experiencing intrinsically good pleasure and intrinsically evil pain. Stated differently, a moral standard presupposes non-moral intrinsic good and evil.

[40] Lionel Adey says the following about Lewis: "He profoundly agrees with St. Thomas... in thinking evil not positive but 'privative', an absence of good." *C. S. Lewis' Great War with Owen Barfield*, 26. In a few places, Lewis did write that evil is privation. For example, in his review of Helen M. Barrett's *Boethius: Some Aspects of His Times and Work*, Lewis said "[e]vil consists not in being, but in failing to be; it is privative, defective, parasitic. In this form the doctrine [that evil is privation] is... the only sound basis for any metaphysic of value. Indeed, the opposite theology that evil is as substantial as good and has a *natura* of its own, invites a desperate dualism and makes the choice between good and evil, in the long run, something like an arbitrary allegiance to one of two parties." C. S. Lewis, *Image and Imagination*, ed. Walter Hooper (Cambridge: Cambridge University Press, 2013), 202.

In light of everything else Lewis had to say about the nature of evil, and to avoid ascribing incompatible views to him (Lewis' review of Barrett's book was written in February, 1941, a year after *The Problem of Pain* was published), it is plausible to maintain that Lewis was affirming the following in his review of Barrett: To avoid a metaphysical dualism of two ultimate substances, one morally good and one morally evil, theology must affirm that ultimately there is only one substance, God, who is perfectly morally good. Moral evil (as I explained above) is privative insofar as it fails to measure up to a standard of choice. Created persons make privative instrumentally evil choices in pursuit of what is intrinsically good (pleasure). If there were no intrinsic good, there would be no reason to perform instrumentally evil actions. In this sense, evil is parasitic on good. Moreover, in affirming that pain is intrinsically evil, Lewis maintained that evil is a property (of pain). A property is not a substance.

Lewis also wrote that evil is privative in *De Bono et Malo*. A careful reading of that text makes clear that he was denying that any group of moral beings can be absolutely morally evil in the sense that its members perform only immoral actions. The members' evil actions presuppose a backdrop of good, cooperative behavior between them. In this sense, evil is parasitic. Lewis wrote that "[t]he impossibility of absolute evil is also shown by Plato (*Republic* Bk I) when he shows that a wicked State (and for Plato the State is the symbol of the soul) perseveres in existence only by the goodness that is in it, and if it were absolutely evil would cease to be. So Jesus said that Satan's kingdom could not stand if it were divided against itself: showing that even if we assume a species of superhumanly evil beings, even they can maintain themselves only in internal concord and good faith: that is, not by their evil, but by such goodness as they have. An error in arithmetic presupposes at least some correctness: if we have some notion of multiplication we can multiply wrongly. But there cannot be an absolute error, because long before we reached it, we should have to destroy the numerical system itself, and thus abolish all arithmetic, and therefore all arithmetical errors. (A cat never gets the wrong answer to a sum). In the same way, before we reach an absolutely evil soul we should have disintegrated soul life altogether and therefore rendered all evil impossible. Therefore there is no absolute evil." Lewis, *De Bono et Malo*, 3."

Aquinas's account of pleasure, happiness, and goodness

Unlike Lewis, Aquinas denied that pain is intrinsically evil and maintained instead that evil is through and through privative in nature. What did he think about happiness and its relationship to pleasure? Was he, like Lewis, a hedonist about happiness? He was not.

According to Thomas, "the essential meaning of the good is that it provides a terminus for appetite [desire], since [as Aristotle said] 'the good is that which all desire.' Therefore every action and motion are for the sake of a good."[41] Now, "the ultimate end of man, and of every intellectual substance, is called felicity or happiness, because this is what every intellectual substance desires as an ultimate end, and for its sake alone."[42] Thus, because desire is aimed at what is good and human beings, as intellectual substances (entities or things), desire happiness as their ultimate end, this happiness must be their ultimate good. According to Aquinas, "everybody is bound to wish for happiness. For it signifies . . . complete goodness. Since the good is the object of the will, the perfect good is that which satisfies it altogether. To desire to be happy is nothing else than to wish for this satisfaction."[43] Each and every person both wishes for happiness and wishes that it would never end, "for an endless duration of the good is naturally desired."[44]

In Aquinas's view, then, our happiness is good and because it is, we desire it. But what is happiness? To understand Thomas' conception of happiness, it is helpful to view it within the context of his belief that a human being has an overall purpose or end that it seeks to achieve, where this end is happiness. In thinking about what happiness is, Aquinas focused on the fact that a human being is a substance that has powers to *act* in different ways. In light of having these powers, this substance is capable of exhibiting virtues, where "[v]irtue denotes a determinate perfection of a power. The perfection of anything, however, is considered especially in its relation to its end [goal, purpose, telos]. Yet the end of a power is its act. A power is said to be perfect, therefore, in so far as it is determined to its act."[45] For example, as I will explain in more detail in a moment, a human being has the power to know (understand) and the exercising of that power is an act of knowing. So an act of knowing is the perfection of the power to know and this perfection that is the act of knowing

---

[41] Aquinas, *Summa Contra Gentiles: Book Three*, 3: 3.
[42] Aquinas, *Summa Contra Gentiles: Book Three*, 25: 14.
[43] St Thomas Aquinas, *Summa Theologiae: Volume 16 (Ia2ae. 1-5), Purpose and Happiness*, trans. Thomas Gilby, O. P. (New York: McGraw-Hill, 1969), Ia2ae. 5, 8 ad.
[44] Aquinas, *Summa Contra Gentiles: Book Three*, Chapter 29: 7.
[45] St Thomas Aquinas, *Summa Theologiae: Volume 23 (Ia2ae. 55-67), Virtue*, trans. W. D. Hughes, O. P. (New York: McGraw-Hill, 1969), Ia2ae. 55, 1 ad.

perfects the person that is its subject and makes him a good human being and, thereby, happy.

At this point, it is helpful to remember the distinction between action and passion and that we are essentially passive with respect to our experiences of pleasure. Experiencing pleasure is not an activity of ours. It is something that happens to us. Thus, on a hedonistic conception of happiness like Lewis's, happiness is something with respect to which a person is passive. For Aquinas, however, "man's happiness has to be an activity."[46] At the heart of an adequate explanation of Aquinas's rejection of a hedonistic conception of happiness is his belief that happiness is an activity. If we think with Aquinas in terms of perfect happiness, "happiness or beatitude, by which a man is made most perfectly conformed to God, and which is the fulfilment of human life, is an activity."[47] The following is Aquinas's concise summation of his view concerning happiness as activity: "Happiness is the final perfection of a human being. But each thing is perfect to the extent to which it is in actuality [is acting], for potentiality is imperfect without actuality. Consequently, happiness must consist in the final actuality of a human being."[48]

Actuality implies activity, and activity implies the perfection both of the power the exercise of which is that activity and of the human being whose activity it is, where that perfection is happiness. But what kind of activity constitutes perfect happiness? According to Thomas, "[t]he ultimate happiness of man consists in his highest activity, which is the exercise of his mind."[49] Thus, "[r]eason or mind . . . is the proper seat of virtue,"[50] because "the act of understanding is the proper operation of an intellectual substance" and "an intelligent being attains his ultimate end by understanding [God]."[51] Thus, *intellectual* virtue is at the heart of perfect happiness. Aquinas called this intellectual virtue "contemplation," where contemplation is essentially "a simple gaze upon a truth,"[52] an immediate non-inferential intellectual

---

[46] Aquinas, *Summa Theologiae: Volume 16 (Ia2ae. 1-50, Purpose and Happiness*, Ia2ae. 3, 2 ad.
[47] Aquinas, *Summa Theologiae: Volume 23 (Ia2ae. 55-67), Virtue*, Ia2ae. 55, 2 ad 3.
[48] Aquinas, *Summa Theologiae: Volume 16 (Ia2ae. 1-5), Purpose and Happiness*, Ia2ae. 3, 2 ad. This is my translation of the Latin: "Est enim beatitudo ultima hominis pefectio. Unumquodque autem intantum perfectum est inquantum est actu; nam potentia sine actu imperfect est. Oportet ergo beatitudinem in ultimo actu hominis consistere." Aquinas could also say that "happiness is the perfection of soul" (beatitudo est perfectio animae). St Thomas Aquinas, *Summa Theologiae: Volume 16 (Ia2ae. 1-5), Purpose and Happiness*, Ia2ae. 4, 5ad 1.
[49] Aquinas, *Summa Theologiae: Volume 3 (Ia. 12-13), Knowing and Naming God*, trans. Herbert McCabe, O. P. (Cambridge: Cambridge University Press), Ia. 12, 1 ad.
[50] Aquinas, *Summa Theologiae: Volume 23 (Ia2ae. 55-67), Virtue*, Ia2ae. 55, 4 ad 3.
[51] Aquinas, *Summa Contra Gentiles: Book Three*, Chapter 25: 3, 5.
[52] Aquinas, *Summa Theolgiae: Volume 46 (2a2ae. 179-182), Action and Contemplation*, trans. Jordan Aumann, O. P. (Cambridge: Cambridge University Press, 2006), 2a2ae. 180, 3 ad 1.

seeing. "[M]an's last and perfect beatitude [happiness], which he expects in the life to come, is wholly centred on contemplation."[53] Perfect happiness is the mental act of contemplating divine truths; it is an exercising of the intellect directed at divine things. Because Aquinas was a Christian, he held that perfect happiness is the contemplative vision of the divine (God's) essence: "Complete happiness requires the mind to come through to the essence itself of the first cause [God]. And so it will have its fulfillment by union with God as its object, for ... in him alone our happiness lies."[54] "[C]ontemplation above all is sought for its own sake."[55]

What about the relationship between pleasure and this contemplative activity? Aquinas is clear that "happiness turns on the mind's act of vision [of God], not on the delight [pleasure]."[56] This act of vision or active contemplation is rooted in the mind's (the man's) desire for its highest good, which is God. Thus, instead of affirming that happiness consists of nothing but experiences of pleasure, Aquinas held that pleasure is not the essence of happiness but results from or is a consequence of being happy: "And so it is manifest that not even the delight [pleasure] resulting from the perfect good is the decisive point of happiness, but a sort of essential property or result of it."[57] Pleasure results from being happy because it is essentially a passion that is the resting of desire in the possession of a desired good,[58] where possession of that good through activity is what makes a person happy. It is true that "as good is desired on its own account, so too is pleasure desired and not on account of anything else."[59] But while pleasure is not pursued as a means to something else (no one seeks it to attain something else), if we think in terms of the motive of our acting then "pleasure is desired on account of something other than itself, namely the good which is the object providing delight...."[60] "Consequently... pleasure is [not] the sovereign and essential

---

[53] Aquinas, *Summa Theologiae: Volume 16 (Ia2ae. 1-5), Purpose and Happiness*, Ia2ae. 3, 5 ad.
[54] Aquinas, *Summa Theologiae: Volume 16 (Ia2ae. 1-5), Purpose and Happiness*, Ia2ae. 3, 8 ad.
[55] Aquinas, *Summa Theologiae: Volume 16 (Ia2ae. 1-5), Purpose and Happiness*, Ia2ae. 3, 5 ad.
[56] Aquinas, *Summa Theologiae: Volume 16 (Ia2ae. 1-5), Purpose and Happiness*, Ia2ae. 4, 2 ad.
[57] Aquinas, *Summa Theologiae: Volume 16 (Ia2ae. 1-5), Purpose and Happiness*, Ia2ae. 2, 6 ad; cf. 3, 4 ad.
[58] Aquinas, *Summa Theologiae: Volume 16 (Ia2ae. 1-5), Purpose and Happiness*, Ia2ae. 4, 1 ad; cf. 2, 6 ad. I take it that the resting of desire is the cessation or quieting of desire because of the having of the desired good. Pleasure is experienced when a desire is united with the good that is its object.
[59] Aquinas, *Summa Theologiae: Volume 16 (Ia2ae. 1-5), Purpose and Happiness*, Ia2ae. 2, 6 ad 1.
[60] Aquinas, *Summa Theologiae: Volume 16 (Ia2ae. 1-5), Purpose and Happiness*, Ia2ae. 2, 6 ad 1.

good, but . . . each pleasure results from some good, and a pleasure from the highest and essential good."[61]

Contemplation, then, results in the experience of pleasure insofar as it (the contemplation) is the resting of intellectual desire in its good object, God.[62] Indeed, according to Aquinas, "contemplation is intrinsically pleasurable."[63] Given that the divine essence is the object of active contemplation that is intrinsically pleasurable, "one may say either, that the ultimate end of man is God himself, the supreme good without any qualification; or, that it is the enjoyment [the act of contemplation] of God, which includes the pleasure of enjoying one's ultimate end."[64] Either way, the goodness of the pleasure that comes with the active contemplative enjoyment of God ultimately is derived from the goodness of the ultimate object that is desired and enjoyed, namely, God. This is in accordance with Aquinas's more general view that "the delight [pleasure] that accompanies good and desirable operations [e.g., contemplation] is good and desirable . . . ."[65] Hence, "pleasure [is not] the ultimate end [which is happiness]; it is its concomitant."[66]

Perfect happiness is active contemplation of the divine essence, and "[t]his contemplation will be perfect in the next life when we shall see God *face to face*; hence it will make us utterly happy."[67] But to talk of perfect happiness suggests that there is also imperfect happiness. Aquinas believed that because the perfect happiness of contemplation of the divine essence must be uninterrupted activity,[68] and, as such, is only available in the beatific vision of God in the afterlife, we must settle in this life for a form of happiness that is imperfect: "there are two stages in happiness, complete and incomplete."[69]

---

[61] Aquinas, *Summa Theologiae: Volume 16 (Ia2ae. 1-5), Purpose and Happiness*, Ia2ae. 2, 6 ad 3.
[62] Aquinas, *Summa Theologiae: Volume 16 (Ia2ae. 1-5), Purpose and Happiness*, Ia2ae. 4, 2 ad.
[63] St Thomas Aquinas, *Summa Theologiae: Volume 20 (Ia2ae. 31-39), Pleasure*, trans. Eric D'arcy (New York: McGraw-Hill, 1975), Ia2ae. 35, 5 ad.
[64] Aquinas, *Summa Theologiae: Volume 20 (Ia2ae. 31-39), Pleasure*, Ia2ae. 34, 3 ad. Aquinas draws the distinction (in *Summa Theologiae: Volume 16 (Ia2ae. 1-5), Purpose and Happiness*, Ia2ae. 3, 1 ad) between the ultimate end of perfect happiness as an object ("man's ultimate end is uncreated good, namely God") and as the possession of that object ("man's ultimate end is a creaturely reality in him, for what is it but *his* coming to God and *his* joy with God").
[65] Aquinas, *Summa Contra Gentiles: Book Three*, Chapter 26: 13.
[66] Aquinas, *Summa Contra Gentiles: Book Three*, Chapter 26: 15.
[67] Aquinas, *Summa Theologiae: Volume 46 (2a2ae. 179-182), Action and Contemplation*, 2a2ae. 180, 4 ad.
[68] Aquinas, *Summa Theologiae: Volume 16 (Ia2ae. 1-5), Purpose and Happiness*, Ia2ae. 3, 2 ad 4.
[69] Aquinas, *Summa Theologiae: Volume 16 (Ia2ae. 1-5), Purpose and Happiness*, Ia2ae. 3, 6 ad.

Imperfect happiness, like that which is perfect, does not consist of experiences of pleasure. But it does involve a form of contemplation. In this life, "the contemplation of divine truth can be ours only imperfectly, *through a glass in a dark manner*. Consequently, it gives us a certain dawning happiness which begins here so as to be continued in the life to come."[70] Aquinas maintained that we can contemplate God in this life by considering the things that He has made. We move intellectually from effects to their cause: "[A]s we read in *Romans, For the invisible things of him are clearly seen, being understood by the things that are made* . . . ."[71] But "human felicity [happiness] does not consist in the knowledge of God gained through demonstration."[72] Josef Pieper summarizes Thomas' view as follows:

> Contemplation is a form of knowing arrived at not by thinking but by seeing, intuition. It is not co-ordinate with the *ratio*, with the power of discursive thinking, but with the *intellectus*, with the capacity for "simple intuition." Intuition is without doubt the perfect form of knowing. For intuition is knowledge of what is actually present . . . . Thinking, on the other hand, is knowledge of what is absent . . .; the subject matter of thinking is investigated by way of something else which is directly present to the mind, but the subject matter is not seen as it is in itself. The validity of thinking, Thomas says, rests upon what we perceive by direct intuition; but the necessity for thinking is due to a failure of intuition. Reason is an imperfect form of *intellectus*. Contemplation, then, is intuition; that is to say, it is a type of knowing which does not merely move toward its object, but already rests in it.[73]

Contemplation and reasoning are the intellect's activity in its theoretical form. However, Aquinas considered the activity of the intellect to be twofold in nature. Thus, the intellect also has its use in the practical realm of daily life, and correspondingly there is not only intellectual virtue but also virtue of a practical nature. It is with regard to intellectual activity in its practical form that Thomas invoked the concept of moral virtue, where moral virtue is

---

[70] Aquinas, *Summa Theologiae: Volume 46 (2a2ae. 179-182), Action and Contemplation*, 2a2ae. 180, 4 ad.
[71] Aquinas, *Summa Theologiae: Volume 46 (2a2ae. 179-182), Action and Contemplation*, 2a2ae. 180, 4 ad.
[72] Aquinas, *Summa Contra Gentiles: Book Three*, Chapter 39. This sentence is the heading of the chapter.
[73] Josef Pieper, *Happiness and Contemplation*, trans. Richard and Clara Winston (New York: Pantheon, 1958), 73–4.

rooted in the soul's intellectually informed desire (appetitive power/appetite) for what is good: "And so, for a man to act well, it is requisite that not only his reason be well disposed through a habit of intellectual virtue, but also that his appetite be well disposed through a habit of moral virtue. . . . [A] moral habit . . . has the nature of human virtue in so far as it is conformed with reason [is reasonable]."[74]

At this juncture, it is helpful to link Aquinas's view of moral virtue with his understanding of goodness and desire. As we saw several paragraphs back, Thomas maintained that something is good insofar as it is actual.[75] An individual human being achieves its perfection (he or she becomes a good human being) by rightly exercising its powers, where the exercising of a power is an act in the sense of being an actualization of that power. We thereby arrive at the idea that the right exercising of a power by a human being contributes to the good of that being. In Aquinas's view, the concept of a power rightly exercised (an exercise of that power that is reasonable) is linked with the idea of the perfection of a human being (where that perfection is desirable). "[D]esirability is consequent upon perfection, for things always desire their perfection."[76] And "'[g]ood' . . . expresses the idea of desirable perfection and thus the notion of something complete. So things [e.g., human beings] are called 'good', without qualification, when they are completely perfect . . . ."[77]

In summary, when Thomas thinks about human activity as good, he thinks about it in terms of the concept of a virtue, where a virtue is a habit that disposes an agent to perform his or her proper operation, where that operation perfects its subject (makes the subject a good member of its kind).[78] "Virtue . . . is a habit which is always for good."[79] Indeed, "virtue makes [the one acting] good . . . ."[80] And again, "virtue is that which makes its possessor good . . . ."[81] In light of the fact that some virtues are moral in nature and are what give rise to morally good action, it follows that these moral virtues dispose a human being to live well. Moral virtues make a human being a good member of its kind (they make a human being a good human being)

---

[74] Aquinas, *Summa Theologiae: Volume 23 (Ia2ae. 55-67), Virtue,* Ia2ae. 58, 2 ad.
[75] Aquinas, *Summa Theologiae: Volume 2 (Ia. 2-11), Existence and Nature of God,* Ia. 5, 1.
[76] Aquinas, *Summa Theologiae: Volume 2 (Ia. 2-11), Existence and Nature of God,* Ia. 5, 1 ad.
[77] Aquinas, *Summa Theologiae: Volume 2 (Ia. 2-11), Existence and Nature of God,* Ia.5, 1ad 1.
[78] St Thomas Aquinas, *Summa Theologiae: Volume 22 (Ia2ae. 49-54), Dispositions,* trans. Anthony Kenny (New York: McGraw-Hill, 1973), Ia2ae. 49, 2.
[79] Aquinas, *Summa Theologiae: Volume 23 (Ia2ae. 55-67), Virtue,* Ia2ae. 55, 4 ad.
[80] Aquinas, *Summa Theologiae: Volume 23 (Ia2ae. 55-67), Virtue,* Ia2ae. 56, 1 ad 2.
[81] Aquinas, *Summa Theologiae: Volume 23 (Ia2ae. 55-67), Virtue,* Ia2ae. 56, 3 ad.

and, in the language of perfection, the exercise of moral virtues perfects a person and makes him happy. So in the final analysis, the imperfect happiness of this life has two components, a primary and a secondary: "As for the imperfect beatitude we can have at present, it is primarily and chiefly centred on contemplation, secondarily on the activity of the practical intelligence governing our deeds and feelings...."[82]

Now all of this might come across as abstract and formulaic. Therefore, to make it more concrete, let us briefly consider what Thomas maintained are the four cardinal moral virtues: prudence, temperance, courage, and justice, all of which are rooted in the proper exercise of reason. Prudence is wisdom or right reason that will enable a person to make good judgments about what will promote his proper end, which is happiness, in different circumstances ("Prudence is of good counsel about matters regarding a man's life in its entirety, and its last end")[83]; temperance involves the use of reason to curb the passions so that "the evil of drunkenness and excessive drinking consists in a failure in the order of reason"[84]; courage is the use of reason to strengthen the passions against fear of dangers or hardships ("a person needs to be steadfast and not run away from what is right; and for this *courage* is named")[85]; and justice is the use of reason to give to people what is due to them: "The proper characteristic of justice, as compared with the other moral virtues, is to govern a man in his dealings towards others.... The other moral virtues ... compose a man for activities which befit him considered in himself."[86] All of these moral virtues, both the self- and other-regarding, if had by an individual, are goods that will perfect him. The having of them will help make him as happy as he can be in this life.

Imperfect happiness consists of both intellectual and moral virtue. There is contemplation and prudence, temperance, courage, and justice. And what, if any, relationship exists between the two kinds of virtue? While "moral virtues do not enter into the contemplative life ... [they] do have their place in the contemplative life as dispositions."[87] Their place is that of enabling an individual to restrain the vehemence of the passions and external distractions so that he can turn his mind to contemplation. Thus, the moral virtue of justice is valuable for contemplation "because one

---

[82] Aquinas, *Summa Theologiae: Volume 16 (Ia2ae. 1-5), Purpose and Happiness*, Ia2ae. 3, 5 ad.
[83] Aquinas, *Summa Theologiae: Volume 23 (Ia2ae. 55-67), Virtue*, Ia2ae. 57, 4 ad 3.
[84] Aquinas, *Summa Theologiae: Volume 23 (Ia2ae. 55-67), Virtue*, Ia2ae. 55, 3 ad 2.
[85] Aquinas, *Summa Theologiae: Volume 23 (Ia2ae. 55-67), Virtue*, Ia2ae. 61, 2 ad.
[86] St Thomas Aquinas, *Summa Theologiae: Volume 37 (2a2ae. 57-62), Justice*, trans. Thomas Gilby, O. P. (Cambridge: Cambridge University Press, 2006), 2a2ae. 57, 1 ad.
[87] Aquinas, *Summa Theologiae: Volume 46 (2a2ae. 179-182), Action and Contemplation*, 2a2ae. 180, 2 ad.

who refrains from wronging others, lessens the occasions of quarrel and disturbance. Thus the moral virtues dispose one to the contemplative life by causing peace . . . ."[88]

Eudaemonism and "Good"

From the foregoing overview of Aquinas's view of intellectual and moral virtue as it relates to human happiness, it is clear that he was a eudaemonist insofar as he thought that virtue, as it is manifested in action, constitutes an agent's happiness, which is itself the overall end of a human being. Moreover, happiness comes in degrees, because a person can be more or less perfect and, thereby, more or less happy. And given that a person is a member of the species "human being," it is possible for a person to be a good or not-so-good member of his kind. This implies that Aquinas thought of the term "good" as primarily a context-dependent word (its use is always restricted, qualified, or conditioned by the subject that it modifies). With "a good human being" as our model, to say that "good" is context-dependent is to say that it is properly used in the grammatical *attributive* position. One thing is a good X, another is a good Y, and yet another is a good Z. As McCabe writes, "whenever we say that something is a good X, the sense of the word 'good' is not independent of the meaning of 'X'."[89] Thus, if X is a pen, then to say that X is a good pen is to say something like X is easy to hold, X writes smoothly, X does not bleed ink, etc. If Y is a pair of shoes, then to say that Y is a good pair of shoes is to say something like Y feels comfortable, Y laces easily, Y is fashionable, etc. Finally, if Z is a human being, then to say that Z is a good human being is to say that Z is prudent, Z is temperate, Z is courageous, Z is just, and Z is contemplative. In short, to say Z is a good human being is to say that Z is virtuous.

And how does the issue of pleasure's goodness relate to this attributive view of "good"? Most generally, good pleasure is the pleasure experienced by a good human being (one who is virtuous and, thereby, happy), while evil (bad) pleasure is that experienced by an evil (bad) human being (one who is vicious). "[T]he delight [pleasure] that accompanies good and desirable operations is good and desirable, but that which accompanies evil deeds is evil and repulsive. So, it owes the fact that it is good and desirable to something

---

[88] Aquinas, *Summa Theologiae: Volume 46 (2a2ae. 179-182), Action and Contemplation*, 2a2ae. 180, 2 ad 2.
[89] McCabe, *God and Evil in the Theology of St Thomas Aquinas*, 53.

else."⁹⁰ When pleasure accompanies virtuous action, whether intellectual or moral, and, thus, the happiness this action comprises, the pleasure gets it goodness from that action. While there is good pleasure, it is a mistake to say "pleasure is intrinsically good."

Lewis and Aquinas

What might Lewis have said in response to Aquinas's position on happiness, pleasure, and the good? Given that I am not familiar with a written work of Lewis's in which he discusses the matter, I will have to engage in a bit of informed conjecture.

The most reasonable place to start is with Lewis's commitment to common sense, which he thought included a belief in the unconditional goodness of pleasure and evilness of pain. In his mind, it was only in light of this belief that the everyday idea of heaven and hell makes any sense: "I have no doubt at all that pleasure is in itself a good and pain in itself an evil; if not, then the whole Christian tradition about heaven and hell and the passion of our Lord seems to have no meaning."⁹¹ Moreover, Lewis believed that the only adequate explanation for why people respectively pursue and avoid pleasure and pain as they do is because pleasure is intrinsically good and pain is intrinsically evil.

Given his adherence to common sense, it is most plausible to think Lewis would have insisted upon the primacy of the context-independent use of "good" in "Pleasure is intrinsically good." Here, "good" appears and is properly used in the grammatical *predicative* position. If "Pleasure is intrinsically good" is true, then pleasure is good when derived from watching a sporting

---

[90] Aquinas, *Summa Contra Gentiles, Book Three*, Chapter 26: 13. Elsewhere, Aquinas wrote that "the pleasures of good actions are good, [and] the pleasures of evil actions are evil." Aquinas, *Summa Theologiae: Volume 20 (1a2ae. 31-39), Pleasure*, Ia2ae. 34, 1 ad.

Two contemporary Thomists, Patrick Lee and Robert P. George, nicely capture the Thomist view of the value of pleasure that accompanies activity: "Virtuous persons find morally good actions pleasant; vicious persons take pleasure in revenge or power, as well as other activities or conditions. In this sense, pleasure . . . refers to the experiential aspect or consequence of an activity, and it is not the (core) good itself, but a consequence of possessing the good or apparent good; though pleasure of this sort *is* a good, when it is a consequence of possessing a real good. We add 'apparent good,' because we hold that someone can take pleasure in something that is not really good, but merely apparently good (fulfilling). That is, one's conscious delight in participating in a good is one type of pleasure, but we hold that one's delight can be misdirected (and in that case is not a good)." *Body-Soul Dualism in Contemporary Ethics and Politics* (Cambridge: Cambridge University Press, 2008), 97.

[91] Lewis, *Christian Reflections*, 21.

event, from playing a musical instrument, from reading a book, and from sexual intercourse (whether licit or not). Pleasure is good independent of its relationship to anything else and, thus, whenever and wherever it is experienced.[92] Pleasure is intrinsically good because goodness is a simple, indefinable, immaterial property that pleasure exemplifies, period.

In insisting upon the context-independent intrinsic goodness of pleasure, Lewis need not and would not have denied the context-dependent use stressed by Aquinas. What Lewis would likely have wanted to know is why it cannot be the case that both uses of "good" are correct. In other words, he might have asked "Why couldn't this be a 'both-and' instead of an 'either-or'?"

However, whenever there are two of anything (in this case, two ways of using "good"), questions arise about how they are related. In the case of the context-independent and context-dependent uses of "good," Lewis would have maintained that it is most plausible to think that the non-contextual use of "good" in "Pleasure is intrinsically good" is more fundamental than and explains the existence of the contextual use of "good" in "X is a good human being." For example, a good novel is good because its good-making properties (e.g., its plot, character development, appropriate length) provide its reader with pleasure. A good kitchen knife is one whose good-making properties (e.g., its sharpness, ease of handling) enable its user to prepare food that will be a source of pleasure. And a good human being is one who has the good-making virtuous properties (e.g., prudence, temperance, courage, and justice) that ultimately enable him to promote experiences of pleasure in others and himself. In other words, "good" in "a good novel," "a good kitchen knife," and "a good human being" refers to instrumental goodness.

At this point, it is helpful to consider an argument against the Lewisian commonsensical view of pleasure and its intrinsic goodness that comes from the pen of the British Thomistic philosopher Peter Geach.[93] Geach developed his argument in response to the claim made by the British philosopher

---

[92] Thus, Lewis would disagree with the following Thomistic position of Lee and George: "[W]hether a pleasure is an intrinsic good or not depends on whether it is associated with a real perfection or a harmful condition. The pleasures of the sadist or child molester are *in themselves* bad . . . ." *Body-Soul Dualism in Contemporary Ethics and Politics*, 113. It is worth re-quoting Lewis here so that it is clear how his view differs from Aquinas': "I think *all* pleasure simply good: what we call bad pleasures are pleasures produced by actions, or inactions, [which] break the moral law, and it is those actions or inactions [which] are bad, not the pleasures." *The Collected Letters of C. S. Lewis: Volume II*, 462–3.

[93] For those with interests in biographical details, Geach was the husband of Elizabeth Anscombe, who was also a Thomist and best known by readers of Lewis for her criticism of his argument from reason, which was discussed in Chapter 2.

G. E. Moore that "good" is like the word "yellow" insofar as each term refers to a simple, nonanalyzable property.[94] Geach argued that nothing can be just plain good in the unqualified way expressed by "pleasure is (intrinsically) good" because all good is good relative to a certain kind of object. He believed we can see this is the case because "good" is unlike "yellow" in the following way: whereas "x is a yellow bird" breaks up into "x is a bird" and "x is yellow," "x is a good singer" does not break up into "x is a singer" and "x is good." Furthermore, from "x is a yellow bird" and "a bird is an animal" we readily infer "x is a yellow animal," but from "x is a good singer" and "a singer is a human being" we cannot infer "x is a good human being."

How might Lewis have responded to this argument? It is not implausible to think that Lewis would have asked us to consider something like the following: "x is a good psychological event" seems to break up into "x is a psychological event" and "x is good," and from "x is a good psychological event" and "a psychological event is an event in a soul" we can infer "x is a good event in a soul." Nothing seems amiss in either of these cases (let "x" be "an experience of pleasure") so that nothing seems amiss with either the claim that an experience of pleasure is good or the assertion that an experience of pleasure is good in an unqualified sense.

Opponents of the non-contextual use of "good" would, however, likely persist with their objections. Some would maintain that *all* good is relative good in the sense that what is *good for* something is relative to the kind of thing that it is, and something is *good for* that kind of thing insofar as it helps that thing to *flourish* or *do well*.[95] Thus, just as water, sunshine, and warm temperatures are *good for* a plant because they help it to grow tall, flower, and smell fragrant (all of which are aspects of its flourishing), so also pleasure is *good for* a human being because it (along with food, water, and a multitude of other things) helps a human being to flourish (possess eudaemonia). Pleasure itself, however, is not intrinsically good and, therefore, the absolute use of "good" is mistaken.

It is hard not to believe that Lewis would have wondered why it could not be that, in the case of a human being, what is most fundamentally good for it is something (pleasure) that is itself good intrinsically. Pleasure's intrinsic goodness by itself is all that is needed to explain why the experience of it is *good for* a person and constitutes his well-being. Instrumental goods that are *good for* persons are properly understood in terms of pleasure's

---

[94] Peter Geach, "Good and Evil." *Analysis* 17 (1956): 32–42; and Moore, *Principia Ethica*, 7. I mentioned Lewis vis-à-vis Moore in Chapter 1.
[95] See Richard Kraut, *What is Good and Why: The Ethics of Well-Being* (Cambridge, MA: Harvard University Press, 2007).

being good for them. Thus, if knowledge, music, and beauty are good for an individual, they are so only because they are instrumental to pleasure. When it is good for a person P1 to have X but not good for a person P2 to have X, this is because X is instrumentally good for P1 but not for P2. But pleasure's intrinsic goodness makes it good for anyone to have because it constitutes a person's well-being. It perfects or makes perfect a person.

What about final or perfect happiness? Here Lewis would have agreed with Aquinas that we obtain pleasure from knowing God. But he would have insisted that happiness consists in the experiences of pleasure that come from knowing God. It does not consist in knowing God, which is the cause of experiences of pleasure. Lewis also would likely have queried why it is appropriate that knowing God be accompanied by experiences of pleasure (indeed, he likely would have queried why it is fitting that virtuous activity of any kind be, as Aquinas held, accompanied by pleasure). He would have answered that the most reasonable explanation for the necessity of this accompaniment is that pleasure is intrinsically good and alone comprises (perfect) happiness. Lewis probably would have added that if pleasure is not itself intrinsically good, then Aquinas's insistence that it accompany contemplation of God (and moral activity) seems completely *ad hoc* in nature.

Aquinas was well aware that it seems as if we desire to perform actions for the sake of the pleasure that they provide: "[D]elight [pleasure] seems to be so much an object of desire for its own sake that it is never desired for the sake of something else; indeed, it is foolish to ask a person why he wishes to be delighted. Now, this is characteristic of the ultimate end: it is sought for its own sake."[96] But "the fact that men desire pleasure for its own sake, and not for the sake of something else, [is not] enough to indicate that pleasure is the ultimate end...."[97]

Given his commitment to common sense, Lewis would have reminded us that a eudaemonist understanding of happiness like Aquinas's dispenses with the commonsensical notion of happiness and is revisionist in nature. He would also have looked for a reason that justified Aquinas making the revision. Perhaps part of the explanation for it was Aquinas's belief that "[a] cause is always more excellent than its effect...."[98] In the case of perfect happiness, the vision (intellectual contemplation) of God is the cause of the pleasure that accompanies the vision, and, therefore, the vision is better than the pleasure: "[D]elight [pleasure] is not the ultimate end. For the very

---

[96] Aquinas, *Summa Contra Gentiles: Volume Three*, Chapter 26: 4.
[97] Aquinas, *Summa Contra Gentiles: Volume Three*, Chapter 26: 19.
[98] Aquinas, *Summa Theologiae: Volume 23 (Ia2ae. 55-67), Virtue*, Ia2ae. 66, 1 ad.

possession of the good is the cause of the delight. . . . So, delight is not the ultimate end."[99]

Given everything that Lewis had to say about pleasure and its intrinsic goodness, it is hard to see how he would have been dissuaded from his belief in the hedonistic view of happiness and the intrinsic goodness of pleasure on which that view rests by an appeal to the nature of the cause-effect relationship. Lewis would have insisted that an experience of pleasure that causally depends on the occurrence of some other event need not derive its goodness from that other event.

It is important to remember that the difference between a commonsense view of pleasure like that of Lewis and Aquinas's eudaemonist revisionary understanding of it is an old one in philosophy. Indeed, it goes all way back to the Greeks. For example, Aristotle was aware of the different views about pleasure's goodness. As I mentioned in Chapter 1, he pointed out that most people would recognize that happiness is the highest good attainable by action, and he added that when it comes to defining "happiness" the common person believes it is identical with an obvious good like pleasure. But Aristotle was not a commoner and in opposition to the ordinary person maintained that happiness consists in action of a certain kind, namely, that which is virtuous: "[T]he good of man is an activity of the soul in conformity with excellence or virtue, and if there are several virtues, in conformity with the best and most complete. . . . [T]he good of man, happiness, is some kind of activity of the soul in conformity with virtue."[100] Given what we have seen of Aquinas's view of happiness in this section, it should not come as a surprise that he drew heavily on the eudaemonist thought of Aristotle.

What did Aristotle say about happiness as an activity and its relationship to pleasure? Like Aquinas, he believed there is a very close connection between virtuous activity and the experience of pleasure. For example, he acknowledged that "[p]leasure is intimately connected with the activity which it completes."[101] Indeed, Aristotle believed that because the connection between pleasure and virtuous action is so close, it is tempting to say that virtuous activity and the experience of pleasure that accompanies it are one and the same event: "[P]leasure is so closely linked to activity and so little distinguished from it that one may dispute whether <or not> activity is identical with pleasure."[102] And again, "because [pleasure and activity] are

---

[99] Aquinas, *Summa Contra Gentiles: Book Three*, Chapter 26: 12. Cf. *Summa Theologiae: Volume 16*, Ia2ae. 4, 2ad.
[100] Aristotle, *Nicomachean Ethics*, 1098a16-17, 1099b26.
[101] Aristotle, *Nicomachean Ethics*, 1175a29-30.
[102] Aristotle, *Nicomachean Ethics*, 1175b33-4.

never found apart, some people get the impression that they are identical."[103] However, Aristotle maintained that it would be absurd to hold that pleasure is identical with an activity.[104] While the pleasure that accompanies a cognitive activity can itself be called cognitive in virtue of its source, it is fundamentally different from that activity as such. But if the two are not identical, what is the relationship between them? Aristotle concluded that the close connection between the two is a perfective relation: the experience of pleasure perfects the activity: "Pleasure completes the activity not as a characteristic completes an activity by being already inherent in it, but as a completeness that superimposes itself upon it, like the bloom of youth in those who are in their prime."[105]

At this point, we would probably find Lewis asking why it is right to think of pleasure as perfecting the activity that it accompanies. As I mentioned a few paragraphs back when discussing Aquinas, Lewis would most likely have answered this question in terms of pleasure's intrinsic goodness: an experience of pleasure perfects an activity because the former itself is intrinsically good. What could be more qualified to play the role of being that which perfects an activity than that which is intrinsically good? But more than perfecting an action, pleasure, because it is intrinsically good, perfects the person who experiences it.

In Chapter 1, I discussed how the philosopher Robert Nozick seeks to tease out the difference between an activity and the pleasure that accompanies it in terms of an experience machine. This machine is an imaginary device to which one can connect and receive nothing but experiences of pleasure without having to act while connected. One point Nozick aims to make clear is that there is no necessary connection between the concept of activity *per se* and that of an experience of pleasure. The Aristotelian scholar Gerd van Riel makes the same point in the following way:

> [W]e never know for sure what to do in order to attain pleasure: it is never guaranteed. As an additional element, pleasure can occur, but it is just as likely to fail to appear. [Consider] Beethoven's fourth piano concerto. It is not certain that I will experience pleasure in attending a performance of this work. Even if all the circumstances are in an optimal state, I cannot be sure that I will enjoy the concert. . . . If this is true, it should be possible that an activity is perfectly performed even without yielding pleasure. But this dismisses the immediate link between pleasure

---

[103] Aristotle, *Nicomachean Ethics*, 1175b35.
[104] Aristotle, *Nicomachean Ethics*, 1175b34-5.
[105] Aristotle, *Nicomachean Ethics*, 1174a32-3.

and a perfect activity, and moreover, it implies that the perfection of an activity is not enough to secure our pleasure. Even if all circumstances are perfectly arranged, and the activity perfectly performed, pleasure is not guaranteed. This "escape from our control" is not an accidental quality of pleasure, dependent on circumstances, but a characteristic of the very essence of pleasure.[106]

What is also of interest for my overall purpose of explaining the differences between Lewis's and Aquinas's views of pleasure and happiness is that van Riel makes clear that we not only have a lack of direct control with respect to experiences of pleasure, but we also have a lack of direct control with respect to happiness:

> But . . . [t]here is no clearcut answer to the question of when and how we will attain pleasure. Like happiness, it is something which we may hope to attain, without ever being sure how to behave in order to guarantee its appearance. Even if we know exactly what to do to perfect the performance of an activity, we cannot be sure that pleasure will be added to it.[107]

Lewis believed happiness in this life is subject to luck. It is something over which a person has no direct control and of which he cannot guarantee possession. Therefore, it is extremely plausible to think Lewis would have maintained that we should not be surprised to find someone like van Riel pointing out to us the similarity between happiness and pleasure in this regard. Because happiness consists in nothing but experiences of pleasure, what is true of pleasure is also true of happiness.[108]

---

[106] Gerd van Riel, "Does Perfect Activity Necessarily Yield Pleasure? An Evaluation of the Relation between Pleasure and Activity in Aristotle, *Nicomachean Ethics* VII and X." *International Journal of Philosophical Studies* 7 (1999): 219–20.

[107] van Riel, "Does Perfect Activity Necessarily Yield Pleasure?," 219.

[108] In maintaining that what is true of experiences of pleasure is true of happiness, because happiness is composed of experiences of pleasure, Lewis need not have committed what is known in informal logic as the "fallacy of composition." Owen Flanagan suggests that hedonists about happiness commit this fallacy with respect to life as a whole: "Happiness is said to have worth in and of itself. Suppose this is true. Would it follow that a life with many happy times in it was worth living? Not necessarily. Properties of parts do not confer the property on the whole. My parts are small, I am large. Happy times, even many of them, might not constitute a worthwhile life." "What Makes Life Worth Living?," in *The Meaning of Life*, 2nd edn. ed. E. D. Klemke (Oxford: Oxford University Press, 2000), 199.

Lewis need not have been assuming that always and everywhere a property of each of the parts of a whole is also a property of the whole. While in some cases a property of each of the parts is not also a property of the whole, in other cases it is. Whether or not it is depends on the property in question. For example, a wall that is made up of nothing

The fact that we have no ultimate control over the occurrence of pleasure and happiness helps to explain why Lewis was not a eudaemonist. In the words of Nicholas Wolterstorff, eudaemonism is the view that "[h]appiness does not consist in what happens to one but in what one makes of what happens to one."[109] For a eudaemonist, happiness is activity and, therefore, cannot be identical with pleasure because pleasure is about what happens to one. With respect to it, one is a patient. One is passive. The differences over this point between Lewis and Aristotle-cum-Aquinas are hard to miss. And as we continue this philosophical walking tour, we will find that there are more differences ahead.

---

but yellow bricks is also yellow. Similarly, if experiences of pleasure are events over whose occurrence we have no direct control (they are subject to luck), then the happiness that is made up of those experiences is also something over whose occurrence we have no direct control.

[109] Wolterstorff, *Justice: Rights and Wrongs*, 152.

4

Body and Soul

There is also, whatever it means, the resurrection of the body. We cannot understand. The best is perhaps what we understand least.[1]

Cartesian dualism

While there is no standard dictionary definition of "Cartesian dualism," the term refers to a position espoused by René Descartes. Roughly, a view of what it is to be a human being is Cartesian in nature only if it includes the idea that there is a soul that is distinct from its material body, where each entity is a substance in its own right that directly causally interacts with the other. Moreover, a Cartesian holds that the soul is the self or person,[2] which together with its physical body comprises a human being. In addition, and in opposition to the standard view of the soul-body relationship up until Descartes's treatment of the topic, a proponent of Cartesian dualism holds that the soul does not give life to its body. Rather, the body, as a substance in its own right, is an organic machine with its own principles of unity and operation that are not derived from the soul. Death is not the soul ceasing to give life to its body but the final, irreparable breakdown of the body which prevents the soul from any longer being causally related to it. Lewis was basically a Cartesian in his views of the soul and body and the relationship between them.

Aquinas, although he lived before Descartes, would have been intellectually uncomfortable with the latter's views of the soul and body. As Eleonore Stump, one of the foremost contemporary interpreters and defenders of

---

[1] Lewis, *A Grief Observed*, 75.
[2] If we assume for the sake of discussion that "soul" and "mind" are synonymous, as Descartes did ("the mind [or soul of man (I make no distinction between them)]"); see his "Synopsis of the Meditations," in *The Philosophical Works of Descartes*, vol. I, trans. E. S. Haldane and G. R. T. Ross (Cambridge: Cambridge University Press, 1967), 141), then Patrick Lee and Robert P. George (*Body-Self Dualism in Contemporary Ethics and Politics*, 5 are right: "substance dualism" is the view that affirms "the identification of mind with an independent spiritual substance."

Aquinas's thought today makes clear, Aquinas was no friend of Cartesian dualism.[3] The goal of this chapter is, in part, to explain why this was the case. And the best way to do this is to concisely set forth Aquinas's view of the soul and body and the relationship between them.[4] Because his view of the body is best understood in light of his view of the soul, I begin with the latter.

Aquinas's view of the soul

According to Aquinas, the soul is the form of the body and gives life to the latter:

> Now it is obvious that the soul is the prime endowment by virtue of which a body has life. Life manifests its presence through different activities at different levels, but the soul is the ultimate principle by which we conduct every one of life's activities; the soul is the ultimate motive factor behind nutrition, sensation and movement from place to place, and the same holds true of the act of understanding [the soul is what explains it]. So this prime factor . . . is the formative principle of the body.[5]

The idea that the soul is the life-giving *form* of the body is not easy to explicate, and for help I draw upon the work of Stump. As she points out, Thomas believed that "all material things are composites of matter and form."[6] For present purposes, I focus on the concept of a substantial form, which is a form in virtue of which a material composite like an animal is a member of its species. In the case of beasts (animals other than human beings), the substantial form is a soul but the soul is not a substance in its own right (the soul-body composite as a whole is a substance). Because the soul is not a substance, it cannot survive the death of the animal organism.[7] But while it cannot survive death, the soul of a beast does give life to the organism. As the

---

[3] See Eleonore Stump, "Non-Cartesian Substance Dualism and Materialism without Reductionism." *Faith and Philosophy* 12 (1995): 505–31.
[4] For a fuller treatment of Aquinas's views on the soul and body, see Stewart Goetz and Charles Taliaferro's *A Brief History of the Soul* (Oxford: Wiley-Blackwell, 2011), Chapter 2.
[5] St Thomas Aquinas, *Summa Theologiae: Volume 11 (Ia.75-83), Man*, trans. Timothy Sutter (New York: McGraw-Hill, 1970), Ia.76, 1ad.
[6] Stump, "Non-Cartesian Substance Dualism and Materialism without Reductionism," 507.
[7] Aquinas, *Summa Theologiae: Volume 11, Man*, Ia.75, 3; and see St Thomas Aquinas, *Questions on the Soul*, trans. James H. Robb (Milwaukee: Marquette University Press, 1984), Question XIV. ad1.

giver of life, the soul of a beast *configures* the matter that constitutes its body. That is, the soul is the organizational principle that guides the development of the beast's body and provides it with its structure. In addition to being a giver of life, the soul also confers upon an animal all the psychological powers that it possesses. In the cases of animals like dogs, cats, and chimpanzees, these psychological powers include the capacities to experience pain and pleasure, the capacities to sense (see, hear, touch, etc.), and the capacities to experience emotions such as fear.

What about the human soul? Aquinas believed it is the life-giving form of the human body and configures the matter that constitutes that body. Thus, as with beastly souls, the soul of a human being is the organizational principle that guides the development of its body and provides it with its structure. Thomas clarified the idea that the soul is the form of its body that makes its parts what they are by contrasting it with the view that the soul is like a sailor in a ship:

> Therefore, a human soul is the form of its body. Again, if a soul were in its body as a sailor is in a ship, it would not give to its body nor to its parts their specific nature; whereas the contrary seems to be true from the fact that when the soul leaves its body, the individual parts of the body do not retain their original names except in an equivocal sense. For the eye of a corpse, like the eye in a portrait or the eye of a statue, is only equivocally called an eye, and the same would be true of any other part of the body. Furthermore, if a soul were in its body as a sailor is in a ship, it would follow that the union of soul and body is accidental. Consequently death, which signifies the separation of soul and body, would not be a substantial corruption [but rather a separation of two substances], and this is obviously false.[8]

In Aquinas's view, death is the separation of soul and body, which occurs when the soul ceases to inform its body. This cessation entails that an eye is no longer an eye (it could not be because it was made to be an eye by the soul that informed the body in which it was an eye), and any other part of the body is no longer what it was, once the body ceases to be informed by its soul. An eye in a corpse is an eye in name only, just as the corpse is a human body in name only.

Although both the souls of human beings and beasts are the organizing principles of their respective bodies, the human soul is unlike beastly souls insofar as the former is able to survive death while the latter are not.

---

[8] Aquinas, *Questions on the Soul*, Question I. ad.

The survival of death by a human soul is possible even though *the human soul is not a substance in its own right*. Aquinas is explicit about the in- or non-substantial nature of the human soul: "[B]ody and soul are not two actually existing substances; rather, the two of them together constitute one actually existing substance."⁹ But though the human soul is not a substance in its own right, it is capable of *subsisting* (existing on its own) apart from the body that it informs. For illustrative purposes, Stump suggests that we liken a human soul as a subsistent form to an unfinished house (e.g., one with no more than its foundation laid and its walls erected). This unfinished house exists on its own but is not a complete member of its species (being a house).[10]

Aquinas believed that one thing that follows from the fact that a human soul is not a substance in its own right is that it is not a person. Thus, he wrote that "[the soul] cannot be called 'this something,' if by this phrase is meant ... [a] person, or an individual situated in a genus or in a species."[11] Elsewhere he wrote that "[n]ot every particular substance is ... a person, but rather, that which has the full nature of the species. Thus a hand or foot cannot be called a ... person. Nor, likewise, can the soul, as it is a part of human nature."[12] And, finally, "The soul is a part of human nature; and hence, although it can exist apart from the body, it ever can be reunited, and therefore cannot be called an 'individual substance,' or a 'hypostasis' or 'first substance' any more than a hand or any other part. So we can neither define it nor speak of it as a 'person.'"[13]

This point about the non-personhood status of the human soul led Aquinas to deny that he is his soul: *Anima autem cum sit pars corporis hominis, non est totus homo, et anima mea non est ego* (However, the soul, since it is part of man's body, it is not the whole man, and I am not my soul.")[14] He reiterated this point in his commentary on Peter Lombard's *Sentences*: "The soul of Abraham is not Abraham himself, properly speaking, but is part of him."[15] But while the human soul as disembodied is not the referent

---

⁹ St Thomas Aquinas, *Summa Contra Gentiles; Book Two: Creation*, trans. James F. Anderson (Notre Dame, IN: University of Notre Dame Press, 1975), Chapter 69: 2.
[10] Stump, "Non-Cartesian Substance Dualism and Materialism without Reductionism," 517.
[11] St Thomas Aquinas, *On Spiritual Creatures*, trans. M. C. Fitzpatrick (Milwaukee: Marquette University Press, 1949), II. ad 16).
[12] Aquinas, *Summa Theologiae, Volume 11, Man*, Ia.75, 4 ad 2.
[13] St Thomas Aquinas, *Summa Theologiae, Volume 6 (Ia.27-32), The Trinity*, trans. Ceslaus Velecky (New York: McGraw-Hill, 1965), Ia. 29, 1 ad 5.
[14] St Thomas Aquinas, *Commentary on the First Epistle to the Corinthians*, Section 924, trans. Fabian Larcher. Available at www.dhspriory.org/thomas/SS1Cor.htm.
[15] This quote comes from Christina van Dyke, "Human Identity, Immanent Causal Relations, and the Principle of Non-Repeatability: Thomas Aquinas on the Bodily Resurrection." *Religious Studies* 43 (2007): 376.

of "I" and is not a person, it will be able to think.[16] Moreover, a disembodied soul will be able to feel joy (pleasure) and sadness (pain) from intellectual, but not bodily, desire and activity.[17] Aquinas touched upon the issues of the "I"-ness and personhood of the disembodied human soul when he discussed prayers to the saints. How can Peter's soul, if it is not Peter, pray for us on earth? Can we call upon St Peter, as opposed to calling upon his soul, to pray for us? In response, Aquinas granted that the soul of St Peter is not St Peter, but added that we invoke a saint like St Peter under the name by which he was known in this life and will be known when re-embodied at the resurrection, which is a name that refers to the whole of the body plus soul.[18]

Aquinas's view of the body

All of us die, and Aquinas maintained that death was the separation of the soul from the body that it informed. According to Thomas, Christ "chose to rise [from the dead] to free us from death."[19] An effect of Christ's resurrection is that "we shall all rise by the power of Christ"[20]:

> Since the soul is united to the body as its form, and since each form has the right matter corresponding to it, the body to which the soul will be reunited must be of the same nature and species as was the body laid down by the soul at death. At the resurrection the soul will not resume a celestial or ethereal body, or the body of some animal, as certain people fancifully prattle [Origen, *Peri Archon*, III, 6]. No, it will resume a human body made up of flesh and bones, and equipped with the same organs it now possesses.
>
> Furthermore, just as the same specific form ought to have the same specific matter, so the same numerical form ought to have the same numerical matter. The soul of an ox cannot be the soul of a horse's body, nor can the soul of this ox be the soul of any other ox. Therefore, since

---

[16] St Thomas Aquinas, *Summa Theologiae: Volume 12 (Ia. 84-89), Human Intelligence*, trans. P. T. Durbin (New York: McGraw-Hill, 1968), Ia. 89.
[17] Aquinas, *Summa Theologiae, Volume 11 (Ia.75-83), Man*, Ia. 77, 5 ad 3. Cf. *Summa Theologiae, Volume 20 (Ia2ae. 31-39), Pleasure*, Ia2ae. 35, 5 ad.
[18] St Thomas Aquinas, *Summa Theologiae, Vols. I-III*, trans. Fathers of the English Dominican Province (Allen, TX: Christian Classics, 1948), IIa.-IIae. 83, 11 ad 5.
[19] St Thomas Aquinas, *Summa Contra Gentiles: Book Four; Salvation*, trans. Charles J. O'Neil (Garden City, NY: Image Books, 1957), Chapter 79: 2.
[20] Aquinas, *Summa Contra Gentiles: Book Four; Salvation*, Chapter 79: 4.

the rational soul that survives remains numerically the same, at the resurrection it must be reunited to numerically the same body.[21]

In other words, not only does the resurrection require the same *kind* of body (the same in species), namely, a human body, but also, as Aquinas indicates in the last paragraph just quoted, it requires the *numerically* same human body (the same particular piece of matter):

> [S]ince the human body substantially dissolves in death, it cannot be restored to numerical identity by the action of nature. But the concept of the resurrection requires such identity.... Consequently the resurrection of man will not be brought about by the action of nature.... No, the restoration of all who rise will be effected solely by divine power.... The fact that ... the resurrection will be effected by divine power, enables us to perceive readily how the same numerical body will be revived. Since all things, even the very least, are included under divine providence, ... the matter composing this human body of ours, whatever form it may take after man's death, evidently does not elude the power or the knowledge of God. Such matter remains numerically the same, in the sense that it exists under quantitative dimensions, by reason of which it can be said to be this particular matter, and is the principle of individuation. If then, this matter remains the same, and if the human body is again fashioned from it by divine power, and if also the rational soul which remains the same in its incorruptibility is united to the same body, the result is that identically the same man is restored to life.[22]

Now during a person's lifetime the material components of his body are continually changing. Thus, there are many more material components that form that individual's body (sequence of bodies) over the course of a lifetime than can be included in the resurrection body:

> If ... a man's identical body is restored to life, by equal reasoning whatever was in the man's body ought to be returned to the same man. But on this something extremely unseemly follows—not only by reason of the beard and the nails and the hair which are openly removed by daily trimming, but also by reason of other parts of the body which are covertly resolved

---

[21] Thomas Aquinas, *Compendium Theologiae*, trans. Cyril Vollert, S. J. (St. Louis: B Herder Book Co., 1947), Chapter 153. http://dhspriory.org/thomas/Compendium.htrr.

[22] Thomas Aquinas, *Compendium Theologiae*, trans. Cyril Vollert, S. J. (St. Louis: B Herder Book Co., 1947), Chapter 154.

by the action of the natural heat—and if these all are restored to the man rising again, an unseemly enormity will rise with him.[23]

In light of this problem of enormity, Aquinas concluded that only some of the material components that passed through a person's body must be part of his resurrection body:

> During the course of the present life, man evidently remains numerically the same from birth to death. Nevertheless the material composition of his parts does not remain the same, but undergoes gradual flux and reflux, in somewhat the way that the same fire is kept up although some logs are consumed and others are fed to the blaze....
>
> God, in restoring the risen body, does not reclaim all the material elements once possessed by man's body. He will supply whatever is wanting to the proper amount of matter.... [T]hose who do not have sufficient quantity may be supplied from outside matter with whatever was lacking to them in this life as regards integrity of natural members or suitable size. Consequently, although some may have lacked certain of their members during this life, or may not have attained to perfect size, the amount of quantity possessed at the moment of death makes no difference; at the resurrection they will receive, through God's power, the due complement of members and quantity.[24]

While God will ensure that some of the material parts that constituted the body in this life will be parts of the resurrection body, not all can or need be, and He will add parts that were not constituents during this life in cases where there were missing limbs or those present were of an inadequate size. What about the problem of cannibalism which, as we saw in Chapter 2, concerned Augustine? Aquinas also saw the need to address it:

> [Objectors] say that a cannibal may have eaten human flesh, and later, thus nourished, may beget a son, who eats the same kind of food. If what is eaten is changed into the substance of the eater's flesh, it seems impossible for both to rise in their full integrity, for the flesh of one has been changed into the flesh of the other.....
>
> But this state of affairs is not incompatible with a general resurrection. ... [N]ot all the material elements ever present in any man need be resumed when he rises; only so much matter is required as suffices to keep up the amount of quantity he ought to have....

[23] Aquinas, *Summa Contra Gentiles: Book Four*, Chapter 80: 4.
[24] Aquinas, *Compendium Theologiae*, Chapters 159 and 160.

> At the general resurrection ... [i]f the same matter existed in different men, it will rise in that one in whom it fulfilled the higher function. If it existed in two men in exactly the same way, it will rise in him who had it first; in the other, the lack will be made up by divine power. And so we can see that the flesh of a man that was devoured by another, will rise not in the cannibal, but in him to whom it belonged originally.[25]

And what about a case in which both the parents have eaten only human flesh so that their seed and, thereby, their offspring, has been generated from the flesh of others? Aquinas said the matter will rise in the body of the offspring, even though it was first in the bodies of the parents:

> Accordingly, if something was in one man as the radical seed from which he was generated, and in another as the superfluity of nourishment, it will rise in him who was generated therefrom as from seed. If something was in one as pertinent to the perfection of the individual, but in another as assigned to the perfection of the species, it will rise in him to whom it belonged as perfection of the individual. Accordingly, seed will arise in the begotten, not in his generator; the rib of Adam will arise in Eve, not in Adam in whom it was present as in a principle of nature.[26]

Like Augustine, then, Aquinas believed the idea of the resurrection of the dead requires that God have rules to follow in situations where there are multiple claimants to shared matter. Given that my reason for discussing this issue is only to provide a contrast between Aquinas's and Lewis's views of the resurrection, I will say nothing further about Aquinas's view of the identity of the resurrection body.[27]

What would Lewis have thought?

Unlike Aquinas, Lewis believed the resurrection of the dead did not require, partially or wholly, the numerical sameness of bodily parts. While

---

[25] Aquinas, *Compendium Theologiae*, Chapter 161. Cf. Aquinas, *Summa Contra Gentiles: Book Four*, Chapter 80: 5.
[26] Aquinas, *Summa Contra Gentiles: Book Four*, Chapter 81: 13.
[27] I believe it is important to note that contemporary Thomists continue to advocate Aquinas' view of the resurrection body. For example, Patrick Lee and Robert George write that "[t]he ... most traditional [interpretation of the resurrection body] ... is the one we favor.... This is the reassembly view. On this proposal, God simply reassembles the matter, or much of the matter, that was in the human being at the point of his death and restores it to life by rejoining his immortal soul to it." *Body-Self Dualism in Contemporary Ethics and Politics*, 79.

Lewis would have found Thomas' intuitions about what is required for the numerical sameness of entities like a human body that are composed of parts very commonsensical (the numerical sameness of a body requires the numerical sameness of its parts), and would therefore have understood Aquinas's concern that a person's resurrection body be composed of at least some of the numerically same parts as his or her earthly body in order to be the numerically same body, Lewis regarded an insistence like Aquinas's that a resurrection body be the same numerically as the earthly body "a foolish fancy."[28] For one thing, Lewis pointed out that "the unity of our bodies, even in this present life, [does not] consist in retaining the same particles. My form remains one, though the matter in it changes continually. I am, in that respect, like a curve of a waterfall."[29] For another, Lewis believed that the commonsense requirement for the numerical sameness of a body, which is the numerical sameness of its parts, simply cannot be met in the resurrection because there would not be enough parts to go around: "we all live in second-hand suits and there are doubtless atoms in my chin which have served many another man, many a dog, many an eel, many a dinosaur."[30]

But in addition to citing commonsense philosophical considerations, Lewis believed the view that the resurrection body must be numerically identical with the earthly body is "not justified by the words of Scripture . . . ."[31] While so far as I know he did not explicitly make the following point, Lewis might have added that no creed of the Christian Church has ever taught or insisted upon the numerical sameness of the resurrection and earthly bodies. And had he pointed this out he would likely have insisted that the commonsense

---

[28] Lewis, Miracles, 246.
[29] Lewis, Miracles, 246-7. In an article entitled "The Soul in Greek Christianity," Kallistos Ware writes that "[i]n the light of current scientific theories concerning the nature of matter, it is difficult to give any clear meaning to [the] assertion [that at the final resurrection the soul will gather together, from the common store of matter, precisely the selfsame physical particles as previously constituted its body]." He then goes on to say the following: "The important thing is not the identity of the material constituents but the continuity of the 'form' supplied by the soul. C. S. Lewis appeals in this context to the example of a waterfall. The drops in a waterfall are continually changing, but the curve assumed by the water remains constant; since the water preserves the same 'form', it is indeed the same waterfall." In From Soul to Self, ed. M. James C. Crabbe (New York: Routledge, 1999), 53. But Lewis did not say that the important thing is the continuity of the form of the human body, on analogy with the form of the waterfall. Moreover, Lewis did not say that because the waterfall retains the same form across time that it is the same waterfall, with the implication being that because the human body retains the same form through time it is the same human body. Lewis addressed only the unity of the body through time, not its sameness. Finally, he did not say that the soul imposed this unity or form.
[30] Lewis, Miracles, 246.
[31] Lewis, Miracles, 246.

philosophical considerations cited in the previous paragraph make clear why the authors of the creeds never insisted upon anything like this.

Lewis said there are no words in Scripture for a view of the resurrection body like Aquinas's that requires the numerical sameness of parts. He also thought that what Scripture says about the resurrection supports the idea that the resurrection body is not the same kind of body as the earthly body. In other words, Lewis doubted that the resurrection body is a human body, if by "human body" is meant a flesh-and-blood organism with the same kinds of parts that function in the same way as they did before death. At this point, he emphasized that "all references to the risen *body* make us uneasy: they raise awkward questions."[32] While he acknowledged that there is no getting away from the fact that the risen body of Jesus was a body, he also insisted it was no ordinary body. It occupied "a wholly new mode of being" and it is both

> like, and yet unlike, the body His friends knew before the execution. It is differently related to space and probably to time, but by no means cut off from all relation to them. It is so related to matter, as we know it, that it can be touched, though at first it had better not be touched. It has also a history before it which is in view from the first moment of the Resurrection; it is presently going to become different or go somewhere else. That is why the story of the Ascension cannot be separated from that of the Resurrection.[33]

> The records represent Christ as passing after death (as no man had passed before) neither into a purely, that is, negatively, "spiritual" mode of existence nor into a "natural" life such as we know, but into a life which has its own, new Nature. It represents Him as withdrawing six weeks later, into some different mode of existence. . . . It is the picture of a new human nature, and a new Nature in general, being brought into existence. We must, indeed, believe the risen body to be extremely different from the mortal body: but the existence, in that new state, of anything that could in any sense be described as "body" at all, involves some sort of spatial relations and in the long run a whole new universe.[34]

> It must be emphasized throughout that we know and can know very little about the New Nature. . . . The New Nature is, in the most troublesome way, interlocked at some points with the Old. Because of its novelty we have to think of it, for the most part, metaphorically . . . .[35]

---

[32] Lewis, *Miracles*, 240.
[33] Lewis, *Miracles*, 241–2.
[34] Lewis, *Miracles*, 243–4.
[35] Lewis, *Miracles*, 250–1.

The resurrection body's relationship to pleasure and happiness

Whatever the kind of body Christ has in the New Nature, Lewis believed there could be no denying that it is a body. He emphasized "that the Resurrection [of Christ] was not regarded simply or chiefly as evidence for the immortality of the soul. . . . Immortality simply as immortality is irrelevant to the Christian claim."[36] And while Lewis insisted that we know very little about the New Nature occupied by the resurrection body, he firmly believed the resurrection body is one that will be conducive to the purpose for which we exist, which is that we experience nothing but pleasure. Lewis stressed that just as "in this life matter would be nothing to us if it were not the source of sensations,"[37] so also we are concerned with the resurrection of the body only because "the soul cries out for . . . the resurrection of the senses."[38] And the soul cries out for the coming back to life of the senses because they are sources of pleasure. Thus, the rationale for the resurrection of the body, whatever that body will be like, is that it provide us with pleasure, just as the rationale for the earthly body is that it provide us with pleasure: "[Christians], of all men, must not conceive spiritual joy and worth as things that need to be rescued or tenderly protected from time and place and matter and the senses. Their God is the God of corn and oil and wine. He is the glad Creator. He has become Himself incarnate."[39]

Lewis's view of the relationship between the earthly body and its actions (whether earthly or resurrection) and pleasure was in tension with that of Aquinas. While Lewis saw the body and its actions as directed toward pleasure, Aquinas saw pleasure as directed toward the body and its actions:

> The life of those who rise will be better ordered than our life. . . . But in the present life it is a disordered and vicious thing to use food and sexual union for mere pleasure and not for the necessity of sustaining life and begetting offspring. And this is reasonable, for the pleasures which are in the activities mentioned are not the ends of those activities. It is, rather, the converse, for nature ordered the pleasure of those acts for this reason: lest the animals, in view of the labor, desist from those acts necessary to nature, which is what would happen if they were not stimulated by pleasure. Therefore, the order is reversed and inharmonious if those

---

[36] Lewis, *Miracles*, 236, 239.
[37] *Letters to Malcolm*, 121.
[38] *Letters to Malcolm*, 121.
[39] Lewis, *Miracles*, 265.

operations are carried out merely for pleasure. By no means, therefore, will such a thing be found among those who rise; their life is held to be the one of perfect order.[40]

Moreover, Aquinas insisted that because the pleasure of a bodily act is not the end to which the bodily act is a means in this life, which is a form of existence wherein we find no more than imperfect happiness, it would be wrongheaded to think that pleasure is the end to which a bodily act is a means in the resurrection life, wherein we experience perfect happiness: "The life of the risen . . . is ordered to the preservation of perfect beatitude. But the beatitude and felicity of man do not consist in bodily pleasures, and such are the pleasures of eating and of sexual union . . . . One should not, therefore, hold that there are pleasures of this kind in the life of those who rise."[41]

What, then, of the resurrection body? From Aquinas's perspective, how is it related to perfect happiness? To be sure, it provides no pleasure that is a part of perfect happiness because no pleasure of any kind, whether its source is mental or bodily, is a constituent of perfect happiness. In Aquinas's view, the soul's perfect happiness is not had in virtue of its being the form of its body:

> Happiness is the perfection of soul on the part of the mind which transcends the organs of body; it is not the perfection of soul precisely as the natural form of the body. A disembodied soul keeps enough natural completeness to be equal to happiness, although the natural completeness of actually being the form of the body has departed.[42]

But because the soul will be reunited with its physical body in the resurrection life, its happiness will overflow into its body to ensure bodily well-being and the avoidance of bodily ills that might impede its happiness:

> Let us declare, then, that happiness complete and entire requires the well-being of the body, both before and during its activity. It is an antecedent condition because, and we quote Augustine, *if the body be such that its governance is difficult and burdensome, like unto the flesh which sickens and weighs upon the soul, then the mind is turned away from that far vision in high heaven.* He concludes that *when the body will no longer be animal but spiritual, then it will match the angels, and that will be glory*

---

[40] Aquinas, *Summa Contra Gentiles: Book Four*, Chapter 83: 10. Cf. Aquinas, *Summa Contra Gentiles: Book Three*, Chapter 26: 14.
[41] Aquinas, *Summa Contra Gentiles: Book Four*, Chapter 83: 11.
[42] Aquinas, *Summa Theologiae: Volume 16 (Ia2ae. 1-5), Purpose and Happiness*, Ia2ae. 4, 5 ad 1.

which erstwhile was a carcass. Bodily well-being, then, is a consequent condition, for happiness of soul overflows into body, which drinks of the fullness of soul.[43]

Even though the body contributes nothing to that activity of mind which sees God's essence, it could prove a drag. And therefore its perfection is required so as not to encumber mind's ascent.[44]

In Aquinas's view, the resurrection body avoids being instrumentally bad insofar as it does not impede the perfect happiness that is the contemplation of God's essence. However, Thomas believed the resurrection body is not instrumentally good as a source of the perfect happiness of the resurrection life. Indeed, Aquinas's denial of this kind of instrumental goodness extended to all external goods (those other than our bodies, which in this life include food, clothing, shelter, etc.). While external goods are necessary for the imperfect happiness of this life, they are not needed for the perfect happiness of the resurrection life:

> External goods are required for the imperfect happiness open to us in this life, not that they lie at the heart of happiness, yet they are tools to serve happiness which lies, says Aristotle, in the activity of virtue. Ownership of them is required in order to lead a life of contemplative virtue, and of active virtue as well, particularly the last, which calls for many more.
> Nowise are they needed for the perfect happiness of seeing God. We need them now to support our animal bodies or to exercise the physical functions proper to our condition. Perfect happiness, however, is for a soul without a body or a soul united to a body which is no longer animal but spiritual.[45]

The Thomist scholar, Georg Wieland, summarizes Aquinas's view of the relationship between the soul and its perfect happiness and the body as follows:

> The essence of complete human happiness does not require the body.... The integral, natural relationship between the body and soul is not abolished; rather, it is completed by the beatific vision. The soul's desire thus rests completely only when this essential relationship is reestablished, and in this the body participates in its own way in the

---

[43] Aquinas, *Summa Theologiae: Volume 16 (Ia2ae. 1-5), Purpose and Happiness*, Ia2ae. 4, 6 ad.
[44] Aquinas, *Summa Theologiae: Volume 16 (Ia2ae. 1-5), Purpose and Happiness*, Ia2ae. 4, 6 ad 2.
[45] Aquinas, *Summa Theologiae: Volume 16 (Ia2ae. 1-5), Purpose and Happiness*, Ia2ae. 4, 7 ad.

fullness of divine wealth.... The body-soul relationship experienced in this life is reversed in complete happiness. In this case, the soul, or more precisely the intellect, is not oriented toward the body. Rather, the soul lets the body participate in its perfection ....[46]

It warrants repeating that Lewis had a decidedly different understanding of the soul-body relationship in heaven as viewed through the lens of happiness. Rather than maintain that the soul allows its perfect happiness to perfect its body, he believed that in the resurrection life the body and external goods will be sources of the intrinsically good pleasure that perfects the soul. Because experiences of pleasure compose happiness both in this and the next life, the soul-body relationship is not, as Aquinas maintained, reversed in perfect happiness. A passage I cited in Chapter 2 merits quoting again here: "Christianity is almost the only one of the great religions which thoroughly approves of the body—which believes that matter is good, that God Himself once took on a human body, that some kind of body is going to be given to us even in Heaven and is going to be an essential part of our happiness . . . ."[47] To make his point, Lewis invoked the idea of riding horses:

> There is in our present pilgrim condition plenty of room (more room than most of us like) for abstinence and renunciation and mortifying our natural desires. But behind all asceticism the thought should be, "Who will trust us with the true wealth if we cannot be trusted even with the wealth that perishes?" Who will trust me with a spiritual body if I cannot control even an earthly body? These small and perishable bodies we now have were given to us as ponies are given to schoolboys. We must learn to manage: not that we may some day be free of horses altogether but that some day we may ride bare-back, confident and rejoicing, those greater mounts, those winged, shining and world-shaking horses which perhaps even now expect us with impatience, pawing and snorting in the King's stables.[48]

In Lewis's view, just as our earthly body is a source of pleasure in this life, so also the spiritual body will be a source of pleasure in the life to come. The resurrection body will be instrumentally good as a source of the intrinsic goodness of pleasure that makes for perfect happiness.

---

[46] Georg Wieland, "Happiness (Ia IIae, qq.1-5)," in *The Ethics of Aquinas*, ed. Stephen J. Pope (Washington, D.C.: Georgetown University Press, 2002), 64.
[47] Lewis, *Mere Christianity*, 98.
[48] Lewis, *Miracles*, 266.

Lewis, Aquinas, and the soul

What would Lewis have thought about Aquinas's view of the soul? Let us begin with the soul's relationship to its body. What is most immediately noticeable is Lewis's silence about the topic. Just as he advocated mere Christianity, so also he seems to have been comfortable with what can reasonably be termed "mere dualism," the view which maintains the existence of a substantial soul and body but refrains from insisting upon any particular account of how they are related. The explanation for his holding this minimalist position is found, at least in part, in his belief that no one had yet proposed a model that makes intelligible the unity of soul and body. For example, immediately under the section heading "Soul and Body" in *The Discarded Image*, Lewis wrote that

> [n]o Model yet devised has made a satisfactory unity between our actual experience of sensation or thought or emotion and any available account of the corporeal processes which they are held to involve.... The chasm between the two points of view is so abrupt that desperate remedies have been adopted. Berkeleyan idealists have denied the physical process; extreme Behaviourists, the mental.[49]

While Lewis himself had idealist leanings, he seems to have always remained a substance dualist, even though he could not succeed where all others had failed by providing an explanation of how the soul and body are related. He thought it unnecessary and ill-advised to advocate a position on an issue that remained shrouded in darkness. Thus, Lewis saw no need to commit to a position on the widely disputed question of whether the soul gives life to its body. As I pointed out earlier in this chapter, Aquinas affirmed that a body is enlivened by its soul. Being a Cartesian about the soul in the sense that he regarded the soul as the self, Lewis seems to have been comfortable with (at least, I am not aware of a denial of) the additional Cartesian idea that the body is an organic mechanical substance in its own right and that the soul ceases to be related to the body when it ceases to function (as opposed to death being the soul's leaving its body).[50] For example, he

---

[49] Lewis, *The Discarded Image*, 165, 166.
[50] Here are two lengthy quotes from Descartes about the body's status as a machine: "And as a clock composed of wheels and counter-weights no less exactly observes the laws of nature when it is badly made, and does not show the time properly, than when it entirely satisfies the wishes of its maker, ... [so also] if I consider the body of a man as being a sort of machine so built up and composed of nerves, muscles, veins, blood and skin, that though there were no mind in it at all, it would not cease to have the same motions as

concisely expressed the Cartesian view in a letter to Mary Willis Shelburne in November 1962, a year before he died: "[Our bodies are like] old automobiles, aren't they? where all sorts of apparently different things keep going wrong, but what they add up to is the plain fact that the machine is wearing out."[51] But while Lewis himself was comfortable with viewing the human body as a machine, this understanding of the human body was not a part of mere dualism, which extended no further than the Cartesian belief in the existence of the soul as a substance in its own right that is the self or "I" and has a substantial body.

As serious contemporary Thomists, Lee and George insist that the soul is not a substance in its own right, that human beings and not souls are persons, and, therefore, "that 'I' refers to a rational animal"[52] and not to the soul alone. But other equally serious Roman Catholics find it hard to avoid the commonsensical view that the soul is the "I." For example, consider the following thoughts of the priest Richard John Neuhaus:

> More common in the history of thought [than views that minimize the significance of death] is the idea of the immortality of the soul. The essential person, it is said, is the soul. . . . Surely we should not deny that there is an "I"—call it the soul—that is distinct from, if not independent from, the body. I am, after all, reliably told that every part of the body, down to the smallest molecule, is replaced several times in my lifetime, and yet "I" persist. . . .
>
> I want to insist upon, if you will forgive the awkward terms, the "I-ness" of the soul. It is not as though I *have* a soul in the way I have a liver or a kidney. . . . The soul is one with the enduring "I" that embraces, that defines, that gives form to my essential identity [as a human being]—an identity that includes my body. And yet I believe, in a faith disposed toward the future that we call hope, that it endures through its temporary separation from the body.[53]

---

at present, exception being made of those movements which are due to the direction of the will, and in consequence depend upon the mind [as opposed to those which operate by the disposition of its organs] . . . ."; and "[L]et us consider that death never comes to pass by reason of the soul, but only because some one of the principal parts of the body decays; and we may judge that the body of a living man differs from that of a dead man just as does a watch or other automation (i.e. a machine that moves of itself), when it is wound up and contains in itself the corporeal principle of those movements for which it is designed along with all that is requisite for its action, from the same watch or other machine when it is broken and when the principle of its movement ceases to act." The quotes come from Descartes, *The Philosophical Works of Descartes*, vol. I, 195, 333.

[51] Lewis, *The Collected Letters of C. S. Lewis: Volume III*, 1384.
[52] Lee and George, *Body-Self Dualism in Contemporary Ethics and Politics*, 28.
[53] Richard John Neuhaus, *As I Lay Dying: Meditations upon Returning* (New York: Basic Books, 2002), 71–2.

And *The Wall Street Journal* political columnist, Peggy Noonan, who is also a Roman Catholic, says this:

> The other day in a seminar at a university, a student of political science asked a sort of complicated question that seemed to be about the predictability of human response to a given set of political stimuli. I answered that if you view people as souls, believe that we have souls within us, that they *are* us, then nothing political is fully predictable, because you never know what a soul will do, how a soul will respond, what truth it will apprehend and react to. I was thinking as I spoke of the headline when the Titanic went down: "1,400 Souls Lost." We used to see people in that larger dimension, which is not a romantic but realistic one. The puniest person is big, and rich. . . .
>
> We were not built to be all about politics. Empires rise and fall, nations come and go, but the man who poured your coffee this morning is eternal, because his soul is eternal. That's C. S. Lewis.[54]

The reasoning behind Noonan's comments here might be as follows: "I am a soul"; there are others like me; therefore, "We are all souls." But whatever the reasoning, it cannot be ignored that not only does she believe that our souls *are* us, but also she thinks this is Lewis's view.

At this juncture, the following rejoinder might be given: "Look, though Noonan is a Roman Catholic, one cannot reasonably expect her to know her Aquinas. Moreover, while Neuhaus was a Roman Catholic priest, he spent the majority of his life within the Lutheran Church and might never have been schooled in the details of Aquinas's view of the soul."

Both points are legitimate. But my claim is not that Neuhaus and Noonan misrepresent Aquinas's teaching concerning the soul, but rather that they express the commonsense view about it. And in Noonan's case, she makes clear that this view was Lewis's.

As I pointed out in Chapter 2, while Lewis believed the soul is the "I" he also wrote the following: "[I]n every human being a more than natural activity (the act of reasoning) and therefore presumably a more than natural agent is thus united with a part of Nature: so united that the composite creature calls itself 'I' and 'Me'."[55] Here, I want to stress that Lewis believed a soul-body composite refers to itself as "I" only because a soul first does this. And the explanation for this extended use of "I" is easy to explain. As someone who well understood the use of words, Lewis knew that in daily

---

[54] Peggy Noonan, "We're More than Political Animals." *The Wall Street Journal* March 3–4, 2012, sec. A.
[55] Lewis, *Miracles*, 177.

life we often ascribe the properties of one object to another because of a close association between them. Thus, if I am driving an automobile and it is hit by another vehicle, I do not hesitate to say "I was hit." And if my doctor asks my height and weight, I do not hesitate to answer "5' 11" and "175 pounds." Given the close association in this life that all of us as souls have with our bodies (indeed, are there any entities with which we are more closely associated than our own bodies?), we naturally refer to our soul-body composite as "I" and "Me."

A section not strictly necessary

I close this chapter with an issue that could be passed over but nevertheless is relevant to Lewis's thought about the soul and happiness. As I indicated in the Introduction and briefly discussed in Chapter 2, scholars in theological circles have argued at length in recent years that the early church wrongfully incorporated soul-body dualism into its anthropological views. According to them, the mistake was made because the early church drew too heavily from Greek philosophical categories of thought to express its own ideas. As I also made clear in these earlier chapters, Lewis would have rejected this suggestion as nothing more than Bulverism. But he would have made an additional point. He would have told the Bulverisers that if they are serious about finding a deleterious Greek influence on early Christianity they should look no further than Greek eudaemonist thought about morality and happiness and the relationship between them.[56] To the extent that Christian intellectuals in the first centuries abandoned commonsense beliefs about these topics and endorsed eudaemonism, they jeopardized connecting intellectually with ordinary people. Soul-body dualism is commonsensical. Eudaemonism is not. Lewis embraced the former and rejected the latter. Aquinas did the opposite. Thus the intellectual divide between them was wide and deep. As I will argue in the next chapter, this difference had significant implications for Lewis's view of Roman Catholicism.

---

[56] Scott MacDonald writes the following about Christianity and Greek moral thought: "For well over a thousand years Greek philosophy provided the framework for the philosophical understanding of the foundations of Christian morality. . . . Aquinas, for instance . . . ." "Egoistic Rationalism: Aquinas's Basis for Christian Morality," in *Christian Theism and the Problems of Philosophy*, ed. Michael D. Beaty (Notre Dame, IN: University of Notre Dame Press, 1990), 327.

Part Three

5

A Rational Journey

Thomas Aquinas and D. H. Lawrence do not divide the universe between them . . . .[1]

Why not Roman Catholicism?

Thomas Howard, after acknowledging that the question "Why Did C. S. Lewis Never Become a Roman Catholic?" is widely and frequently asked, says the following:

> On the surface of things, the question might be dismissed as frivolous. Why didn't Tillich become Orthodox? Why didn't Karl Barth become Wesleyan? . . . There seems something odd about such a line of question—odd, perhaps slightly impertinent, and very likely irrelevant. The rejoinder in each case might well be, "Why should he have?"
>
> In the case of Lewis and the Catholic Church, however, different elements come into play. For one thing, there is the nature of the Catholic Church itself. No other ecclesial entity in the world can lay such a sure claim to immense dominical, apostolic, historical, and theological origins and fabric. Hence, as a corollary to this, we assume that anyone as vastly literate in matters Christian as was Lewis will most assuredly have been obliged to face the claims of Rome at some point or another in his reading and conversation.[2]

Howard goes on to suggest that it is extremely hard to grasp how a person with a mind like Lewis's could have viewed the Anglican Church as anything other than an anomaly. But Lewis was and until the very end remained an Anglican. So what answer does Howard give to the question of why Lewis did not become Roman Catholic? "'He didn't want to' is, in some serious sense, pretty much the answer."[3] Andrew Cuneo says that this answer is hardly

---

[1] Lewis, "Early Prose Joy," 13.
[2] Thomas Howard, "Why Did C. S. Lewis Never Become a Roman Catholic?," *Lay Witness*, November, 1998, 8.
[3] Howard, "Why Did C. S. Lewis Never Become a Roman Catholic?," 8.

sufficient. Obviously what we want to know is the answer to the following question: "*Why* did [Lewis] not want to?"[4] Howard believes that Lewis simply "thought Rome was wrong."[5]

But wrong about what? Howard never mentions the fundamental component in the explanation of why Lewis believed Rome was wrong. As background for treatment of this issue, I begin where so many others have, which is with Lewis's commitment to mere Christianity.

Conversion and mere Christianity

The details of C. S. Lewis's religious journey are fairly well known. In barest outline, by his own account he lost his Christian faith in his early teens while away from home in 1911–12 at a British preparatory school named "Cherbourg".[6] Lewis then remained an atheist for almost two decades. His return to Christianity was in the most general terms a two-step process. The first step involved a return to theism, which occurred in his room in Magdalen College, Oxford, in either the Trinity Term of 1929 or 1930 (roughly late April through mid-to-late June of both years).[7] The following are his memorable words:

> You must picture me alone in that room in Magdalen, night after night, feeling, whenever my mind lifted even for a second from my work, the steady, unrelenting approach of Him whom I so earnestly desired not to meet. That which I greatly feared had at last come upon me. In the Trinity Term of 1929 I gave in, and admitted that God was God, and knelt and prayed: perhaps, that night, the most dejected and reluctant convert in all England.[8]

The second step in his conversion did not occur for (perhaps) another two years. According to Lewis, his brother Warren and he took a picnic lunch to

---

[4] Andrew P. Cuneo, "Review of *C. S. Lewis and the Catholic Church*, by Joseph Pearce; and *C. S. Lewis and the Blessed Virgin Mary: Uncovering a "Marian Attitude"*, by Rev. Arthur Mastrolia." *Seven* 21 (2004): 101–4.
[5] Howard, "Why Did C. S. Lewis Never Become a Roman Catholic?," 9.
[6] A preparatory school is one designed for the purpose of getting a student ready for a British public school, which is the equivalent of an American private school.
[7] The traditional date for Lewis' conversion to theism is the 1929 date. However, McGrath has recently argued that the traditional view is likely wrong and the correct date is that of 1930. McGrath, *C. S. Lewis: A Life*, 141–6. For my purposes, the date of Lewis's conversion is not important.
[8] Lewis, *Surprised by Joy*, 228–9.

A Rational Journey

Whipsnade Zoo in September 1931. Warren was driving his motor cycle and Lewis was riding in the side-car. In Lewis's words:

> When we set out I did not believe that Jesus Christ is the Son of God, and when we reached the zoo I did. Yet I had not exactly spent the journey in thought. Nor in great emotion. "Emotional" is perhaps the last word we can apply to some of the most important events. It was more like when a man, after long sleep, still lying motionless in bed, becomes aware that he is now awake.[9]

Ten years later, the British Broadcasting Corporation engaged Lewis to give a series of radio talks on Christianity to the British public during the Second World War. The talks subsequently formed the best-selling book *Mere Christianity*. In the preface to *Mere Christianity*, Lewis wrote:

> I offer no help to anyone who is hesitating between two Christian "denominations". You will not learn from me whether you ought to become an Anglican, a Methodist, a Presbyterian, or a Roman Catholic. This omission is intentional . . . . There is no mystery about my own position. I am a very ordinary layman of the Church of England, not especially "high", nor especially "low", nor especially anything else. . . . Ever since I became a Christian I have thought that the best, perhaps the only, service I could do for my unbelieving neighbours was to explain and defend the belief that has been common to nearly all Christians at all times. . . . [T]he questions which divide Christians from one another often involve points of high Theology . . . . I think we must admit that the discussion of these disputed points has no tendency at all to bring an outsider into the Christian fold. . . . [I have written] in the defence of what Baxter calls "mere" Christianity.[10]

Elsewhere, Lewis said the following about mere Christianity:

> But if any man is tempted to think—as one might be tempted who read only contemporaries—that "Christianity" is a word of so many meanings that it means nothing at all, he can learn beyond all doubt, by stepping out of his own century, that this is not so. Measured against the ages

---

[9] Lewis, *Surprised by Joy*, 237.
[10] Lewis, *Mere Christianity*, viii–ix. Richard Baxter was a prominent English churchman of the seventeenth century. Within the Anglican Church, he found common ground with the Puritans, a group that opposed the Church's episcopacy—but was itself dividing into factions. Baxter sought common ground, a "mere" Christianity, between Anglicans, Presbyterians, Congregationalists, and other denominations.

"mere Christianity" turns out to be no insipid interdenominational transparency, but something positive, self-consistent, and inexhaustible. . . .

We are all rightly distressed, and ashamed also, at the divisions of Christendom. But those who have always lived within the Christian fold may be too easily dispirited by them. They are bad, but such people do not know what it looks like from without. Seen from there, what is left intact, despite all the divisions, still appears (as it truly is) an immensely formidable unity.[11]

Firmly an Anglican

Lewis spoke and wrote in defense of mere Christianity as that which is commonly owned by all Christians. Nevertheless, some of his more specific comments have encouraged and enabled many to claim that certain of his views represent the position of one Christian denomination to the exclusion of others. In one of its most general (and, perhaps, controversial) forms, the denominational issue manifests itself in terms of Protestantism versus Roman Catholicism. For example, Gilbert Meilaender detects Roman Catholic leanings in Lewis:

> When, in the theological struggles to which the Reformation gave rise, Protestants depicted a nature so thoroughly corrupted by sin that death and rebirth were necessary, Catholics sometimes thought that this demonstrated an insufficient appreciation of the continuing goodness of creation, of its ability to point us to God. And so, Catholics responded by saying that "grace does not destroy nature, but perfects it." . . .
>
> Lewis, mere Christian that he seeks to be, sees the worth of both pictures of the Christian life—and sees it quite profoundly. As always in his view, the real truth of things is captured in the Catholic formulation: The natural life is God's good gift; he will not destroy but perfect it.[12]

However, Meilaender's claim that "As always in [Lewis'] view, the real truth of things is captured in the Catholic formulation" has at least one major consideration working against it: Lewis never became a Roman Catholic. It is fair to conclude that Lewis, contrary to what Meilaender says, did not always think that the Roman Catholic formulation captured the real truth of things.

---

[11] Lewis, *God in the Dock*, 203–4.
[12] Gilbert Meilander, "The Everyday C. S. Lewis." *First Things* 85 (August/September 1998): 32–3.

A Rational Journey 155

While Lewis believed Roman Catholicism did not always capture the truth of the matter, he was, as Christopher Derrick points out,[13] reluctant to talk about his not going to Rome. For example, Lewis wrote to Mrs Halmbacher in March of 1951, that

> [t]he question for me (naturally) is not "Why should I not be a Roman Catholic?" but "Why should I?" But I don't like discussing such matters, because it emphasises differences and endangers charity. By the time I had really explained my objection to certain doctrines which differentiate you from us (and also in my opinion from the Apostolic and even the Medieval Church), you would like me less.[14]

Similarly, to Dom Bede Griffiths, a former pupil and converted Roman Catholic priest and monk, Lewis wrote in April of 1951 that "I am no nearer to your Church than I was but I don't feel [very] inclined to re-open a discussion. I think it only widens [and] sharpens differences."[15] This was seventeen years after he had written the following to Griffiths in April of 1934:

> And while I am on the subject, I had better say once and for all that I do not intend to discuss with you in future, if I can help it, any of the questions at issue between our respective churches. It would have the same unreality as those absurd conversations in which we are invited to speak frankly to a woman about some indelicate matter—[which] means that she can say what she likes and we can't. I could not, now that you are a monk, use that freedom in attacking your position which you undoubtedly would use in attacking mine. I do not think there is any thing distressing for either of us in agreeing to be silent on this matter: I have had a Catholic [J. R. R. Tolkien] among my most intimate friends for many years and a great deal of our conversation has been religious. When all is said (and truly said) about the divisions of Christendom,

---

[13] Derrick, *C. S. Lewis and the Church of Rome*, 94.
[14] Lewis, *The Collected Letters of C. S. Lewis: Volume III*, 106. Interestingly, Dorothy L. Sayers, the British novelist and sometimes correspondent with Lewis, also faced the issue of becoming Roman Catholic. In a letter to V. A. Demant from October 2, 1941, she wrote: "The Romans seem to have taken a great fancy to [*The Mind of the Maker*]— the *Universe* emitting the usual dark mumble about hoping to see me follow G. K. [Chesterton] into the arms of Mother Church. I have no doubt it is their job to say these things, but I do dislike being made to feel like a rabbit exposed to the slow fascination of a waiting serpent." Dorothy L. Sayers, *The Letters of Dorothy L. Sayers: Volume II; 1937 to 1943*, ed. Barbara Reynolds (New York: St. Martin's Press, 1997), 306.
[15] Lewis, *The Collected Letters of C. S. Lewis: Volume III*, 112.

there remains, by God's mercy, an enormous common ground. It is abstaining from one tree in the whole garden.[16]

In yet another letter to Griffiths, this one from February 1936, Lewis again played down the importance of differences between Protestants and Catholics:

> As to the main issue I can only repeat what I have said before. One of the most important differences between us is our estimate of the importance of the differences. You, in your charity, are anxious to convert me: but I am not in the least anxious to convert you. You think my specifically Protestant beliefs a tissue of damnable errors: I think your specifically Catholic beliefs a mass of comparatively harmless human tradition which may be fatal to certain souls under special conditions, but which I think suitable for you. I therefore feel no *duty* to attack you: and certainly feel no *inclination* to add to my other works an epistolary controversy with one of the toughest dialecticians of my acquaintance, to which he can devote as much time and reading as he likes and I can devote very little. As well—who wants to debate with a man who begins by saying that no argument can possibly move him? Talk sense, man! With other Catholics I find no difficulty in deriving much edification from religious talk on the common ground: but you refuse to show any interest except in differences.[17]

As is evident from the last sentence of this quote, Lewis believed Christians of different denominations could receive edification from each other. In a letter from November 1952, to Mary Willis Shelburne, who had recently left Anglicanism for Roman Catholicism, Lewis wrote that "[though] you have taken a way which is not for me I nevertheless can congratulate you—I suppose because your faith and joy are so obviously increased. Naturally, I do not draw from that the same conclusions as you—but there is no need for us to start a controversial correspondence!"[18] And in a letter from January 1950 to Sister Mary Rose, Lewis said the following:

> I am sorry if I misunderstood your letter: and I think that you misunderstood mine. What I meant was that if I replied to your original question (why I am not a member of the Roman Church), I [should] have to write a [very] long letter. It would of course be answerable: and your answer would be answerable by me . . . and so on. The resulting

---

[16] Lewis, *The Collected Letters of C. S. Lewis, Volume II*, 135–6.
[17] Lewis, *The Collected Letters of C. S. Lewis, Volume II*, 178–9.
[18] Lewis, *The Collected Letters of C. S. Lewis: Volume III*, 248–9.

correspondence would certainly not, of course, be in excess of the importance of the subject: but haven't you and I both probably more pressing duties? For a real correspondence on such a subject [would] be nearly a wholetime job. I thought we [could] both discuss the matter more usefully with people nearer at hand.[19]

From the foregoing letters, it is clear that Lewis sought to emphasize the common ground shared by Protestants and Roman Catholics and to affirm those individuals who were members of the Roman church. Not to do so endangered charity. Moreover, Lewis also believed that many people were unaware of just how much the two groups shared in common. About his own books, Lewis said the following in a letter to Father Don Giovanni Calabria in September 1947:

> Be assured that for me too the schism in the Body of Christ is both a source of grief and a matter of prayers, being a most serious stumbling block to those coming in and one which makes even the faithful weaker in repelling the common foe. However, I am a layman, indeed the most lay of laymen, and least skilled in the deeper questions of sacred theology. I have tried to do the only thing that I think myself able to do: that is, to leave completely aside the subtler questions about which the Roman Church and Protestants disagree among themselves—things which are to be treated by bishops and learned men—and in my own books to expound, rather, those things which still, by God's grace, after so many sins and errors, are shared by us. Nor is this a pointless task; for I find that people are unaware how many matters we even now agree on . . . . Over and above that work, it has always seemed to me that I should maintain as much fraternal intercourse as possible with all those who call themselves Christians. If all were actively to do this, might we not hope that this unity of love and action over many years would precede—not to say foster—an eventual reunification of doctrines.[20]

While Lewis was clearly averse to entering into serious discussions about his relationship to Roman Catholicism, he did open up to some individuals. For example, the door was ajar just slightly in the following letter to Father Peter Milward, from May 1963:

> You ask me in effect why I am not an R. C. If it comes to that, why am I not—and why are you *not*—a Presbyterian, a Quaker, a Mohammedan,

---

[19] Lewis, *The Collected Letters of C. S. Lewis: Volume III*, 8–9.
[20] Lewis, *The Collected Letters of C. S. Lewis: Volume II*, 801.

a Hindoo, or a Confucianist? After how prolonged and sympathetic study and on what grounds have we rejected these religions? I think those who press a man to desert the religion in which he has been bred and in which he believes he has found the means of Grace ought to produce positive reasons for the change—not demand from him reasons *against* all other religions. It [would] have to be *all*, wouldn't it? . . . [A] great many of my closest friends are your co-religionists, some of them priests. If I am to embark on a disputation—[which] could not be a short one, I [would] much sooner do it with them than by correspondence.[21]

Lewis provided a bit more information concerning what stood in the way of his becoming Roman Catholic in a letter from November 1947 to Father Calabria. There, Lewis stated that "we disagree about nothing more than the authority of the Pope: on which disagreement almost all others depend."[22] In another letter from May 1945 to the layman Hart Lyman Stebbins, Lewis explained that his position about the different Christian churches could be clarified by an imaginary example:

> Suppose that I want to find out the correct interpretation of Plato's teaching. What I am most confident in accepting is that interpretation [which] is common to all the Platonists down all the centuries: what Aristotle and the Renaissance scholars and Paul Elmer More agree on I take to be true Platonism. And purely modern views [which] claim to have discovered for the first time what [Plato] meant, and say that everyone from Aristotle down has misunderstood him, I reject out of hand. . . .
>
> I do the same with Xtianity. What is most certain is the vast mass of doctrine [which] I find agreed on by Scripture, the Fathers, the Middle Ages, modern [Roman Catholics], modern Protestants. That is true "catholic" doctrine. Mere "modernism" I reject at once.
>
> The Roman Church where it differs from this universal tradition and specially from apostolic Xtianity I reject. Thus their theology about the [Blessed Virgin Mary] I reject because it seems utterly foreign to the New Testament: where indeed the words "Blessed is the womb that bore thee" receive a rejoinder pointing in exactly the opposite direction [Jesus' rejoinder is "blessed are they that hear the word of God, and keep it" (Luke 11:27-8)]. Their papalism seems equally foreign to the attitude of St Paul towards Peter in the Epistles. The doctrine of Transubstantiation insists in defining in a way [what] the [New Testament] seems to me

---

[21] Lewis, *The Collected Letters of C. S. Lewis, Volume III*, 1425–6.
[22] Lewis, *The Collected Letters of C. S. Lewis, Volume II*, 815–16.

not to countenance. In a word, the whole set-up of modern Romanism seems to me to be as much a provincial or local *variation* from the central, ancient tradition as any particular Protestant sect is. I must therefore reject their *claim*: tho' this does not mean rejecting particular things they say.[23]

In a letter to Mary van Deusen in June 1952, Lewis provided some further thoughts about the Blessed Virgin Mary in a discussion of Hail Marys:

Hail Marys raise a *doctrinal* question: whether it is lawful to address devotions to any *creature*, however holy. My own view would be that a *salute* to any saint (or angel) cannot in itself be wrong any more than taking off one's hat to a friend: but that there is always some danger lest such practices start one on the road to a state (sometimes found in [Roman Catholics]) where the [Blessed Virgin Mary] is treated really as a deity and even becomes the centre of the religion. I therefore think that such salutes are better avoided. And if the Blessed Virgin is as good as the best mothers I have known, she does not *want* any of the attention which might have gone to her Son diverted to herself.[24]

Though Lewis was intellectually at odds with what he called "papalism" in the above-mentioned letter to Stebbins,[25] he shared in a letter with Griffiths in May of 1939 that "[n]othing [would] give such strong support to the Papal claims as the spectacle of a Pope actually functioning as head of Christendom."[26] Moreover, Lewis was not in disagreement with everything Roman Catholic. As examples of some Roman Catholic practices that Lewis embraced, Pearce cites Lewis's conviction that Holy Communion and baptism are physical means of grace beyond a purely mental act like belief[27]; the fact

---

[23] Lewis, *The Collected Letters of C. S. Lewis, Volume II*, 645–7.
[24] Lewis, *The Collected Letters of C. S. Lewis: Volume III*, 209.
[25] In writing about the Reformation in *Poetry and Prose in the Sixteenth Century*, 157, Lewis made clear that he intended nothing disrespectful to Roman Catholics with his use of the term "Papists": "I ask my readers to believe that I have at least intended to be impartial. Unfortunately the very names we have to use in describing this controversy [between Rome and Reformers] are themselves controversial. To call one party Catholics implicitly grants their claim; to call them Roman Catholics implicitly denies it. I shall therefore call them Papists: the word, I believe, is not now used dyslogistically except in Ulster, and it is certain not so intended here." So his use of the term "papalism" was in no way intended to be derogatory.
[26] Lewis, *The Collected Letters of C. S. Lewis: Volume II*, 257.
[27] Pearce, *C. S. Lewis and the Catholic Church*, xxi. James Como points out that Lewis believed in the Real Presence of Christ in the bread and wine of Holy Communion, "though not in any one theory, such as transubstantiation, purporting to explain it." *Branches to Heaven*, 105–6. Como goes on to quote Lewis from *Letters to Malcolm*, 104: "The command, after all, was Take, eat: not Take, understand."

that Lewis regularly went to confession[28]; and Lewis's belief in the reality of purgatory.[29] About purgatory, in March of 1955 Lewis wrote the following to Mr Allcock:

> The doctrine of purgation after death is one of the many held by the Roman Church which I consider to be intrinsically probable but which, since it is not clearly stated in Scripture, nor included in the early creeds, I do not think they have any warrant for enforcing. I repudiate their practice of defining and systematising and continually enumerating the list of things that *must* be accepted. But that is quite consistent with my believing, as private speculations, some of the things they accept as revealed certainties. For of course one may "assert" (in the sense "hold as private opinion") lots that one does not "believe" in the sense of holding as faith.
>
> I'd be a wicked idiot if I went about putting this forward as an article of faith: nor [would] it make the slightest difference to my religious life if I found my opinion to be wrong.[30]

Beyond these Romish particulars that Lewis accepted,[31] what might also have favorably disposed him to embrace Roman Catholicism was his attraction to what he called a "hierarchical" view of the world. For example, he wrote: "I do not believe that God created an egalitarian world. I believe the authority of parent over child, husband over wife, learned over simple to have been as much a part of the original plan as the authority of man over beast. I believe that if we had not fallen, Filmer would be right, and patriarchal monarchy would be the sole lawful government."[32] But as Lewis went on to add, "we have learned sin," and because "as Lord Acton says . . . 'all power corrupts and absolute power corrupts absolutely [,]' [t]he only remedy has been to take away the powers and substitute a legal fiction of equality."[33] One might surmise that Lewis believed this "legal fiction of equality" applied to the Christian church and, therefore, that any vesting of power in a single man (the Pope) and those around him (the cardinals and bishops) was suspect. What weakens this position, however, is the fact that Lewis was a member of

---

[28] Pearce, *C. S. Lewis and the Catholic Church*, 138–40. Lewis' confessor was Father Adams. See Lewis, *The Collected Letters of C. S. Lewis: Volume II*, 482.

[29] Pearce, *C. S. Lewis and the Catholic Church*, xix–xx.

[30] Lewis, *The Collected Letters of C. S. Lewis: Volume III*, 587–8.

[31] Though concerning purgatory, it should be stressed that Lewis thought of it as a process of purification from sinful habits and inclinations and not either the earning of merit or the payment for the guilt of venial sin or the suffering of punishment. See Lewis, *Letters to Malcolm*, 108–9; and Meilaender, *The Taste for the Other*, 110–17.

[32] Lewis, *The Weight of Glory*, 168. Sir Robert Filmer, a sixteenth-seventeenth century Englishman, believed that the civil state is like a family with a patriarchal king as its head, to whom submission is due.

[33] Lewis, *The Weight of Glory*, 168.

the hierarchical Anglican Communion and he argued against the ordination of women as priests.³⁴

The issue of hierarchicalism, or at least the issue of well-defined responsibilities, is raised in some comments by Alan Jacobs about Tolkien's dissatisfaction with Lewis's public status as a Christian apologist. According to Jacobs,

> [p]erhaps deeper than anything else in Tolkien's mind was a simple and straightforward disagreement with the course his friend's [Lewis's] career had taken. For more than he disagreed with any particular idea or element in Lewis's writings, he repudiated the very idea of a *layman* serving as a popular apologist for the Christian faith. This view stemmed from the insistence of Tolkien's Catholic tradition on the very different roles of clergy and laity. What Lewis took upon himself was, in Tolkien's judgment, none of Lewis's business: the defense of the Christian faith was the province of the ordained priesthood.³⁵

However, as Jacobs goes on to point out, Lewis's own view was that he would have been happy to cede the responsibility of defending Christianity to the clergy. According to Lewis, the problem was that the clergy was not doing its job of writing books to defend the faith. Thus, in a letter from May 20, 1956 to Katharine Farrer, whose husband, Austin, was an Anglican priest and author of a book on popular spirituality, Lewis wrote that if more priests had authored such popular books "a little earlier, the world [would] have been spared C. S. L."³⁶

These excerpted letters confirm that Lewis chose to be seen as "a very ordinary layman" who defended the "immense formidable unity" of Christendom while admitting and occasionally briefly explaining his disagreements with Rome. Lewis's explanations, or the lack thereof, have prompted many to offer more detailed reasons for his disinclination to travel to Rome. I will now survey some of what I regard as less-than-adequate explanations for why Lewis did not find a home in Rome.

Lack of exposure

If Christopher Derrick, a former student of Lewis, is right, Lewis had trouble giving Roman Catholicism the serious consideration it deserves because he

---

³⁴ Lewis, *God in the Dock*, 234–9.
³⁵ Jacobs, *The Narnian*, 199.
³⁶ Lewis, *The Collected Letters of C. S. Lewis, Volume III*, 754.

had not traveled enough, especially to the Continent. To make his point, Derrick contrasts Lewis's lack of travel with the journeys of the Roman Catholic Cardinal Newman:

> Resembling Lewis in being a scholar and a Christian, [Cardinal] Newman differed from him in having travelled and seen something of Europe. Lewis's insularity is in fact one of the most remarkable things about him. . . . A childhood holiday in France, a subaltern's experience of the wartime trenches, a brief and very late visit to Greece—these represent the sum total of his foreign travels. . . .
> This geographical narrowness of his horizons meant that in certain senses, he never "met" Catholicism at all. He met it in certain Oxford friends, but he knew them to be untypical; he met it in Ireland, but only in the context of certain old antagonisms with which he himself had been embroiled since childhood. He never had the experience of it which the open-minded traveller can receive in Poland, in Bavaria, in Italy or Spain or even in Boston or Rhode Island; as a living alternative to Anglicanism, it never came his way.[37]

Now this explanation of Lewis's not becoming a Roman Catholic is surely as remarkable as what Derrick regards as Lewis's insularity. One can only wonder what J. R. R. Tolkien, who was a devout Roman Catholic and for many years a close friend of Lewis, would have thought about Derrick's hypothesis that Tolkien provided Lewis with an "untypical" experience of Catholicism. It is difficult to take Derrick's proposed explanation seriously.

Homegrown prejudices

A slightly more plausible explanation than Derrick's of Lewis's not becoming a Roman Catholic, but only a bit more plausible, is that Lewis grew up in Belfast, Northern Ireland and could never escape the anti-Catholic prejudices of his youth. Thus, according to Joseph Pearce,

> [i]t would be a grave mistake to ignore the importance of Lewis's place of birth on the subsequent shaping of his mind, heart and life. It would also be a mistake to ignore the extent to which the poisonous twins of pride and prejudice exert a vice-like grip on those brought up in the sectarian shadow of Ulster in general, and Belfast in particular. For those who have

---

[37] Derrick, *C. S. Lewis and the Church of Rome*, 168–9.

never been to Belfast, and who have never savoured the bitterness that descends like an omnipresent fog over its war-weary and war-worried inhabitants, no words will convey the power that all-pervasive prejudice wields on both sides of the religious divide.[38]

Pearce notes that Lewis himself took offence at this proposed explanation.[39] But he did more than this. In an essay entitled "Christian Reunion: An Anglican Speaks to Roman Catholics," written at the invitation of Roman Catholic friends, Lewis admitted he had been exposed to the disunity between Ulster Protestants and Roman Catholics but insisted that this barrier no longer existed and, thus, by implication did not explain his not becoming a Roman Catholic:

> I grew up in a very archaic society—that of Northern Ireland—amidst conditions which had even then long since passed away in England. I have thus had a glimpse of the *old* disunity—the kind that descended from the sixteenth century. In it the strictly theological differences were hopelessly entangled with differences of nationality, class, politics, and the less essential differences of ritual. (I do not suggest that all differences of ritual are unessential.) They were also very embittered. A Protestant mother whose son turned from Atheism to Rome, or a Roman mother whose son turned from Atheism to Protestantism, would both have felt (I think) simple grief.
>
> That state of affairs has passed away. . . . Whatever the barrier now is, it is no longer a barrier of candles [a matter of ritual]: whatever the fog, it is not a fog of incense.[40]

In fairness to Pearce, he does concede that it would be wrong to claim that Lewis's geographical roots provide a complete explanation for his not having embraced Roman Catholicism. But he apparently believes that those roots must be part of the story. James Como agrees. In his "C. S. Lewis' Quantum Church: An Uneasy Meditation," he states that

> The possibility . . . of Lewis having become a Catholic, or a crypto-Catholic, is not idle. In fact, maybe the question should be why wasn't he? Surely the inventory above shows that he could *not* have been, say, a Baptist, or even a Presbyterian. I know there is a small bookshelf of answers to the question. Mine is this: for reasons having nothing

---

[38] Pearce, *C. S. Lewis and the Catholic Church*, 2. Cf. 99–100.
[39] Pearce, *C. S. Lewis and the Catholic Church*, 61–2.
[40] C. S. Lewis, *C. S. Lewis: Essay Collection and Other Short Pieces*, ed. Lesley Walmsley (London: Harper Collins, 2000), 395.

to do with intelligence or rationality—but everything to do with the interanimation of certain shortcomings of character ("prejudices instilled" [against Roman Catholicism from his youth in Ulster]) and temperament, . . . [Lewis] *simply could not have been* [Roman Catholic].[41]

While it is hard to provide a decisive refutation of Pearce's and Como's claim about the explanatory relevance of Lewis's upbringing in Northern Ireland to his not becoming Roman Catholic,[42] the fact that Lewis took offence at the claim should at least make us pause before accepting it. In the just-quoted paragraph, Como states that Lewis's reason for not becoming Roman Catholic had nothing to do with intelligence or rationality. But surely this is precisely why Lewis would have taken offence at both of the proposed explanations that have been considered so far. The fact that they have nothing to do with rationality makes them instances of what Lewis called "Bulverism," which in the present context is the idea Lewis did not become a Roman Catholic either because he was from Northern Ireland or because he did not travel to the Continent.

Vocational aspirations

A bit earlier in his essay from which I just quoted, Como conjectures (without, he points out, in any way trying to be rude) that had Lewis preserved the "jots and tittles" of his work but become a Roman Catholic, he would have significantly undermined his vocation as an apologist for Christianity: "Book sales would be lower, the amount of scholarship more paltry, documentaries mostly unmade."[43] In Como's estimation, Lewis's awareness of this gave him a reason for remaining an Anglican.

---

[41] James Como, "C. S. Lewis' Quantum Church: An Uneasy Meditation," in *C. S. Lewis and the Church: Essays in Honour of Walter Hooper*, eds. Judith Wolfe and Brendan N. Wolfe (London: Bloomsbury, 2011), 95.

[42] It is appropriate to mention here that J. R. R. Tolkien also appealed to Lewis's Ulster origins to explain the latter's not becoming Roman Catholic. In an unpublished essay entitled "The Ulsterior Motive," written in 1964 after Lewis' death as a critique of Lewis' book *Letters to Malcolm*, Tolkien said the following: "It was not for some time that I realized that there was more in the title *Pilgrim's Regress* [see C. S. Lewis, *The Pilgrim's Regress* [Grand Rapids, MI: Eerdmans, 1981)] than I had understood (or the author either, maybe). Lewis would regress. He would not re-enter Christianity by a new door, but by the old one: at least in the sense that in taking it up again he would also take up, or reawaken, the prejudices so sedulously planted in boyhood. He would become again a Northern Ireland protestant." See Carpenter's *The Inklings*, 50.

[43] Como, "C. S. Lewis' Quantum Church: An Uneasy Meditation," 93.

From personal correspondence, we know Lewis did believe that were he to have taken a stance on interdenominational questions it would have negatively impacted his defense of mere Christianity. In a letter from February 11, 1960, to Michael Edwards, Lewis wrote "I have never said anything in print [on interdenominational questions] except that I am *not* offering guidance on it. . . . Whatever utility I have as a defender of 'mere' Christianity would be lost if I did, and I should become only one more participant in the dog-fight."[44] The following comments of Tolkien vividly make clear why Lewis did not want to participate publicly in the counterproductive "dog fight":

> We were coming down the steps of Magdalen Hall . . . long ago in the days of our unclouded association, before there was anything, as it seemed, that must be withheld or passed over in silence. I said that I had a special devotion to St John. Lewis stiffened, his head went back, and he said in the brusque harsh tones which I was later to hear him use again when dismissing something he disapproved of: "I can't imagine any two persons more dissimilar." We stumped along the cloisters, and I followed feeling like a shabby little Catholic caught by the eye of an "Evangelical clergyman of a good family" taking holy water at the door of a church. A door had slammed.[45]

So what about Como's conjecture? Is he right when he suggests that Lewis's book sales and popular appeal would have suffered, had he written what he did but as a Roman Catholic? The suggestion presupposes not only that Lewis was to some extent "in it for the money" but also that as a Roman Catholic he could have penned the same things about mere Christianity. By the end of this chapter, it will be obvious that the latter half of the supposition is highly questionable.

Ignorance of history

The Roman Catholic John Randolph Willis, S. J., writes the following: "My concluding judgment is that it was due to Lewis's having no sense of, and no interest in, history [that he did not become a Roman Catholic]. His literary criticisms were divorced from concurrent political history. And the larger social, economic, cultural and church history he missed altogether."[46]

---

[44] Lewis, *The Collected Letters of C. S. Lewis: Volume III*, 1133.
[45] Carpenter, *The Inklings*, 51–2.
[46] Willis, *Pleasures Forevermore*, 84.

It is extremely hard not to be amazed by Willis's claim. Lewis had no sense of and interest in history? Without trying to be derogatory in any way, is it not accurate to say that with Willis's assertion about why Lewis did not become a Roman Catholic we have an instance of the absolutely ludicrous, what Lewis's brother Warren would have referred to as "silly"?[47] The fact that Lewis was a classicist of the first order, that he read Augustine, Aquinas, Boethius, Athanasius, and countless other pillars of Christian thought, that he was as well read as anyone else in medieval thought and called upon by Oxford University Press to write *Poetry and Prose in the Sixteenth Century*, all underscore his deep interest in and sense of history.

Difficulties based in reason

All of the explanations for Lewis not journeying to Rome in the four preceding sections are ultimately unconvincing. To help us think further about Lewis's relationship with Roman Catholicism, consider Michael Ward's *Planet Narnia: The Seven Heavens in the Imagination of C. S. Lewis*. Ward opens his fascinating book with the claim that he has "stumbled upon the secret imaginative key" that unlocks the door to the intellectual space which contains the idea that unites the Narnia stories into a coherent whole.[48] He acknowledges that looking for and finding such "secret codes" is the favorite pastime of conspiracy theorists, charlatans, and obsessives. Thus by claiming to have discovered the secret imaginative key that unlocks the door to the world of Narnia, Ward knows he runs the risk of being relegated to the circles of cranks.[49] But run the risk he does. Skeptical questions will be numerous, says Ward. First and foremost will be the query about why Lewis did not, so far as we know, tell someone about this "plan" behind the Narnia tales. After all, Lewis was not a secretive man, so surely he would have told his closest friends about it, if it existed.

Ward believes otherwise about Lewis's openness and points out that friends of Lewis (e.g., George Sayer and Humphrey Havard) knew that he could be quite secretive (Havard said that Lewis's autobiography *Surprised by Joy* should have been entitled *Suppressed by Jack*).[50] Ward goes on to

---

[47] Warren Lewis referred to Charles Moorman's book *The Precincts of Felicity: The Augustinian City of the Oxford Christians* as "not a stupid book, nor a dull one, but I think a silly one." Lewis, *Brothers and Friends: The Diaries of Major Warren Hamilton Lewis*, 268. My judgment of Willis's comment is the same: it is neither stupid, nor dull, but just silly.

[48] Michael Ward, *Planet Narnia: The Seven Heavens in the Imagination of C. S. Lewis* (Oxford: Oxford University Press, 2008), 5.

[49] Ward, *Planet Narnia*, 5.

[50] Ward, *Planet Narnia*, 7.

make clear that to the extent that Lewis did talk about the Narnia series, his explanations were breezy, abbreviated, and different for different people.[51] Ward says that many persons over the years have been left with the sense that Lewis never disclosed the hidden thread woven into the Narnia tales and have speculated about what it might be.[52]

We know that Lewis never became a Roman Catholic, but as with the issue of the thread uniting the Narnia stories, it is not as if he never said anything about why he did not make the journey to Rome. He did make a few comments. Nevertheless, just as Ward and others have been unable to shake the conviction that there was a hidden plan for the Narnia stories, so also I, like others, have been unable to shake the conviction that Lewis never in one place, including his personal correspondence, completely explained why he did not become a Roman Catholic.[53] However, unlike what Ward maintains about the secretive nature of the thread that ties together the Narnia stories, it is plausible to hold that Lewis believed the fundamental part of the multilayered explanation for why he did not become a Roman Catholic was never a secret. It was never a secret because Lewis thought it was there to be had in his published work by anyone who seriously read that work and knew something significant about Roman Catholicism.

Where, then, shall we go to find an explanation for Lewis's not heading to Rome? I recommend trying to understand why Lewis did not become a Roman Catholic in terms of intelligence and rationality. With a person of Lewis's intellectual capability and great learning, this is surely the most natural place to look. A hint that rationality had at least something to do with Lewis's declining to enter the Roman Church can be found in a letter that he wrote to his friend Arthur Greeves in December of 1931 about why he (Lewis) distrusted the Puritanism that counted for so much of what he regarded as Greeves' psychological "make up":

> All I feel that I can say with absolute certainty is this: that if you ever feel that the *whole spirit and system* in which you were brought up was, after all, right and good, then you may be quite sure that that feeling is

---

[51] Ward, *Planet Narnia*, 13–15.
[52] Ward, *Planet Narnia*, 10–11.
[53] I say Lewis "never in one place" provided such an explanation for his not becoming Roman Catholic because I think he did reveal in bits and pieces in private correspondence (cited later in this chapter) a fairly complete explanation. What no one has yet done is gather the bits and pieces together. The late Christopher Mitchell, the former director of the Wade Center at Wheaton College in Wheaton, Illinois, which along with the Bodleian Library in Oxford houses most things Lewisian, upon meeting me and hearing of my interest in the issue of why Lewis did not become a Roman Catholic, immediately said "No one has satisfactorily answered THAT question."

a mistake .... [One of my] reasons for this [is that] the system denied pleasures *to others* as well as to the votaries themselves: whatever the merits of *self*-denial, this is unpardonable interference.⁵⁴

This letter is of interest for two reasons. First, rather than being blinded by and beholden to the Protestant Christianity of Northern Ireland, we see that Lewis could be critical of it.⁵⁵ Second, the reason for Lewis's criticism is of particular interest: the Puritan denomination's unwarranted denial of pleasures. Given that Lewis raised the issue of pleasure when critiquing Northern Ireland Puritanism and held views about pleasure that were at odds with those of Thomas Aquinas, it would not be the least bit surprising if intellectual concerns about it and other related issues provided the foundational reasons for his not becoming a Roman Catholic. From the comments in his letters about the Pope and the Blessed Virgin Mary, we know Lewis believed that the Roman Catholic Church advocated and taught positions that were in tension, if not outright contradiction, with those found in Scripture. This disagreement was a matter of the intellect. But it was the tip of the iceberg and secondary in nature. At this point, it is helpful to turn once again to Lewis's personal correspondence.⁵⁶

Thomas Aquinas and Roman Catholicism

In the letter quoted earlier to Mr Allcock, Lewis wrote "I repudiate their [Roman Catholics'] practice of defining and systematizing and continually enumerating the list of things that *must* be accepted." In the essay entitled

---

⁵⁴ Lewis, *The Collected Letters of C. S. Lewis: Volume II*, 23.
⁵⁵ A. N. Wilson writes that "Lewis had a very distinct loathing of Ulster Protestantism" and that the first time he attended St Mark's Dundela, the church where his parents were married and his mother's father had been parson, "he was repelled by the sense that [those attending] went there to express party solidarity rather than religious feeling ...." *C. S. Lewis: A Biography*, 136. If Wilson is right, then we can see clearly why, as Pearce pointed out above, Lewis took offence at the suggestion that his Ulster upbringing provided an explanation for his not becoming Roman Catholic.
⁵⁶ Some have admonished me to take Lewis "at his word" about the intellectual problems that he had with theological issues concerning the Virgin Mary and the Pope. I want to make clear that I do take Lewis at his word concerning these issues. My argument in the rest of this chapter is not in any way intended to minimize or contradict Lewis' word. What I am seeking to make clear is that Lewis' concerns about Roman Catholicism went beyond and much deeper than those about Mary and the Pope that he mentioned in his personal correspondence. Lewis, as a philosopher, had pre-theological and epistemologically more basic disagreements with Rome that stemmed from its philosophical orientation.

"Christian Reunion: An Anglican Speaks to Roman Catholics," from which I have already quoted, Lewis wrote that

> the real reason why I cannot be in communion with you is not my disagreement with this or that Roman doctrine, but that to accept your Church means, not to accept a given body of doctrine, but to accept in advance any doctrine your Church hereafter produces. It is like being asked to agree not only to what a man has said but to what he's going to say. . . . To us the terrible thing about Rome is the recklessness (as we hold) with which she has added to the *depositum fidei* [deposit of faith]—the tropical fertility, the proliferation, of *credenda* [what must be believed] . . . . [W]e see in Rome the Faith smothered in a jungle.[57]

For Lewis, Roman Catholicism was too willing to systematize "add-ons" to the deposit of the faith. While I have no formal definition of a theological "add-on," I believe it is plausible to think of one as a position adopted by the Roman Catholic Church that (in Lewis's mind) was neither implicit in nor a natural extension of the data of Scripture. Given this notion of a theological add-on, we should consider what particular add-ons besides those already mentioned might have been of special concern to Lewis. But more on this in a moment.

Also of interest at this point is an additional hypothesis of Derrick's about why Lewis did not become Roman Catholic. To get at it, consider what Lewis had to say about the difference between Roman Catholics and Protestants in *The Allegory of Love*:

> Catholicism is allegorical. Allegory consists in giving an imagined body to the immaterial . . . . The whip of Penaunce is an excellent example. No Christian ever doubted that repentance involved "penaunce" and "whips" on the spiritual plane; it is when you come to material whips— to Tartuffe's *discipline* in his closet—that the controversy begins. It is the same with the "House" of Holinesse. No Christian doubts that those who have offered themselves to God are cut off *as if* by a wall from the World, are placed under a *regula vitae* [rule of life], and "laid in easy bed" by "meek Obedience"; but when the wall becomes one of real bricks and mortar, and the Rule one in real ink, superintended by disciplinary officials and reinforced (at times) by the power of the State, then we have reached that sort of actuality which Catholics aim at and Protestants deliberately avoid. Indeed, this difference is the root out of which all other differences between the two religions grow.

---

[57] Lewis, *C. S. Lewis: Essay Collection and Other Short Pieces*, 396.

The one suspects that all spiritual gifts are falsely claimed if they cannot be embodied in bricks and mortar, or official positions, or institutions: the other, that nothing retains its spirituality if incarnation is pushed to that degree and in that way. The difference about Papal infallibility is simply a form of this. The proper corruptions of each Church tell the same tale. When Catholicism goes bad it becomes the world-old, world-wide *religio* of amulets and holy places and priestcraft: Protestantism, in its corresponding decay, becomes a vague mist of ethical platitudes. . . . Hence Plato, with his transcendent Forms, is the doctor of Protestants; Aristotle, with his immanent Forms, the doctor of Catholics. . . . In the world of matter, Catholics and Protestants disagree as to the kind and degree of incarnation or embodiment which we can safely try to give to the spiritual . . . .[58]

In commenting on this passage, Derrick acknowledges that Lewis was on to a significant difference between Protestants and Roman Catholics:

[T]he interesting thing here is that Lewis saw the difference between Catholicism and Protestantism *radically* ("the root out of which all other differences between the two religions grow") in terms of the extent to which the incarnational principle ought to be pressed. A Catholic will not necessarily disagree violently; he can see that a question of that kind does arise. He can go a little further than that: he can point out, for example, that the question of how far the incarnational principle ought to be pressed is itself a kind of doctrinal question . . . .[59]

For the sake of simplicity, I will assume that the incarnational principle is about the manner and degree to which the spiritual and, more broadly speaking, the immaterial (nonphysical) is "fleshed out" or embodied in, or even reduced to or eliminated by, what is material (physical).[60] In the *theological* realm, the incarnational principle is concerned with issues like how the Word is present in the Eucharist and to what extent Christ's true church is visible as opposed to invisible. Derrick is correct to remind us that Lewis believed the incarnational principle comes in to play when considering theological (doctrinal) differences between Roman Catholicism

---

[58] C. S. Lewis, *The Allegory of Love* (Oxford: Oxford University Press, 1936), 322–3.
[59] Derrick, *C. S. Lewis and the Church of Rome*, 71.
[60] A reader should not confuse the incarnational principle with the Incarnation. Lewis had problems with the former, while fully embracing the latter. He did not have a problem with the latter because it does not reduce or eliminate the immaterial. In the Incarnation, God the Son as an immaterial being remains immaterial and takes on a human body.

and Protestantism. However, people like him err if they believe that Lewis's own problem with the incarnational principle was principally theological. A good case can be made that for Lewis the incarnational principle, when pressed too far, had fundamental *philosophical* applications that he believed were erroneous.[61]

Where, or better yet, in which person or persons in Roman Catholicism do we find the incarnational principle developed in a philosophically materialistic way? In the large block quote above from *The Allegory of Love*, Lewis knew full well that "Plato, with his transcendent Forms, is the doctor of Protestants; Aristotle, with his immanent Forms, the doctor of Catholics." Moreover, Lewis also knew full well that Aquinas had, by his time, as I will show momentarily, become the central philosophical and theological spokesman for truth in Roman Catholicism and that Aquinas's philosophy was through and through Aristotelian in character. Thus Aquinas, by embracing the spirit, if not always the specific views, of Aristotle, advocated a more materialistic (i.e., incarnational) philosophical perspective than Lewis, who was attracted to the immaterialism of Platonism and Idealism. Lewis, then, was most fundamentally philosophically distanced from Rome because of the manner and degree to which it, by embracing the philosophical thought of Aquinas, in turn embraced the incarnational principle and views that were too materialistic (incarnational).

The arguments of the previous chapters support this thesis. Philosophically, Lewis understood that if pleasure is not intrinsically good, where both pleasure itself and its goodness are immaterial in nature, then a hedonistic conception of happiness would be threatened and hard to take seriously. A hedonistic conception of happiness requires a certain understanding of goodness that the Roman Catholic Church rejected because of its adoption of Aquinas's view of goodness, which was infused with the incarnational principle. In Lewis's illustrative language, Rome, through Aquinas, took the spiritual (the immaterial) out of pleasure and its goodness and made them too much like bricks and mortar. Rome walked us too close to the precipice of materialism, just as she did when she embraced Aquinas's view that "I" does not primarily refer to the immaterial soul alone but instead fundamentally picks out a human being as a soul-body composite.

But the problem for Lewis concerning Thomas Aquinas was not just one of fundamental philosophical disagreement. There was also the fact of Aquinas himself being an add-on. Pope Pius V pronounced Thomas

---

[61] Of Lewis' observation about Rome pressing the incarnational principle too far, Derrick says that it "was never a very weighty accusation." *C. S. Lewis and the Church of Rome*, 94. Here, I believe Derrick could not be more wrong.

the "Angelic Doctor" in 1567 (and here, it is plausible to think we have an instance of Lewis's problem with the authority of the Pope). In the words of Josef Pieper, Aquinas "subsequently became a veritable institution."[62] Pope Leo XIII, in his 1879 encyclical on the restoration of Christian philosophy entitled *Aeterni Patris*, reminded readers that "the Fathers of Trent made it part of the order of conclave to lay upon the altar, together with sacred Scripture and the decrees of the supreme Pontiffs, the Summa of Thomas Aquinas, whence to seek counsel, reason, and inspiration,"[63] and commended the patriarchs, archbishops, and bishops of the Roman Catholic world to "furnish to studious youth a generous and copious supply of those purest streams of wisdom flowing inexhaustibly from the precious fountainhead of the Angelic Doctor."[64] Moreover, Leo XIII exhorted the venerable brethren "to restore the golden wisdom of St. Thomas, and to spread it far and wide for the defense and beauty of the Catholic faith, for the good of society, and for the advantage of all the sciences. . . . Let carefully selected teachers endeavor to implant the doctrine of St. Thomas in the minds of students, and set forth clearly his solidity and excellence over others."[65] In keeping with the spirit and letter of *Aeterni Patris*, in 1917 Aquinas was, in the words of Pieper, "incorporated into one of the great law books of history, the *Codex Juris Canonici*, which directed that the priests of the Catholic Church should receive their theological and philosophical education according to the method, doctrines, and principles of Thomas Aquinas."[66] Canon 252 of the *Codex* declared that "[t]here are to be classes in dogmatic theology, always grounded in the written word of God together with sacred tradition; through these, students are to learn to penetrate more intimately the mysteries of salvation, especially with St. Thomas as teacher."[67]

---

[62] Josef Pieper, *Guide to Thomas Aquinas* (New York: Mentor-Omega Books, 1964), 24.
[63] *Aeterni Patris: Encyclical of Pope Leo XIII on the Restoration of Christian Philosophy*, Section 22. www.vatican.va/.../hf_l-xiii_enc_04081879_aeterni-patris_en.html.
[64] *Aeterni Patris: Encyclical of Pope Leo XIII on the Restoration of Christian Philosophy*, Section 26.
[65] *Aeterni Patris: Encyclical of Pope Leo XIII on the Restoration of Christian Philosophy*, Section 31.
[66] Pieper, *Guide to Thomas Aquinas*, 24.
[67] John P. Beal, James A. Coriden, and Thomas J. Green (eds), *New Commentary on The Code of Canon Law* (New York, NY/Mahwah, NJ: Paulist Press, 2000), 321. Earlier in this chapter, I quoted (and dismissed) James Como's suggestion that Lewis did not become Roman Catholic because it would have significantly undermined his vocation as a Christian apologist, his book sales, and his scholarship. Como also says the following about Lewis: "[he] did not follow schools . . . ." (Como, *Branches to Heaven*, 116). Como is surely right about this. And because Lewis did not follow schools, he did not follow the school of Thomas Aquinas. In Lewis' mind, however, to have become a Roman Catholic would have meant that he would have had to follow the school of Thomas.

A Rational Journey 173

It is clear, then, that by the time (1917) Lewis was in his late teens, Aquinas had been accorded an authoritative teaching position in the Roman Catholic Church.[68] We know from Lewis's letters that after he became a Christian, the special status of Aquinas caused him consternation. For example, at the end of his letter of February 1936 to Griffiths, from which I quoted earlier, Lewis expressed dismay when he thought (erroneously) that a belief in the views of Thomas had actually become necessary for salvation according to the Catholic church: "It was a great shock to learn that Thomism is now *de fide* [a matter of faith] for your Church—if that is what you mean. But is that really so? I should welcome a letter clearing the matter up—I don't mean clearing up the content of Thomism but the degree to which it has been made necessary to salvation."[69]

Even though, contrary to what Lewis thought, it was not the case that an acceptance of Thomism had become a prerequisite for salvation within the Roman Catholic Church, the fact that Lewis was under the impression that it had and his reaction to what he believed is evidence for his unease with and dislike of the status that Aquinas had come to occupy within the Church. The add-on of Aquinas would have been particularly problematic for Lewis if he were at that time seriously considering becoming Roman Catholic. And he would not have been irrational to wonder about his freedom to express views that he knew were in conflict with those of Thomas Aquinas.

Lest I be charged at this point with placing too much weight on Lewis's problems with Aquinas,[70] it is important to note that the philosopher and biographer of Lewis, Richard Purtill, says that "Lewis had certain misgivings about scholastic philosophy . . . ."[71] Purtill suggests that this in part was because of Lewis's low estimate of the cosmological argument for God's existence, which "scholastic philosophy [e.g., Thomas Aquinas] . . . has traditionally put a good deal of weight on . . . ."[72] James Patrick also

---

[68] Anthony Kenny introduces the thought of Aquinas on the soul and body in the following way: "St Thomas Aquinas, who in the twentieth century has been considered an official spokesman for Roman Catholic Orthodoxy . . . ." Anthony Kenny, "Body, Soul, and Intellect in Aquinas," in *From Soul to Self*, ed. M. James C. Crabbe (New York: Routledge, 1999), 33.
[69] Lewis, *The Collected Letters of C. S. Lewis: Volume II*, 179. In Roman Catholicism, a matter that is *de fide* is something that one is required to believe.
[70] I once shared with a knowledgeable Roman Catholic friend Lewis' view of Aquinas and my belief that it played a significant role in explaining why Lewis did not make the journey to Rome. His response was curt: "You CAN'T be serious!"
[71] Purtill, *C. S. Lewis's Case for the Christian Faith*, 17.
[72] Purtill, *C. S. Lewis's Case for the Christian Faith*, 17.

discusses Lewis's less-than-appreciative attitude toward Neo-Scholasticism. According to Patrick,

> [a] philosophical movement for which . . . Lewis expressed distaste was Neo-Scholasticism, the movement begun on the Continent after Leo XIII recommended in 1879 that the study of St. Thomas . . . be renewed. . . . To the degree that Neo-Scholasticism encouraged the study of medieval writers by a strictly historical method, it necessarily earned the approval of Lewis . . . . On the other side, whenever Neo-Scholasticism was presented as a system claiming philosophic certainty, or in its connection with Catholic dogma, [Lewis] found it biased and unhistorical.[73]

And Derrick describes Lewis's relationship to scholasticism and Thomism in the following way: "The 1920s and 1930s saw a vigorous revival of scholastic and Thomist thought among Catholics, and this made itself very definitely felt at Oxford, where the newly restored Dominican priory of Blackfriars gave it a kind of headquarters. Lewis appears to have been out of sympathy with this movement as a whole . . . ."[74] Derrick goes on to say that "there was something in [Lewis] which revolted instinctively from the scholastic method and mentality, and it may not be fanciful to associate this with his total incapacity in mathematics. Scholasticism may resemble mathematics in seeming to be a cold, arid, and heartless manner of proceeding . . . ."[75] But Derrick gets it wrong here. Lewis's problem was not with the scholastic method and mentality. It was with the content of Aquinas's views about the fundamental philosophical topics of this book that guaranteed his disagreements with Roman Catholicism ran very deep.

---

[73] Patrick, *The Magdalen Metaphysicals: Idealism and Orthodoxy at Oxford 1901–1945*, 140–1.
[74] Derrick, *C. S. Lewis and the Church of Rome*, 76. In describing his conversion to theism in 1929 or 1930 (see footnote 7), Lewis said that he "arrived at God by induction" and distinguished this "method" of conversion "from that of many [of his] contemporaries. It is, for instance, noticeably out {of} harmony with the association lately established among us between . . . catholicism in religion . . . . There is a *via media* between syllogisms and psychoses: Thomas Aquinas and D. H. Lawrence do not divide the universe between them: God has made n{o} decree to hide Himself from those who love the literature of the Romantic Revival." Lewis continued by saying that he had "no quarrel against . . . catholics." "Early Prose Joy," 13. So it is clear that by 1929 or 1930 Lewis knew the work of Thomas Aquinas, of the revival of Thomism, and of its importance in the Roman Catholic Church. And he made clear that his conversion to theism did not go through Aquinas to Rome. All the evidence supports the position that Lewis never fundamentally changed his view of Aquinas and this explains at the deepest level why he did not become a Roman Catholic.
[75] Derrick, *C. S. Lewis and the Church of Rome*, 77.

For support of my suggestion that Lewis, were he to have become Roman Catholic, would have had reason to be concerned about having the freedom to express views that he knew were in conflict with those of Aquinas, it is helpful to consider the recent comments of Brian Davies about the Roman Catholic Dominican friar, Herbert McCabe, who was for years the editor of the Roman Catholic journal *New Blackfriars* and an "indefatigable exponent of and commentator on the thought of Thomas Aquinas."[76] McCabe died in 2001, and Davies says the following about McCabe's exposition in 1957 of Aquinas's work in *God and Evil in the Theology of St Thomas Aquinas*, which is an edited version of McCabe's thesis for a License in Sacred Theology (STL):

> One problem with the text (and this is another reason why I was initially hesitant about offering it for publication) is that in it exposition of Aquinas and evaluation of him are sometimes blurred in a way that was never the case in what Herbert later came to write. He nearly always made it clear what Aquinas actually said and where he did and did not agree with him. His STL thesis, however, sometimes provides accounts of Aquinas's teachings without holding them out at arm's length as matters to be defended or attacked. Though the thesis has plenty to say about the worth of Aquinas's thinking, it sometimes seems to treat Aquinas as an authority in a way that Herbert did not in his subsequent writings. I have no doubt that it did so because the work was, as I have explained, something to be examined by a panel of Dominicans.[77]

Davies' comments are of interest in the present context because they indicate the authoritative status of Aquinas, McCabe's concern in his younger years to acknowledge this authority before his STL thesis examining board, and McCabe's openness in his later years about his disagreements with Aquinas. It is this concern about the status of Thomas in Roman Catholicism and the pressure of agreeing with his philosophical positions that were at the foundation of Lewis's rational rejection of the Roman Church. Pieper points out that "the pre-eminent position assigned to St. Thomas . . . may now and then strike people as strange . . . ."[78] Lewis did find it strange and an extremely troubling intellectual add-on.

There is additional evidence for Lewis's less-than-favorable view of Aquinas and (neo-) Scholasticism that comes from comments of his own and those who knew him. To begin, Lewis said he read Aquinas, Augustine,

---

[76] McCabe, *God and Evil in the Theology of St Thomas Aquinas*, xiii.
[77] McCabe, *God and Evil in the Theology of St Thomas Aquinas*, xvii–xviii.
[78] Pieper, *Guide to Thomas Aquinas*, 25.

Boethius, and Dante "because they were 'influences',"[79] by which he seems to have meant that these individuals had a significant impact on Christian thought and practice. But while Aquinas was an influence, Chad Walsh, a friend and biographer of Lewis, says that Lewis told him that he (Lewis) used "Thomas Aquinas as a convenient reference work but [was not] greatly influenced by him in general . . . ."[80] Dom Bede Griffiths, who has already been mentioned several times as the recipient of letters from Lewis, writes that Lewis "was most unsympathetic to the revival of Thomism, which was taking place during the thirties and forties. I don't think that he found Saint Thomas himself very attractive (though, of course, he appreciated the Thomist elements in the poetry of Dante), and neo-Thomism he objected to most strongly."[81] Griffiths adds that Lewis "was not attracted to [Scholasticism] himself, and with considerable prescience he regarded it as a movement in philosophy that was destined to pass along with others."[82] Lewis wrote to Griffiths in January 1936, that "in the Oxford world 'Neo-Scholasticism' has become such a fashion among ignorant undergrads. that I am sick of the sound of it. A man who was an atheist two terms ago, and admitted into your Church last term, and who had never read a word of philosophy, comes to me urging me to read the *Summa* and offering to lend me a copy!"[83] In this context, it should not be overlooked that Lewis described himself as "a very poor Thomist."[84] Perhaps of only anecdotal value, but nevertheless consistent with what I have emphasized in this section about the intellectual disagreement Lewis had with Aquinas, is the fact that upon retiring from Cambridge Lewis had to sell a good many of his books because of a lack of space at the Kilns (his home). According to Walter Hooper, "[a]mongst those [Lewis] parted with were St Thomas Aquinas' *Summa Theologica* . . . ."[85]

---

[79] Lewis, *God in the Dock*, 203.
[80] Walsh, *C. S. Lewis: Apostle to the Skeptics*, 138.
[81] Alan Bede Griffiths, "The Adventure of Faith," in *Remembering C S. Lewis: Recollections of Those Who Knew Him*, ed. James T. Como (San Francisco: Ignatius, 2005), 90.
[82] Griffiths, "The Adventures of Faith," 90.
[83] Lewis, *The Collected Letters of C. S. Lewis: Volume II*, 176.
[84] Lewis, *Christian Reflections*, 17.
[85] Hooper, *C. S. Lewis: A Companion and Guide*, 770. Despite all of the evidence for Lewis' intellectual difficulties with Aquinas and Thomism, some still think that Lewis was a Thomist. Carnell points out that "Lewis's insistence on reason has led some to regard him as essentially Thomist in his Theology." (*Bright Shadow of Reality*, 70) But evidence for Aquinas's direct influence on Lewis is hard to come by. Some suggest it is indirect and perhaps even unknown to Lewis. For example, Pearce maintains that Dante is the conduit for this influence. In discussing Lewis' *The Pilgrim's Regress*, Pearce points out how Lewis's placing the sins "of the head" to the north and those "of the heart" to the south mirrors Dante's locating (in his *Inferno*) the former in the lower and the latter in the upper regions of hell. "Since Dante himself was merely following the categorization

Common sense, mere Christianity, and Roman Catholicism

Lewis was committed to common sense and advocated what he called "mere Christianity." Was there any significant relationship between these two elements of Lewis's thought?

Lewis regarded mere Christianity as that which is "common to nearly all Christians at all times."[86] However, Pearce reminds us that "[t]he question that confronts any conscientious student of Lewis is the extent to which his definition of 'mere Christianity' conforms to objective criteria...."[87] Just what is and is not part of mere Christianity? Pearce goes on to suggest that Lewis was clearer about the things that stand outside mere Christianity, which in Pearce's estimation include "questions of authority, or the role and meaning of the Church, or the place of the Blessed Virgin, or the role of the sacraments, or that of the saints, or the liturgy...."[88] Pearce believes that Lewis's failure to include these things in mere Christianity without any objective justification amounts to his "confecting 'mere Christianity' in his own image"[89] and for all intents and purposes renders the notion worthless.

There is something to Pearce's charge. But there is also a minimalist response that Lewis would have given to Pearce. Here, it is fruitful to consider the issues of happiness, pleasure, pain, and the soul, body, and person which Lewis believed were the subject matter of commonsense beliefs. Lewis thought commonsense beliefs are foundational in nature and shared by all people at all times. And he saw mere Christianity as the theological counterpart to common sense in that mere Christianity is the foundation shared by any and every legitimate expression of Christianity.

---

of these sins by his mentor, Saint Thomas Aquinas, ... it can be seen that Saint Thomas Aquinas emerges as the preeminent and towering influence on the structure of Lewis's allegorical 'Regress'. Whether Lewis was consciously aware of Aquinas's centrality is perhaps open to question. It is at least possible that Dante has succeeded in 'smuggling' the theology of his Master into the thoughts of Lewis without Lewis's fully realizing the fact." C. S. Lewis and the Catholic Church, 49–50.

Let us concede this influence of categorization. Three points are in order. First, if Lewis did not know that the source of this categorization was Aquinas, then this is a strike against the idea that Lewis was in any robust sense a Thomist. Second, Lewis's use of this categorization is thoroughly consistent with my claim that his views of happiness, pleasure, and pain, which are the conceptual building blocks of our concepts of heaven and hell, were at odds with Thomas's positions concerning them. Third, given that Lewis was so well read in ancient and medieval thought, it is hard to believe that Lewis was unaware that Dante was drawing upon Aquinas's thought.

[86] Lewis, Mere Christianity, viii.
[87] Pearce, C. S. Lewis and the Catholic Church, 119.
[88] Pearce, C. S. Lewis and the Catholic Church, 121.
[89] Pearce, C. S. Lewis and the Catholic Church, 121.

But Lewis believed that mere Christianity was more than just the counterpart to common sense. He also thought that its most fundamental components are drawn from the contents of commonsense beliefs like those just listed. For example, Lewis held that mere Christianity is concerned with heaven and hell, the understanding of which is rooted in the commonsense idea of perfect happiness and the lack thereof, as well as that of ordinary morality. Because the concepts of pleasure and pain are at the heart of the ideas of heaven and hell, Lewis held that there was simply no way to understand the latter without a grasp of the former: "I have no doubt at all that pleasure is in itself a good and pain in itself an evil; if not, then the whole Christian tradition about heaven and hell and the passion of our Lord seems to have no meaning."[90]

Lewis believed that things were no different vis-à-vis heaven and hell when it came to the self (being a person), the soul, and its body. Heaven and hell are concepts that presuppose the numerical identity (sameness) of a person (soul) in this life with an individual in the afterlife. Common sense identifies the self with the soul and affirms the soul's persistence from this life into the next. Stated slightly differently, common sense embraces the idea that "I" refers to the soul and it is the soul, a substance in its own right, which survives death and the dissolution of its material body. Once again then, mere Christianity draws upon concepts that are rooted in common sense. The fact that Christianity also affirms that the afterlife will be bodily in nature in no way undercuts the idea that the commonsensical identification of self and soul is at the core of mere Christianity. Indeed, Lewis believed that it is precisely because the body is composite and constantly takes on and loses parts that it cannot be wholly or partly identified with the self in this life. And Lewis also thought that the idea that the resurrection body would be or needed to be identical with a part or the whole of the earthly body was simply misguided.

As Pearce points out, Lewis believed that mere Christianity is about more than heaven and hell and, therefore, by implication, about more than happiness, pleasure, pain, ordinary morality, the self, and soul and body.

---

[90] Lewis, *Christian Reflections*, 21. At this point one might object that because the ideas of heaven and hell are not specifically Christian in nature, Lewis could not have considered them parts of mere Christianity. He must have regarded them as no more than broadly theistic concepts. But the textual evidence indicates otherwise. Thus, Lewis wrote in *Mere Christianity* that "the view which simply says there is a good God in Heaven and everything is all right—leaving out all the difficult and terrible doctrines about sin and hell and the devil, and the redemption" is "the view I call Christianity-and-water." (40) The implication is that mere Christianity includes the ideas of both heaven and hell, which, as we have seen in the quote above, Lewis asserted presuppose the notions of pleasure and pain and their respective intrinsic goodness and evilness.

It is also about things such as baptism and the Eucharist.[91] But however conceptually rich Lewis believed the notion was, it is clear he believed that the merest of mere Christianity was about the issues that have been the subject matter of this book.

What then of Roman Catholicism? Lewis ultimately rejected it for himself because he rationally could not accept the philosophical thought of Thomas Aquinas about happiness, pleasure, pain, the self, soul, and body. And Lewis could not embrace Aquinas's philosophical thought about these issues because it conflicted with common sense. Given this conflict, Lewis was convinced that Thomistic Roman Catholicism, while it theologically espoused mere Christianity, put its integrity at risk philosophically, because mere Christianity requires the integrity of common sense. Hence, Lewis could not have written in defense of mere Christianity as a member of the Roman Catholic Church.[92] And there was no need for secrecy about this issue on Lewis's part here. The matter would have been readily understood by anyone familiar with the views of both Aquinas and Lewis. The difficulty for Lewis would have been explaining to those unfamiliar with Aquinas's thought his reasons for not becoming Roman Catholic. To appreciate that explanation would have required that they take a philosophical walking tour with him of a much greater length than they were prepared to make.

Conclusion

Lewis believed that for Christians the Scriptures "are 'holy', or 'inspired', or, as St Paul says, 'the Oracles of God'."[93] He admonished that the "total result is not 'the word of God' in the sense that every passage, in itself, gives impeccable science or history. It carries the Word of God; and we . . . receive that word from it not by using it as an encyclopedia or an encyclical but by steeping ourselves in its tone or temper and so learning its overall message."[94] I purposefully avoided reading C. S. Lewis for years because it seemed to me that many people participated in a cultish devotion to him and

---

[91] Pearce, *C. S. Lewis and the Catholic Church*, 127.
[92] Corbin Scott Carnell rightly points out that Lewis "does not see Christianity as dependent upon any philosophical system, though various systems have certainly lent themselves to interpreting the faith." *Bright Shadow of Reality*, 70. It is because Roman Catholicism ties Christianity too intimately to Aquinas's philosophical system and as a result threatens what Lewis thought of as mere Christianity that he concluded he could not find a home in Rome.
[93] Lewis, *Reflections on the Psalms*, 109.
[94] Lewis, *Reflections on the Psalms*, 112.

his written work. They often quoted *his* writings as if they were an inspired encyclopedia on anything and everything. They are not. But they are a well of deep insights and a great source of pleasure. I have tried to steep myself in the tone and temper of his work, and I highly recommend that you, the reader, pick up some books by Lewis and read him for yourself. I suspect you will find yourself embarking on a pleasurable philosophical walking tour that will last a lifetime.

Bibliography

Adey, Lionel. *C. S. Lewis' 'Great War' with Owen Barfield*. Great Britain: Ink Books, 2002.

Aeschliman, Michael D. *The Restitution of Man: C. S. Lewis and the Case against Scientism*. Grand Rapids, MI: Eerdmans, 1983.

Aeterni Patris: Encyclical of Pope Leo XIII on the Restoration of Christian Philosophy. www.vatican.va/.../hf_l-xiii_enc_04081879_aeterni-patris_en.html.

Annas, Julia. *The Morality of Happiness*. Oxford: Oxford University Press, 1993.

—. "Virtue Ethics and the Charge of Egoism." In *Morality and Self-Interest*, edited by Paul Bloomfield. Oxford: Oxford University Press, 2008, 205–21.

Aquinas, Saint Thomas. *Commentary on the First Epistle to the Corinthians*. Translated by Fabian Larcher. www.dhspriory.org/thomas/SS1Cor.htm.

—. *Compendium Theologiae*. Translated by Cyril Vollert, S. J. St. Louis: B. Herder Book Co. http://dhspriory.org/thomas/Compendium.htrr. 1948.

—. *Summa Theologiae: Vols. I-III*. Translated by Fathers of the English Dominican Province. Allen, TX: Christian Classics, 1948.

—. *On Spiritual Creatures*. Translated by M. C. Fitzpatrick. Milwaukee, WI: Marquette University Press, 1949.

—. *Summa Contra Gentiles: Book Four*. Translated by Charles J. O'Neill. Garden City, NY: Image Books, 1957.

—. *Summa Theologiae: Vol. 2 (Ia. 2-11), Existence and Nature of God*. Translated by Timothy McDermott, O. P. New York: McGraw-Hill, 1964.

—. *Summa Theologiae: Vol. 6 (Ia. 27-32), The Trinity*. Translated by Ceslaus Velecky. New York: McGraw-Hill, 1965.

—. *Summa Theologiae: Vol. 8 (Ia. 44-49), Creation, Variety, and Evil*. Translated by Thomas Gilby, O. P. New York: McGraw-Hill, 1967.

—. *Summa Theologiae: Vol. 12 (Ia. 84-89), Human Intelligence*. Translated by P. T. Durbin. New York: McGraw-Hill, 1968.

—. *Summa Theologiae: Vol. 16 (Ia2ae. 1-5), Purpose and Happiness*. Translated by Thomas Gilby, O. P. New York: McGraw-Hill, 1969.

—. *Summa Theologiae: Vol. 23 (Ia2ae. 55-57), Virtue*. Translated by W. D. Hughes, O. P. New York: McGraw-Hill, 1969.

—. *Summa Theologiae: Vol. 11 (Ia. 75-83), Man*. Translated by Timothy Sutter. New York: McGraw-Hill, 1970.

—. *Summa Theologiae: Vol. 22 (Ia2ae. 49-54), Dispositions*. Translated by Anthony Kenny. New York: McGraw-Hill, 1973.

—. *Summa Contra Gentiles: Book Two*. Translated by James F. Anderson. Notre Dame: IN: University of Notre Dame Press, 1975.

—. *Summa Contra Gentiles: Book Three*. Translated by Vernon J. Bourke. Notre Dame: IN: University of Notre Dame Press, 1975.

—. *Summa Theologiae: Vol. 20 (Ia2ae. 31-39), Pleasure*. Translated by Eric D'arcy. New York: McGraw-Hill, 1975.
—. *Questions on the Soul*. Translated by James H. Robb. Milwaukee, WI: Marquette University Press, 1984.
—. *Summa Theologiae: Vol. 3 (Ia.12-13), Knowing and Naming God*. Translated by Herbert McCabe. Cambridge: Cambridge University Press, 2006.
—. *Summa Theologiae: Vol. 37 (2a2ae. 57-62), Justice*. Translated by Thomas Gilby, O. P. Cambridge: Cambridge University Press, 2006.
—. *Summa Theologiae: Vol. 46 (2a2ae. 179-182), Action and Contemplation*. Translated by Jordan Aumann, O. P. Cambridge: Cambridge University Press, 2006.
Aristotle. *Nicomachean Ethics*. Translated by Martin Ostwald. Indianapolis: Bobbs-Merrill, 1962.
Armstrong, David. "Naturalism, Materialism, and First Philosophy." *Philosophia* 8 (1978): 261–76.
Augustine, St. *The Nature of the Good*. Translated by John H. S. Burleigh. Philadelphia, PA: The Westminster Press, 1953.
—. *The City of God*. Translated by Marcus Dods. New York: The Modern Library, 1993.
—. *Confessions*. Translated by William Watts. Cambridge, MA: Harvard University Press, 1995.
—. *The Enchiridion of Faith, Hope, and Love*. Translated by Bruce Harbert. Hyde Park, NY: New City Press, 1999.
Baggett, David, Gary R. Habermas, and Jerry Walls (eds), *C. S. Lewis as Philosopher: Truth, Goodness and Beauty*. Downers Grove, IL: InterVarsity Press, 2008.
Baker, Mark and Stewart Goetz (eds), *The Soul Hypothesis*. New York: Continuum, 2011.
Barkman, Adam. *C. S. Lewis and Philosophy as a Way of Life*. Allentown, PA: Zossima Press, 2009.
Beal, John P., James A. Coriden, and Thomas J. Green (eds), *New Commentary on the Code of Canon Law*. New York, NY/Mahwah, NJ: Paulist Press, 2000.
Bennett, J. A. W. "The Humane Medievalist." In *Critical Essays on C. S. Lewis*, edited by George Watson. Aldershot: Scolar Press, 1992, 52–75.
Bering, Jesse. "The Folk Psychology of Souls." *Behavioral and Brain Sciences* 29 (2006): 453–62.
Beversluis, John. *C. S. Lewis and the Search for Rational Religion*. Grand Rapids, MI: Eerdmans, 1985.
Bloom, Paul. *Descartes' Baby: How the Science of Child Development Explains What Makes Us Human*. New York: Basic Books, 2004.
Brentano, Franz. *Psychology from an Empirical Standpoint*. Translated by Antos C. Rancurello, D. B. Tyrrell, and Linda L. McAlister. New York: Routledge, 1995.
Brown, Warren S., Nancey Murphy and H. Newton Maloney (eds), *Whatever Happened to the Soul?* Minneapolis, MN: Fortress Press, 1998.

Carnell, Corbin Scott. *Bright Shadow of Reality: Spiritual Longing in C. S. Lewis.* Grand Rapids, MI: Eerdmans, 1999.
Carpenter, Humphrey. *The Inklings: C. S. Lewis, J. R. R. Tolkien, Charles Williams, and Their Friends.* London: Harper Collins, 1997.
Catholic Church. *Catechism of the Catholic Church.* New York: Doubleday, 1995.
Chalmers, David. *The Conscious Mind: In Search of a Fundamental Theory.* Oxford: Oxford University Press, 1996.
Como, James. *Branches to Heaven: The Geniuses of C. S. Lewis.* Dallas, TX: Spence Publishing Company, 1998.
—. "C. S. Lewis' Quantum Church: An Uneasy Meditation." In *C. S. Lewis and the Church: Essays in Honour of Walter Hooper,* edited by Judith Wolfe and Brendan N. Wolfe. London: Bloomsbury, 2011, 90–102.
Cuneo, Andrew P. "Review of *C. S. Lewis and the Catholic Church,* by Joseph Pearce, and *C. S. Lewis and the Blessed Virgin Mary: Uncovering a "Marian Attitude",* by Rev Arthur Mastrolia. *Seven* 21 (2004): 101–4.
Dennett, Daniel. *Consciousness Explained.* Boston, MA: Little, Brown, 1991.
Derrick, Christopher. *C. S. Lewis and the Church of Rome: A Study in Proto-Ecumenism.* San Francisco: Ignatius Press, 1981.
Descartes, René. *Discourse on Method.* Translated by Laurence J. LaFleur. Upper Saddle River, NJ: Prentice-Hall, 1956.
—. *Descartes' Philosophical Writings.* Translated by Norman Kemp Smith. New York: The Modern Library, 1958.
—. *The Philosophical Works of Descartes.* Volume 1. Translated by Elizabeth S. Haldane and G. R. T. Ross. Cambridge: Cambridge University Press, 1967.
Doyle, Sir Arthur Conan. *The Complete Sherlock Holmes.* New York: Doubleday, 1939.
Dunckel, Mona. "C. S. Lewis as Allegorist: The Pilgrim's Regress." In *C. S. Lewis: Life, Works, and Legacy; Volume 3: Apologist, Philosopher, and Theologian,* edited by Bruce Edwards. Westport, CN: Praeger, 2007, 29–49.
Flanagan, Owen. "What Makes Life Worth Living?" In *The Meaning of Life,* 2nd edn, edited by E. D. Klemke. Oxford: Oxford University Press, 2000, 198–206.
Geach, Peter. "Good and Evil." *Analysis* 17 (1956): 32–42.
Gilson, Etienne. *The Christian Philosophy of Saint Augustine.* Translated by L. E. M. Lynch. New York: Random House, 1960.
Goetz, Stewart. "Mere Dualism." *Touchstone* (April 2007): 9.
—. "C. S. Lewis on Pleasure and Happiness." *Christian Scholar's Review* 40 (2011): 283–302.
—. "Making Things Happen: Souls in Action." In *The Soul Hypothesis,* edited by Mark Baker and Stewart Goetz. London: Continuum, 2011, 99–117.
—. "Purposeful Explanation and Causal Gaps." *European Journal for Philosophy of Religion* 5 (2012): 141–56.
Goetz, Stewart and Charles Taliaferro. *Naturalism.* Grand Rapids, MI: Eerdmans, 2008.
—. *A Brief History of the Soul.* Oxford: Wiley-Blackwell, 2011.

Green, Roger Lancelyn and Walter Hooper. *C. S. Lewis: A Biography*. Rev. edn. London: HarperCollins, 2003.
Griffiths, Alan Bede. "The Adventure of Faith." In *Remembering C. S. Lewis: Recollections of Those Who Knew Him*, edited by James. T. Como. San Francisco: Ignatius Press, 2005, 76–95.
Groothuis, Douglas. Review of Dinesh D'Souza's *God Forsaken: Bad Things Happen. Is There a God Who Cares? Yes. Here's Proof*, by Dinesh D'Souza, *Christianity Today* (March 2012): 47–9.
Haldane, J. B. S. *Possible Worlds*. New York: Harper and Brothers, 1928.
Hooper, Walter. *C. S. Lewis: Companion and Guide*. New York: Harper Collins, 1996.
Horne, Brian. "A Peculiar Debt: the Influence of Charles Williams on C. S. Lewis." In *Rumours of Heaven: Essays in Celebration of C. S. Lewis*, edited by Andrew Walker and James Patrick. Surrey: Eagle, 1998, 83–97.
Horner, David. "The Pursuit of Happiness: C. S. Lewis's Eudaimonistic Understanding of Ethics." *In Pursuit of Truth/A Journal of Christian Scholarship*. April 21, 2009. http://www.cslewis.org/journal.
—. "C. S. Lewis is a Eudaimonist." *Christian Scholar's Review* 40 (2011): 303–10.
Howard, Thomas. "Why Did C. S. Lewis Never Become a Roman Catholic?" *Lay Witness*, November 1998, 8–9.
Hume, David. *The Philosophy of David Hume*, edited by V. C. Chappell. New York: The Modern Library, 1963.
Humphrey, Nicholas. *Soul Dust*. Princeton: Princeton University Press, 2011.
Jacobs, Alan. *The Narnian: The Life and Imagination of C. S. Lewis*. New York: HarperSanFrancisco, 2005.
Johnson, Keith, Tom Fowler, and Cassandra Sweet. "President Details Sweeping Climate Policies." *The Wall Street Journal*, June 26, 2012, sec. A.
Kenny, Anthony. "Body, Soul, and Intellect in Aquinas." In *From Soul to Self*, edited by James C. Crabbe. New York: Routledge, 1999, 33–48.
—. "Faith in Lions." *The Times Literary Supplement* Number 5751, June 21, 2013, 3–4.
Kilby, Clyde S. *The Christian World of C. S. Lewis*. Grand Rapids, MI: Eerdmans, 1964.
Kilby, Clyde S. and Marjorie Mead (eds), *Brothers and Friends: The Diaries of Major Warren Hamilton Lewis*. San Francisco: Harper and Row, 1982.
Kim, Jaegwon. *Physicalism, Or Something Near Enough*. Princeton, NJ: Princeton University Press, 2005.
Kraut, Richard. *What is Good and Why: The Ethics of Well-Being*. Cambridge, MA: Harvard University Press, 2007.
Kreeft, Peter. *C. S. Lewis: A Critical Essay*. Grand Rapids, MI: Eerdmans, 1969.
—. "C. S. Lewis's Argument from Desire." In *G. K. Chesterton and C. S. Lewis: The Riddle of Joy*, edited by Michael H. Macdonald and Andrew A. Tadie. Grand Rapids, MI: Eerdmans, 1989, 249–72.
Lawlor, John. *C. S. Lewis: Memories and Reflections*. Dallas, TX: Spence Publishing Company, 1998.

Lee, Patrick and Robert P. George. *Body-Soul Dualism in Contemporary Ethics and Politics*. Cambridge: Cambridge University Press, 2008.
Levine, Joseph. *Purple Haze: The Puzzle of Consciousness*. Oxford: Oxford University Press, 2001.
Lewis, C. S. "The Moral Good—Its Place among the Values." CSL/MS—76. Wheaton College, Wheaton, IL: The Marion E. Wade Center, 1924.
—. "Summa Metaphysices contra Anthroposophos." CSL/MS-29/X. Wheaton College, Wheaton, IL: The Marion E. Wade Center, 1928.
—. "*De Bono et Malo*." CSL/MS-34/X. Wheaton College, Wheaton, IL: The Marion E. Wade Center, 1930.
—. *The Allegory of Love*. Oxford: Oxford University Press, 1936.
—. *Rehabilitations and Other Essays*. Oxford: Oxford University Press, 1939.
—. *A Preface to Paradise Lost*. New York: Oxford University Press, 1942.
—. *Surprised by Joy*. New York: Harcourt, 1955.
—. *An Experiment in Criticism*. Cambridge: Cambridge University Press, 1961a.
—. *The Screwtape Letters*. New York: Macmillan, 1961b.
—. *The Problem of Pain*. New York: Macmillan, 1962.
—. *The Discarded Image: An Introduction to Medieval and Renaissance Literature*. Cambridge: Cambridge University Press, 1964.
—. *Christian Reflections*. Grand Rapids, MI: Eerdmans, 1967.
—. *Selected Literary Essays*, edited by Walter Hooper. Cambridge: Cambridge University Press, 1969.
—. *God in the Dock*. Grand Rapids, MI: Eerdmans, 1970.
—. *The Last Battle*. New York: Harper Collins, 1984.
—. *Present Concerns*. New York: Harcourt, 1986a.
—. *Reflections on the Psalms*. New York: Harcourt, 1986b.
—. *The Four Loves*. New York: Harcourt, 1988.
—. *All My Road Before Me*. New York: Harcourt, 1991.
—. *Letters to Malcolm: Chiefly on Prayer*. New York: Harcourt, 1992a.
—. *The Pilgrim's Regress*. Grand Rapids, MI: Eerdmans, 1992b.
—. *C. S. Lewis: Essay Collection and Other Short Pieces*. Edited by Lesley Walmsley. London: Harper Collins, 2000.
—. *A Grief Observed*. New York: HarperSanFrancisco, 2001a.
—. *Mere Christianity*. New York: HarperSanFrancisco, 2001b.
—. *Miracles*. New York: Harper Collins, 2001c.
—. *The Abolition of Man*. New York: HarperSanFrancisco, 2001d.
—. *The Great Divorce*. New York: HarperSanFrancisco, 2001e.
—. *The Weight of Glory and Other Essays*. New York: Harper Collins, 2001f.
—. *Poetry and Prose in the Sixteenth Century*. Oxford: Clarendon Press, 2002.
—. *Out of the Silent Planet*. New York: Scribner, 2003a.
—. *Perelandra*. New York: Scribner, 2003b.
—. *That Hideous Strength*. New York: Scribner, 2003c.
—. *The Collected Letters of C. S. Lewis: Volume I; Family Letters 1905–1931*, edited by Walter Hooper. New York: HarperSanFrancisco, 2004a.

—. *The Collected Letters of C. S. Lewis: Volume II; Books, Broadcasts, and The War 1931-1949*, edited by Walter Hooper. New York: HarperSanFrancisco, 2004b.
—. *The Collected Letters of C. S. Lewis: Volume III; Narnia, Cambridge, and Joy, 1950-1963*, edited by Walter Hooper. New York: HarperSanFrancisco, 2007.
—. "'Early Prose Joy': C. S. Lewis's Early Draft of an Autobiographical Manuscript." *Seven* 30 (2013): 13–49.
—. *Image and Imagination*, edited by Walter Hooper. Cambridge: Cambridge University Press, 2013.
Lewis, C. S. and E. M. W. Tillyard. *The Personal Heresy: A Controversy*. London: Oxford University Press, 1939.
Logan, Stephen. "Literary Theorist." In *The Cambridge Companion to C. S. Lewis*, edited by Robert McSwain and Michael Ward. Cambridge: Cambridge University Press, 2010, 29–42.
MacDonald, Scott. "Egoistic Rationalism: Aquinas's Basis for Christian Morality." In *Christian Theism and the Problems of Philosophy*, edited by Michael D. Beaty. Notre Dame, IN: University of Notre Dame Press, 1990, 327–54.
McCabe, Herbert. *God and Evil in the Theology of St. Thomas Aquinas*, edited by Brian Davies. London: Continuum, 2010.
McGrath, Alister E. *Justification by Faith*. Grand Rapids, MI: Zondervan, 1988.
—. *Surprised by Meaning*. Louisville, KY: Westminster John Knox Press, 2011.
—. *The Intellectual World of C. S. Lewis*. Oxford: Wiley-Blackwell, 2013.
—. *C. S. Lewis: A Life; Eccentric Genius, Reluctant Prophet*. Carol Stream, IL: Tyndale House, 2013.
Meilaender, Gilbert. "Broken Bodies Redeemed." www.touchstonemag.com/archives/issue.php?id=126.
—. "The Everyday C. S. Lewis." *First Things* 87 (August/September 1998): 32–3.
—. *The Taste for the Other*. Grand Rapids, MI: Eerdmans, 1998.
Moore, G. E. *Principia Ethica*. Cambridge: Cambridge University Press, 1968.
Mouw, Richard J. "Surprised by Calvin." *First Things* 191 (March 2009): 15–17.
Murray, Michael. *Nature Red in Tooth and Claw: Theism and the Problem of Animal Suffering*. Oxford: Oxford University Press, 2008.
Neuhaus, Richard John. *As I Lay Dying: Meditations Upon Returning*. New York: Basic Books, 2002.
Noonan, Peggy. "We're More than Political Animals." *The Wall Street Journal*, March 3–4, 2012, sec. A.
Nozick, Robert. *Anarchy, State, and Utopia*. New York: Basic Books, 1974.
Nuttall, A. D. "Jack the Giant Killer." In *Critical Essays on C. S. Lewis*, edited by George Watson. Aldershot: Scolar Press, 1992, 269–84.
Papineau, David. *Philosophical Naturalism*. Oxford: Blackwell, 1993.
Patrick, James. *The Magdalen Metaphysicals: Idealism and Orthodoxy at Oxford 1901-1945*. Mercer Press, 1985.
—. "The Heart's Desire and the Landlord's Rules: C. S. Lewis as a Moral Philosopher." In *The Pilgrim's Guide: C. S. Lewis and the Art of Witness*, edited by David Mills. Grand Rapids, MI: Eerdmans, 1998, 70–85.

Pearce, Joseph. *C. S. Lewis and the Catholic Church*. San Francisco: Ignatius Press, 2003.
Pieper, Josef. *Happiness and Contemplation*. Translated by Richard and Clara Winston. New York: Pantheon, 1958.
—. *Guide to Thomas Aquinas*. Translated by Richard and Clara Winston. New York: Mentor-Omega Books, 1964.
Puckett, Joe, Jr. *The Apologetics of Joy: A Case for the Existence of God from C. S. Lewis's Argument from Desire*. Eugene, OR: Wipf and Stock, 2012.
Purtill, Richard. *C. S. Lewis' Case for the Christian Faith*. San Francisco: Harper and Row, 1981.
Reppert, Victor. *C. S. Lewis' Dangerous Idea: In Defense of the Argument from Reason*. Downers Grove, IL: InterVarsity Press, 2003.
—. "The Ecumenical Apologist: Understanding C. S. Lewis' Defense of Christianity." In *C. S. Lewis: Life, Works, and Legacy; Volume 3: Apologist, Philosopher, and Theologian*, edited by Bruce Edwards. Westport, CN: Praeger, 2007, 1–28.
Rey, Georges. *Contemporary Philosophy of Mind*. Oxford: Blackwell, 1997.
Root, Jerry. *C. S. Lewis and a Problem of Evil: An Investigation of a Pervasive Theme*. Eugene, OR: Pickwick Publications, 2009.
Russell, Burton. *Inventing the Flat Earth*. New York: Praeger, 1991.
Sayers, Dorothy L. *The Letters of Dorothy L. Sayers: Volume Two: 1937–1943; Volume Two; From Novelist to Playwright*, edited by Barbara Reynolds. New York: St. Martin's Press, 1998.
—. *The Letters of Dorothy L. Sayers: Volume Three: 1944–1950; A Noble Daring*, edited by Barbara Reynolds. Great Britain: The Dorothy L. Sayers Society, 1998.
Stoll, Elmer Edgar. "Give the Devil His Due: A Reply to Mr. Lewis." In *Critical Essays on C. S. Lewis*, edited by George Watson. Aldershot: Scolar Press, 1992, 177–93.
Stroud, Barry. "The Charm of Naturalism." In *Naturalism in Question*, edited by Mario De Caro and David Macarthur. Cambridge, MA: Harvard University Press, 2004, 21–35.
Stump, Eleonore. "Non-Cartesian Substance Dualism and Materialism without Reductionism." *Faith and Philosophy* 12 (1995): 505–31.
Van Dyke, Christina. "Human Identity, Immanent Causal Relations, and the Principle of Non-Repeatability: Thomas Aquinas on the Bodily Resurrection." *Religious Studies* 43 (2007): 373–94.
Te Velde, Rudi A. "Evil, Sin, and Death: Thomas Aquinas on Original Sin." In *The Theology of Thomas Aquinas*, edited by Rik van Nieuwenhove and Joseph Wawrykow. Notre Dame, IN: University of Notre Dame Press, 2005, 143–66.
Von Riel, Gerd. "Does Perfect Activity Necessarily Yield Pleasure? An Evaluation of the Relation between Pleasure and Activity in Aristotle, *Nicomachean Ethics* VII and X." *International Journal of Philosophical Studies* 7 (1999): 211–41.
Walsh, Chad. *C. S. Lewis: Apostle to the Skeptics*. New York: Macmillan, 1949.

Ward, Michael. *Planet Narnia: The Seven Heavens in the Imagination of C. S. Lewis.* Oxford: Oxford University Press, 2008.
Ware, Kallistos. "The Soul in Greek Christianity." In *From Soul to Self,* edited by James C. Crabbe. New York: Routledge, 1999, 49–69.
White, Nicholas. *A Brief History of Happiness.* Oxford: Blackwell, 2006.
Wieland, Georg. "Happiness (Ia IIae, qq. 1-5." In *The Ethics of Aquinas,* edited by Stephen J. Pope. Washington, D.C.: Georgetown University Press, 2002, 57–68.
Willis, John Randolph, S. J. *Pleasures Forevermore: The Theology of C. S. Lewis.* Chicago: Loyola University Press, 1983.
Wilson, A. N. *C. S. Lewis: A Biography.* New York: W. W. Norton, 1990.
Wolterstorff, Nicholas. *Justice: Rights and Wrongs.* Princeton, NJ: Princeton University Press, 2008.
Wright, N. T. *Surprised by Hope: Rethinking Heaven, the Resurrection, and the Mission of the Church.* New York: HarperOne, 2008.
—. "Mind, Spirit, Soul and Body: All for One and One for All; Reflections on Paul's Anthropology in His Complex Contexts." Paper presented at the Society of Christian Philosophers Eastern Meetisng, March 18, 2011. http//www.ntwrightpage.com/Wright_SCP_MindSpiritSoulBody.htm.

Author Index

Adey, Lionel   86, 113n. 40
Annas, Julia   39n. 84, 50–1
Anscombe, Elizabeth   77, 123n. 93
Aristotle   7n. 21, 22, 31, 39n. 84, 46, 48, 51, 53, 103, 126–7, 129, 143, 158, 170, 171
Armstrong, David   82–3
Augustine   12, 64, 71, 103–6, 107, 108, 111, 137, 138, 142, 166, 175

Baggett, David   4n. 5
Baker, Mark   80n. 44
Barfield, Owen   26n. 31, 48n. 114, 86
Barkman, Adam   29n. 43, 46, 103
Bennett, J. A. W.   5, 19
Bering, Jesse   9n. 26, 87
Beversluis, John   64
Bloom, Paul   9n. 26, 87
Brentano, Franz   78n. 35
Broks, Paul   87
Brown, Warren S.   8n. 24

Carnell, Corbin Scott   59–60, 176n. 85, 179n. 92
Carpenter, Humphrey   70n. 4
Chalmers, David   76n. 27
Chesterton, G. K.   6, 155n. 14
Como, James T.   3, 159n. 27, 163–5, 172n. 67
Conan Doyle, Arthur   95–6
Cuneo, Andrew   151–2

Davidman, Joy   30
Davies, Brian   175
Dennett, Daniel   76n. 26
Derrick, Christopher   2n. 2, 11n. 28, 20, 155, 161–2, 169–70, 171n. 61, 174

Descartes, René   76, 79n. 39, 86, 131, 145–6
Dunckel, Mona   21n. 13

Epicurus   21

Flanagan, Owen   128n. 108

Geach, Peter   123–4
Gell, Alfred   87
George, Robert   122n. 90, 123n. 92, 131n. 2, 138n. 27, 146
Gilson, Etienne   106
Goetz, Stewart   47n. 111, 79n. 41, 80n. 44, 90n. 79, 132n. 4
Green, Roger Lancelyn   5
Greeves, Arthur   95n. 100, 167
Griffiths, Dom Bede   3, 155–6, 159, 173, 176
Groothuis, Douglas   103–4, 111

Habermas, Gary   4n. 5
Haldane, J. B. S.   84
Havard, Humphrey   166
Hooper, Walter   2, 5, 14, 176
Horne, Brian   104, 111
Horner, David   47, 48n. 111, 49
Howard, Thomas   151–2
Hume, David   21–2
Humphrey, Nicholas   9n. 26, 87

Jacobs, Alan   13, 23, 161

Kant, Immanuel   48, 49n. 114
Kenny, Anthony   6, 173n. 68
Kilby, Clyde S.   5n. 13, 66n. 180
Kim, Jaegwon   98–9
Kraut, Richard   124n. 95
Kreeft, Peter   64, 103

Lawlor, John   21
Lee, Patrick   122n. 90, 123n. 92,
    131n. 2, 138n. 27, 146
Levine, Joseph   76n. 27
Lewis, Albert   4
Lewis, Warren   vi, 5, 74, 152, 166
Logan, Stephen   61

McCabe, Herbert   108–9, 121, 175
MacDonald, Scott   148n. 56
McGrath, Alister E.   4, 6, 7, 8, 20,
    42–4, 62, 63, 152n. 7
Maloney, H. Newton   8n. 24
Mead, Marjorie Lamp   5n. 13
Meilaender, Gilbert   3, 8, 56, 90–1,
    93, 103, 154, 160n. 31
Milton, John   18–19, 103
Mitchell, Christopher   167n. 53
Moore, G. E.   28, 29, 124
Morris, William   40, 62n. 160
Mouw, Richard J.   37n. 77
Murphy, Nancey   8n. 24
Murray, Michael   13n. 30

Neuhaus, Richard John   146
Noonan, Peggy   147
Nozick, Robert   55, 127
Nuttall, A. D.   20–1, 28, 29

Obama, Barak   94

Papineau, David   81–2
Patrick, James   4, 29n. 43,
    46, 173–4
Pearce, Joseph   2n. 2, 152n. 4,
    159–60, 162–3, 164, 168n. 55,
    176n. 85, 177, 178–9
Pieper, Josef   118, 172, 175
Plato   9, 29–30, 46, 67, 88, 89–90,
    113n. 40, 158, 170, 171
Princess Elizabeth of Bohemia   86
Puckett, Joe, Jr.   25n. 29
Purtill, Richard   6–7, 173

Quick, Canon Oliver Chase   7, 26,
    35–6

Reppert, Victor   13n. 30, 21n. 13,
    77n. 31
Rey, Georges   83
Root, Jerry   25, 27
Russell, Jeffrey Burton   95n. 99

Sayer, George   166
Sayers, Dorothy L.   104n. 7, 155n. 14
Spenser, Edmund   63
Stoll, Elmer Edgar   19
Stroud, Barry   81
Stump, Eleonore   131–2, 134

Taliaferro, Charles   79n. 41, 80n. 44,
    132n. 4
Te Velde, Rudi A.   109
Tillyard, E. M. W.   7
Tolkien, J. R. R.   1, 2, 6, 155, 161,
    162, 164n. 42, 165

Vanauken, Sheldon   1, 70
Van Dyke, Christina   134n. 15
Van Riel, Gerd   127–8

Walls, Jerry   4n. 5, 73n. 17
Walsh, Chad   53–4, 176
Ward, Michael   166–7
Ware, Kallistos   139n. 29
White, Nicholas   23, 48n. 111,
    58nn. 140–1
Wieland, Georg   143–4
Willis, John Randolph, S. J.   110–11,
    165–6
Wilson, A. N.   4, 168n. 55
Wolterstorff, Nicholas   47n. 110, 50,
    51n. 119, 129
Wright, N. T.   8n. 24, 66n. 183,
    88–9, 90

Yeats, W. B.   62n. 160